Praise for *The New Saints*

"*The New Saints* will challenge your current understanding and offer fresh inspiration about ways, together, we can bring healing to our beautiful and broken world. This is a bold and powerful offering—one that attunes to our times with great lucidity, wisdom, and heart."

Tara Brach
author of *Radical Acceptance* and *Radical Compassion*

"*The New Saints* is Lama Rod Owens's literary embodiment of his compassionately brave, authentic, loving, and fierce essence. Opening our broken hearts is not easy, but disrupting the reigning terror is necessary without becoming the entities we seek to eradicate. Lama Rod's compelling storytelling and sacred teachings remind and teach us that it is through acknowledging and facing our pain, our trauma, and, yes, the often-complex contradictions in our lives that we will create opportunities to cultivate compassion for ourselves and all beings everywhere without exception."

Aishah Shahidah Simmons
editor of *Love WITH Accountability*, producer and director of *NO! The Rape Documentary*

"Step-by-step, Lama Rod Owens prods us to be bold and outrageous, to give up on the idea of justice and instead commit to the wild and arduous task of embodied liberation. In this, we find freedom and power. In this, our hearts begin to heal. In this work, we discover that in all our messy, inspired humanity, we are, indeed, the New Saints."

Swami Jaya Devi
author of *Embodied*

"In *The New Saints*, Lama Rod Owens offers revelation. The loving support demonstrated in this important book provides a model of liberated spiritual practice that helps us through the accidental feedback loops of confirmation bias and spiritual bypassing so that we can step into becoming a deeply embodied New Saint. *The New Saints*, like Lama Rod himself, exists for these times—and the world, and all of us, are so much better off because of this."

Lama Justin von Bujdoss
author of *Modern Tantric Buddhism*

"With finesse and honesty, Lama Rod Owens keeps the dharma radical by transforming the vocabulary of Buddhism into contemporary American terms steeped in social justice—incarceration and freedom, systemic oppression and suffering, abolition and liberation, work and fierceness, joy and love. What an accomplishment *The New Saints* is, opening the doors of the dharma to new generations!"

Sarah Jacoby
author of *Love and Liberation*

The New Saints

Also by Lama Rod Owens

Love and Rage:
The Path of Liberation Through Anger

Radical Dharma:
Talking Race, Love, and Liberation,
with Rev. angel Kyodo williams
and Jasmine Syedullah, PhD

The New Saints

From Broken Hearts to Spiritual Warriors

Lama Rod Owens

 sounds true
BOULDER, COLORADO

Sounds True
Boulder, CO

This book is not intended as a substitute for the medical recommendations of
physicians, mental health professionals, or other health-care providers. Rather, it is
intended to offer information to help the reader cooperate with physicians, mental
health professionals, and health-care providers in a mutual quest for optimal well-
being. We advise readers to carefully review and understand the ideas presented and
to seek the advice of a qualified professional before attempting to use them.

Published 2023

Cover design by Charli Barnes
Book design by Constance Poole
Cover image © Marcus Rogers
Cover photo © Brooks Freehill

Printed in the United States of America

BK06538

Library of Congress Cataloging-in-Publication Data

Names: Owens, Lama Rod, 1979- author.
Title: The new saints : from broken hearts to spiritual warriors / Lama Rod Owens.
Description: Boulder, CO : Sounds True, 2023.
Identifiers: LCCN 2023005442 (print) | LCCN 2023005443 (ebook) | ISBN
9781649630001 (paperback) | ISBN 9781649630018 (ebook)
    Subjects: LCSH: Social justice—Religious aspects—Buddhism. | Buddhist
    sociology. | Buddhist ethics.
Classification: LCC HN40.B8 O94 2023 (print) | LCC HN40.B8 (ebook) | DDC
294.3/376—dc23/eng/20230214
LC record available at https://lccn.loc.gov/2023005442
LC ebook record available at https://lccn.loc.gov/2023005443

10 9 8 7 6 5 4 3 2 1

This work is dedicated to my dear brother, friend, teacher, and barber Allah Mathematics Allah. May the labor he offered in life continue to help us get free.

Contents

Prologue

The old saying is true: freaks come out at night. Since I am half freak (on my mother's side), I journey outside to see what trouble there is for me to get into.

I find myself sitting on my front porch. The land is grateful for my company. The street hushes itself into silence while people settle into sleep, journeying into the realms their needs take them. I take out my pipe along with the tobacco the medicine men told me to grow in my backyard.

I listen to the land whisper bedtime stories. Across the street, a giant magnolia tree towers over the block. Though ignored and misunderstood, it is an ancient spirit guarding the land and its people. It reminds me of age and history, of change and death. My Indigenous elders honor Elder Magnolia and ask me to continue to do the same. From my porch, while staring up into its branches, moon and starlight streaming through its leaves, I ask it questions. It reminds me of the great tree Yggdrasil from Norse mythology, which is said to bind all the worlds together. I am left in silent awe, considering that Elder Magnolia may bind so much existence together.

I light the tobacco and inhale deeply, connecting to the elements of earth and fire, opening to the consciousness of the tobacco and inhaling the energy of gratitude and remembrance in with the smoke: gratitude for the land that has held so much violence and remembrance of the Cherokee, Creek, and Muscogee people who were forced off this land and of my ancestors who were forced to work it, gratitude for the night and its kindness and stillness, and gratitude for all the beings of the unseen world who care for us in this community. I exhale and watch the thick white plumes of smoke hover in front of me before lifting and scattering upward, dissolving into the spirit realm where they will take my gratitude.

In the distance, the siren of a fire truck, dispatched from the station a few blocks up, slices through the stillness of this midnight ceremony. I stop what I'm doing to offer prayers for the people these emergency vehicles are going to help.

On nights like this I tend to make sure I am who I pretend to be by recalling myself as if ticking off a checklist: I am a Black queer middle-aged man, six foot four, two hundred and some-thing pounds (a lady does not disclose her weight!), with broad shoulders, eyes like dark brown pools, thick lips, a wide nose, and a shaved head with a healthy, thick beard spotted with patches of gray. I haven't decided if I am handsome or sexy and maybe that doesn't matter. What I know is that I am moving quickly into my elder years, the same years that many gay and queer men of the generation before me never made it to. I am grateful that I survived, though I mourn for those who did not make it. I offer smoke for those beautiful ones as well.

During my college years I gave myself the nickname Slick Hot Chocolate Rod—melts in your mouth, not in your hand. (Actually, I considered the name to be much grander, like a sobriquet with user instructions attached.) Although in my mind the nickname was quite accurate, it did not survive my early twenties.

These days, although I fantasize about going out to the clubs or having random hookups and engaging in wild, uninhibited group sex, there is nothing more exciting than a nice quiet dinner, a glass of sweet red wine, a few episodes of *The Golden Girls*, and a late-night pipe of tobacco. Sometimes I think I am a modern-day hobbit.

I am also a holy man or, more precisely, a lama—a Tibetan Buddhist title I earned after spending a little over three years in silent, cloistered retreat. *Lama* means "teacher" but carries the connotation of spiritual heaviness, a profound gravitas. Supposedly, I am heavy with spiritual realization. When I tell people I am a lama, they ask, "Oh, like the animal?" In my mind, I respond, *No, like fuck you*. Maybe this response, though not voiced, isn't so spiritual.

Before I earned my gravitas, I was an activist, living in an intentional community, trying to do what Jesus did—feeding folks, trying to stop wars, and struggling to educate people about systems of violence—while at the same time being young and idealistic and doing my best to have fun and drink all the drinks, laugh all the laughs, kiss all the boys, go to all the parties, and, most importantly, experience all the drama. It was a busy time that was interrupted by a sudden emotional crash into hopelessness followed by the calling of the holy Buddhist life.

Back on the porch, my headphones have made their way to my ears. Sister Rosetta Tharpe is singing "Precious Memories" to me in her heavy, bluesy belt that wears the mask of traditional gospel but underneath carries the hard thump of rock 'n' roll. My own precious memories flood my soul and threaten to trap me back in a time when everything seemed simpler and easier.

When I pay attention, I notice that my neighborhood is full of many things, including the ghosts of dead Confederate soldiers lumbering up and down the street. Their roaming is aimless, slow, and melancholic. I am not afraid. I'm pissed off. I remind them that they gave their lives for a stupid, vile cause, and that they can go to hell. But eventually I remember what a good Buddhist is supposed to do, and I offer prayers that they be released from being earth-bound. I offer them smoke from my pipe. Some of them appreciate it and begin to huddle on the sidewalk in front of me. They cannot come closer without an invitation from me, and I do not invite them. The only way I survive both the physical and spirit worlds is by saying no.

I wonder what it is like for them to be stuck in a world that has no more use for them, to be rendered illusions or figments of an overactive imagination. I wonder what it is like to give your life to something, only to be forgotten, and for houses to be built on top of your unmarked grave. I wonder about the twin brutalities of desecration and erasure. I begin to feel sorry for them. Suddenly, I begin to feel sorry for myself, as I realize that I have been reflecting on my own plight and that of my ancestors the whole time.

All this reminds me of how lonely I have been all my life. I have dwelled so deeply inside of myself and developed such a decadent spiritual life that most people can't begin to relate to me. And because of this decadence, I have developed the capacity to see and experience the complexity of people as well as the world we have created. My loneliness stems from not being able to articulate everything I experience to others because they have not developed the same capacity to understand this complexity. So, often I choose to keep these experiences to myself and pretend the world is as simple as people think it is.

I haven't been sleeping well the past few nights. Sometimes, I feel as if I am the only person in the world exhausted from navigating an ocean of trauma and grief that mostly isn't mine. But so many people are drowning in this ocean. They normalize the experience and call it life.

I have two recurring dreams. The first is about shopping at Target. This is a dream I make a reality as often as possible. The second recurring dream is about zombies. I find myself in the middle of a zombie apocalypse, trying to help people get to safety, which often means hiding in abandoned buildings or around corners as undead mobs mill about. Although this sounds like a nightmare, I am never frightened. I always know that the zombies are metaphors for how we move through the world: extremely disassociated from our lived experience of suffering and struggle. Our hiding in the dream echoes our hiding from the grief and trauma we don't know how to tend to.

Things are falling apart. I am being called into the dense confusion of people and the world our confusion has created. All around us the loud, violent clamoring of histories refusing to be settled distracts us. Light and dark maintain a precarious balance. The wind carries troubling news from other realms of existence, and the earth is foretelling a hard winter. However, ancient, powerful magic is awakening, forgotten gods are returning, and people are being shaken awake and directed to the front lines to fight. The world is still full of potential, and it is from this potential that I offer what I can now.

I have finished my pipe and said all my prayers, and I feel complete for the night. I leave a final offering of grains, water, light, and incense on the porch as a bribe for those beings who may be pissed at me, hoping they accept this offering instead of fucking with me.

The New Saint

An Introduction

I am a New Saint. (I am also a queen. However, that may be subject matter for another book!) Traditionally, people do not ordain themselves saints unless they are leaders of a cult. Whether or not someone is a saint (or cult leader) is up to others to discern. In the case of a saint, a spiritual community recognizes the divine qualities of a person and their extraordinary activities, usually after their death. Cult members are not so good at recognizing that they are in a cult or that they have a cult leader. Those labels are applied by others outside of the cult, who are actually members of larger cults that have become mainstreamed and normalized, like academic institutions, pop star fan/stan communities, political parties, royal families, or our favorite online retailers whose products magically appear on our doorstep when we press a button on an app.

This is not a book about cults . . . yet.

I am not a New Saint because I feel divine or extraordinary. I am a New Saint because I have chosen to give a shit about myself and everyone around me and because I have figured out much of the work I need to do to help people experience the freedom to be their most authentic selves, I do that work, and I keep showing up to do that work. This may sound extraordinary, but I don't want it to be because I need you to join me on this path. We no longer have a choice. I want you to become a New Saint so that we can together make this work ordinary and accessible. Just as many of us are trained to do simple tasks to function in our lives, I want us to train to free each other from suffering while we train to reduce our own suffering.

This book is about how to do that. But first I should explain where the notion of New Saints came from.

The Apocalypse

Let's start with something fun and light, like the apocalypse.

To begin with, we are not experiencing the end of the world, but we are experiencing the end of some provocative and desperately enduring lies we have told ourselves. With the end of lies comes the awakening of truth. And so we are living in a period when we are confronting truth—truth about ourselves and our relationship to death and dying, to systems and institutions of violence, to transhistorical trauma, to the health of our planet, to capitalism, and, ultimately, to the fact that we can no longer continue living like we have in the past. Real truth is unrelenting, like the sun piercing the clouds on an overcast day, and it doesn't go away just because we can't handle it. Truth uncovers everything—all the shit that we have spent our lives running away from. And when something is uncovered, even if it's the most intense individual or collective trauma, it demands to be taken care of.

Although the apocalypse can be defined as unveiling and truth telling, it is perhaps experienced by many of us as an invasive anxiety, worry, fear, or even terror. This anxiety can be so intense that we don't even experience it as anxiety, either because we have become disassociated (our nervous system has shut down our capacity to feel because the sensation is too intense for us to process) or because the energy of the anxiety is manifesting as another sensation, like physical pain, fatigue, anger, or sadness.

For me, living through the apocalypse feels like trying to stand on ground that is constantly shifting, like making plans for tomorrow while having little faith that there will be a tomorrow. It is the feeling of the bottom falling out from under me. It is struggling to deal with the great Buddhist law of impermanence, which teaches that everything is always changing and in flux. Impermanence is sometimes excruciating if you, like me, are addicted to stability.

The apocalypse has been happening for a long time, and it started well before the death of Prince and Betty White, the emergence of the coronavirus and its subsequent quarantine, the election of Donald Trump, the January 6 insurrection, Brexit, 9/11, the Newtown and Columbine shootings, the AIDS epidemic, the destruction of the Greenwood Community, or the Holocaust and WWII. Maybe it started when Portuguese sailors reached the coast of Ghana or when Christopher Columbus landed in the Caribbean and my ancestors were later enslaved or with the genocide and relocation of Indigenous peoples all over the world or further back than that with the Spanish Inquisition or the Crusades. Maybe the apocalypse started with the evolution of race into hierarchies of power, with whiteness as the expression of a moral attitude that came to violently repress all other racial groups. Or perhaps the apocalypse began with the transition into modernity, from the agricultural age to the industrial revolution, or even with the violent patrilineal overthrow of matrilineal cultures in the Indus Valley civilizations. Perhaps it started in the Garden of Eden when the forbidden fruit was eaten. My own practices and beliefs suggest that it may have begun when we forgot we were expressions of the Divine and started identifying with the pain of separateness and began feeling overwhelmed by the delusion.

Regardless of when the apocalypse started, we are knee deep in it now! And it may be strange to read this, but I believe the apocalypse is a blessing. There's nothing like a crisis to wake us up and force us to start getting serious about change.

A New Age and New Saints

That the days are becoming indistinguishable from each other is a sign of eternity. The new world isn't that of waiting for the old order to reopen or the old economy to restart. It's to realize that the Messianic Age begins when we see that the essential labor is to love and feed each other and to revel in the feeling of endless resurrection when we wake up and have nothing to do that we don't have to do unless we choose it and choose it in love.

—*Carrie Sealine*

I have often noticed that those who are loudest about how we are doomed are those who have never had to struggle in collective survival. I am not glorifying descending from communities that have had to survive systems created to annihilate us, because the transgenerational trauma has been heavy. When you or your community have not known this struggle, chances are you will not know or embody resilience. You will not understand how important and powerful collective cooperation and care can be. Those of us who are descendants of people who have survived slavery, genocide, wars, plagues, or any expression of warfare carry the seeds of survival in our DNA. We harbor ancestral memories of what it has meant for our people to make a way out of no way. My ancestry has taught me to look deeply into this period and understand that there is potential for not just surviving but flourishing.

In one of his most famous poems, "The Second Coming," W. B. Yeats wrote, "The best lack all conviction, while the worst / Are full of passionate intensity." To meet the apocalypse, you must embody an intention that this experience will not consume you, that this experience is calling you into a deeper labor of transformation and creativity. There are so many people full of "passionate intensity," but this passion is actually intense reactivity to the fear of being consumed as well as to the helplessness we feel confronting something that cannot be organized or bypassed.

Carrie Sealine, a Jewish mystic, scholar, and practitioner of Thelema, an esoteric religious tradition founded by Aleister Crowley, was the first person who offered me a beautiful and generative vision of what the ongoing apocalypse was opening into. As is often the case with people who become my teachers, I never knew of Carrie Sealine until very shortly after her passing in 2020, when a close mutual friend sent me some of her work. I was moved by how she spoke of the days blending into one another and about reveling in eternity, which is a revelation expressed first in my life by our great pop philosopher Lauryn Hill when she said that everything was everything to my generation.

Carrie speaks of the need not to return to our old ways but to expand bravely into the age that is coming, the Messianic Age, or the Golden Age, when we will experience universal peace. I understand peace as the embodiment of the abolitionist dream of a world grounded in personal freedom, collective care, conflicts held in love, and communities where we live in the truth of things held in compassion, as opposed to in avoidance of the violence of our past and present.

Listening to Carrie, I was reminded of the great Indian guru Neem Karoli Baba (or Maharaji), who during the height of his teaching life in the mid-1900s taught, "Love everyone, serve everyone, remember God, and tell the truth." The Messianic Age will be as Carrie envisioned: a time when we must love everyone. This is the essential labor that Maharaji taught as well: to just love and be loved, to feed and allow yourself to be fed, to do what is only done out of love, and to embrace the imperative labor of resting as taught by my sister and comrade Tricia Hersey, the founder and bishop of the Nap Ministry. This is what the rebalancing work of the apocalypse is propelling us toward: a life where the concept of labor is not linked to capitalist production and consumption but to the essential well-being of our hearts, minds, and bodies, where we will know how to choose love over resentment, rest over exhaustion, silence over noise, and stillness over busyness.

The present apocalypse is one thing that has awakened this new path of sainthood for me. The other was getting sick and tired of performative goodness.

Faking It

I have only seen a few seconds of the video of George Floyd being slowly murdered, but it was enough to remind me again that America does not love Black people. The murder of George Floyd ignited a renewed movement for Black lives that saw mass marches and actions not just in the country but around the world. Not only were many of us on the streets, but we were also reeducating ourselves. The quarantine went from an opportunity to explore baking bread and making cakes to learning Marxist theory and becoming abolitionist scholars wanting to defund the police.

On social media, White people were falling over themselves to promote and throw money at Black activists, healers, and scholars, while posting their hot takes and Black Lives Matter memes and calling other White people out. I lost count of how many "you need to follow this Black person now!" lists I was on. On Instagram, I shot up to forty thousand followers from barely six thousand, which was weird for someone like me, who has a strong dislike of social media outside of sharing humorous memes and staying connected to friends and family.

After Floyd's murder, my book *Love and Rage*, which explored anger and its vital role in healing and justice work, was published. It became popular due to its timeliness, and I found myself featured in major publications like the *Washington Post*, educating folks on the need for engaged, compassionate social action that embraces the power of anger while acknowledging our broken hearts.

But something was bothering me. So much of the activity on social media felt performative. It felt like White people were trying to look good and in doing so were desperate to feel good about their unwillingness to do the serious labor of disrupting white supremacy. None of these performative acts, such as posting black squares on Instagram, has done anything to stop the systematic disposal of Black and Brown people. What bothered and hurt me most was when this renewed support from White folks evaporated after the summer of 2020.

But it wasn't just White people. It was queer people talking freedom but still investing in gender policing and conformist notions of sexuality and relationships. It was other Black folks talking about freedom with no anticapitalist analysis. It was new abolitionists reducing abolitionist organizing to only defunding the police instead of engaging in the revolutionary work of dreaming up a new world—one grounded in freedom, love, and care and just as much about abolishing the violence of policing in our interpersonal and community relationships as it is about abolishing the carceral systems that our world seems to depend on. It was people talking about liberation but not showing interest in taking risks, choosing discomfort, and entering the subversive work of fugitivity. It was people wanting freedom while still desperately worshipping comfort and trying to look good.

We Don't Need Another Hero

In observance of Pride that June, I ended up moderating a small online panel for the New York Public Library, during which we explored millennial engagement with various justice movements. It was during that panel that I started wondering what it meant to be good. There were and still are so many people who, inspired by the great changemakers that have come before or are working tirelessly now to free us all, are trying to do what is good and helpful. These same people have risked so much to teach and lead us out of the experience of suffering.

In a sense, this book began introducing itself to me after the panel, as I reflected on the conversation and on everything that had been happening during the pandemic. So much has changed for me and everyone. By now, it's clear that there is no "normal" worth returning to. This loss of our old lives, coupled with facing the work of establishing a new normal, is painful for many of us. Each generation living now must dream up a new world beyond the violence and chaos we were born into. We must choose the end of delusion and embrace a vision that leads us into the Messianic Age of love. To get there, we must return to the truth of who we are, to journey back through the trauma and forgetfulness to reconcile histories of violence and to tend to our broken hearts.

After the panel, I kept asking myself what we need to do this work. How do we excel beyond performative goodness and earn the experience of goodness? How do we let our hearts break and understand we can survive the breaking? How can we hold the complex experiences of being human and how do we care for our humanness? What is freedom for us, as individuals, and for our communities? What does it mean to practice true abolition?

And then: how can we look to the great people—the saints from various spiritual and religious paths as well as the social change agents who have touched this world through profound acts of love and liberation—whom I love and have been changed and inspired by?

I realized that if I loved the saints so much, and if I had committed to the path of becoming a spiritual leader concerned with justice, I had to say out loud, regardless of how it made me look, that this was as much a time of spiritual warfare as it was a time of political and social warfare and that the struggle of the unseen world was at the root of the political and social struggle.

Then, suddenly, in my head, Tina Turner began singing about how we didn't need another hero. And I agreed. Besides no one can save us from ourselves. No one can take our suffering away and instantly endow us with goodness. Instead, we must become our own heroes. We must remember our sainthood—not a sainthood of the past but a sainthood that responds to the urgency of this period of crisis. This new sainthood must be based in courage, hope, vision, and an authentic desire for all beings and everything to be free. We must become New Saints.

The New Saint Is Not a Good Person

So many of us are obsessed with being good because the performance and pursuit of goodness are tied to many cultural and religious ideas of being a person or human. If we are not good, we are not considered human. If we are not human, we are considered bad, flawed, or invalid, which means that we lose our humanity and become othered. In this otherness, we no longer receive the basic care that good people get. This logic fuels the prison industrial complex. When people break the law, they become bad and thus othered and punished without any regard to care because they no longer deserve it. Without care, bad people become the reciprocals of violence masked as justice.

Thus, we learn that being good is how we maintain our humanity and get the resources we need, especially love. But this politics of goodness is linked to one of the most violent expressions of care: conditional love. Many of us have traded actual goodness for a performance of goodness because we are trying to get the care we need to survive. If being good requires us to perform heteronormativity over our innate and authentic queerness, we do that. If it means pretending to agree with someone because they hold the resources we need, we do that, too.

For most of my life, goodness was something used to keep me in line. To be a good boy meant that I adhered to certain etiquettes that have been mostly informed by anti-Blackness, anti-queerness, ableism, class, and capitalism. Being good meant making other people happy through conforming to these etiquettes, which required my silence and complicity in the harm others were causing me.

Systems of dominance have co-opted the work of goodness to keep people from disrupting systemic violence. In this sense, goodness is understood to be an expression of virtue if it does not challenge the power imbalance and does not make the people who benefit the most from that power imbalance uncomfortable. When you are good, you are not causing trouble. Here I define *trouble* as creating discomfort for others.

I am no longer interested in being a good person. Performative goodness, conditional love, and shame are a violent trinity that has functioned to silence and repress countless beings and which I believe belies so much of the violence we deal with each day. I have long known that conditional love and shame are effective weapons of interpersonal and cultural warfare, but we never think of the weaponization of goodness as violence used to harm people by suppressing and silencing them.

I am not a good person. I can't be a good person because goodness is more than something we perform or something we are. It is not an identity location we settle into. Goodness is the choice I am making each moment to do what is conducive to freedom for me and others. Goodness is a verb that I am actively engaging with: I like to say, "I am gooding" as opposed to "I am being good."

We practice goodness not because we want to be seen as good or because we want to experience happiness or even because it is what we are supposed to be doing. We choose goodness because it's how we get free while inviting others to join us.

Voting, educating ourselves, highlighting the voices of the most underrepresented folks, being at least liberal, recycling, carrying people's groceries, reading the current justice books, never saying "Candyman" into a mirror, putting up Black Lives Matter signs, saying please and thank you, paying taxes, not wearing white shoes after Labor Day, supporting charities, avoiding cracks and walking under ladders, and offering thoughts and prayers are all wonderful things to do, but they are more about feeling good about ourselves and making sure others view us favorably. Which one of these beloved labors will actually get us free?

In the past few years, we have been obsessed with voting. According to popular liberal opinion, if you don't vote Democrat, you are a bad person who doesn't give a shit about the rights of others. But there are just as many racists, capitalists, ableists, rapists, and misogynists voting Democrat as there are voting Republican. And voting is no longer going to save us and set us free. I do not consent to anyone voting for me to be free. Voting never freed my ancestors.

Our labor, love, magic, and acting up offered us whatever freedoms we have today, and it is these same tools we and all oppressed communities will continue to rely on.

There are two expressions of goodness: relative and absolute. Relative goodness is how I choose goodness in order to be happy, suffer less, and help others suffer less. Absolute goodness is choosing goodness because we want to get free and help others do the same. For goodness to be sustainable in our lives, we must turn our practice toward the absolute and train in goodness that lights the path into real freedom while showing others how to do this as well.

Practicing goodness also means that I must experience the grief of what it means to align myself with freedom and away from chaos and drama. We must recognize that we have built our lives and identities on the experience of conflict and distraction, which makes sense because although we may talk a good game about freedom, we still use drama in order to distract ourselves from the real work of getting free, which is the work of figuring out who we are through the rage and brokenheartedness. With drama and silliness, we have no idea who we are.

Some of us get into goodness because we want people to like us, while others choose goodness to avoid the shit in our lives by using the pleasure we get from good experiences to cover up the pain of unpleasant ones. These motivations for choosing goodness will lead to more suffering because we are not choosing to be with the truth of who we are. Freedom is only discovered through truth—not through comfortable stories that make us feel good.

To choose goodness does not mean we are performing, documenting, or broadcasting goodness. Goodness isn't a show for others to influence how they think about us. Seeking the approval of others will always enable those others to dictate our freedom. But it may be the case that folks around us don't want to be free, and the choices we make may trigger them. Freedom doesn't require validation; it is a personal choice we must make on our own, even when others around us do not consent. To choose goodness is to choose freedom: first for ourselves and then for our communities.

Goodness also means that I acknowledge the duality of light and dark, which is the practice of acknowledging balance. Balance is one of the laws of the relative world experiencing itself as the idea that there cannot be *this* without *that*. There is no light without dark, no up without down, or maybe no understanding of liberation without the discomfort of incarceration.

To choose goodness we must also know what it has meant to choose the dark. Some of the most influential change leaders and healers have been people who once chose what wasn't conducive to freedom. John Fire Lame Deer believed that in order to really help others as a medicine man, he had to know his trauma, get lost in it, and eventually emerge from it so he could understand how to help others move through their trauma. Or I think about Malcolm X who, after years of struggling to figure out who he was beyond the pain and confusion, came to understand freedom while he was physically incarcerated by the state.

But choosing goodness in this context doesn't mean I stand in opposition to darkness. It means that I recognize that darkness is asking to be held in care and awareness. If I can hold darkness like this, then it becomes a teacher. When I can't hold it, then it holds me, and this is the beginning of evil.

When we realize that goodness is a choice we are making to be free, and that choice becomes a habitual process, we start experiencing the state of virtue. I am practicing virtue when everything in my life is grounded in the pursuit of freedom. I am not trying to be a virtuous person. I am trying to choose what is conducive to freedom, and that continuous choice slowly begins to orient my life toward freedom.

The Old Saints

New Saint is a contemporary expression of an ancient Buddhist tradition that understands the saint as a bodhisattva. *Bodhisattva* is roughly translated as "spiritual warrior" and is one who is motivated by the energy of bodhicitta, or a profound altruistic wish to free all beings from suffering. I feel that the world is desperate for a reframing of this tradition that is contemporary, direct, simple, and accessible to all folks, especially those who do not identify as Buddhist.

Saints are people from various spiritual and religious traditions who have deeply embodied love and compassion and whose embodiment has inspired countless others to aspire to that same practice. However, for most of us, sainthood seems a lofty and vague endeavor that is more divine and religious than practical. This current era is calling for saints — New Saints — who are from this time and place, who speak the language of this time and place, and, most importantly, who embrace the integration of both social and ultimate liberation. New Saints can surrender into the Divine or spiritual while disrupting systems of violence. I believe that we all can and must become New Saints for ourselves and our communities.

The first saint I knew of was Jesus, who walked on water, turned water into wine, healed people, and raised folks from the dead. And then there was Moses, who led his people out of Egypt by dividing the Dead Sea, and the Buddha, who cut out a path of liberation by realizing the dreamlike nature of reality. Later, I found myself laughing with Mary Magdalene (who I call Mary Mags) and Milarepa, the great Tibetan saint and yogi of one of my root lineages, who obtained a staggering kind of enlightenment after struggling with an adolescent trauma and a few very bad decisions. There was also Machig Labdron, a female Tibetan master who offered the profound practice of Chö, and her guru Padampa Sangye, the Black Indian master to whom I have felt very close since one of my teachers confided how I reminded him of Sangye.

Then there were saints like Saint John of the Cross, who wrote "The Dark Night of the Soul," a poem that has shaped my relationship to the loneliness of spiritual awakening. And there was Saint Teresa of Avila, whose passion for life gave way to a deep devotion to the Divine and whom I still dance and sing with as she teaches me how to listen more deeply to the Divine in pleasure. Later in my life, there were teachers whom I considered saints as well.

And there were the great social change saints like W. E. B. Du Bois, Malcolm X, Dr. Martin Luther King, Jr., Harriet Tubman, and Toussaint L'Ouverture, all of whom, early in my life, led me to focus my labor on freedom. Later in my teens came Audre Lorde and the Black Panthers, and moving into my young adult years there was Essex Hemphill, James Baldwin, Dorothy Day, Marsha P. Johnson, Emma Goldman, bell hooks, Samuel Delaney, and others. These writers, thinkers, and activists helped me to understand the responsibility we have to help others experience freedom and safety and how to be Black and proud — to understand that the purpose of being Black is not to be consumed by trauma from perpetual anti-Black racism but to choose joy and care for myself and my community and to allow that joy to reflect back to our oppressors their own deep insecurities and traumas, so they can see and tend to them instead of weaponizing them against us.

Who are your saints or teachers? How have they inspired you? Do you really believe that you can do the same work they did? Can you listen to God or the Divine or your mind and spirit to do the work they did?

The New Saint

First, the work of the New Saint is grounded in radical dharma, teachings that emphasize that there is no ultimate liberation without a commitment to social liberation. To bypass the struggle of people surviving systems of violence in favor of an anesthetic life is itself an act of violence. The New Saint is a being in the world and in a body with identities. Liberation is allowing the confusion of our relative experience to point us into the clarity of ultimate experience while guiding others who suffer into that same realization without bypassing anything.

Second, the New Saint understands that this is a time of spiritual warfare and that spiritual warfare is a cosmic struggle between light and dark, or the struggle between liberation and delusion. The activities of the New Saint may look secular, but the work is driven by the spiritual commitment to liberate beings so that they might return to the experience of the essence, which is the most liberated nature of all phenomena, exhausting the illusion of dualities like light and dark or even comfort and discomfort. There is no secular path to ultimate liberation, and without belief in the essence, we find ourselves circling deeper into the suffering and darkness instead of being propelled out of it.

Third, as a spiritual project, the New Saint works between and/or in collaboration with the unseen world. The New Saint allies with their ancestors, deities, and other benevolent beings to further the work of liberation while strategizing against harmful forces. The New Saint is a spiritual warrior who learns to hold the complexities of multiple realms and realities, and who leverages this work to benefit others.

Fourth, the New Saint embraces—rather than bypasses—the complexity of identity. The New Saint uses their identities as a way for other beings to connect with them and as a way to build trust in liberation work. Identity becomes an expression of the sacred. The New Saint experiences the space and fluidity of identity. They know they are more than their identities while also embracing the realness of identities in the present moment.

Fifth, the New Saint, being situated in identities, speaks in the language of the times—the language that is accessible to people. There is no one way to communicate with beings. Beings are countless and diverse, and New Saints must speak the language of the people they are trying to free. It is hard to help people who can't relate to you or understand what you are trying to communicate.

Sixth, the New Saint is not afraid of taking risks, knowing that real liberation only happens through the discomfort of change—not through the comfort of staying safe. Discomfort forces us to grow, to think differently, and to develop a deeper sense of who we are and what we need. If you are afraid of making mistakes, then liberation work will be impossible.

Seventh, the New Saint is not fearless. On the contrary, the New Saint is full of fear. Fear is important because it is a sign that we are taking risks in the work. Over time, the New Saint can develop a spiritual confidence that helps them enter liberation work with faith that they have what they need to accomplish their goals. However, the New Saint learns to not react to fear and to instead choose courageousness, allowing clarity, love, joy, and compassion to guide liberation work.

Eighth, the New Saint will not free everyone, but they will, if they are authentic, inspire others to do the work of liberation. The New Saint's tradition is like a liberatory pyramid scheme where everyone wins. The New Saint may inspire a handful of people to do liberation work, and that handful may each inspire their own handful of people to do the work, and on and on, in the same way the Buddha emerged, embodying the work of liberation and therefore inspiring, to this day, countless beings to continue the work while everyone continues to be benefited and cared for.

Ninth, the New Saint is a prophet, which means that the New Saint reveals what is happening right now. Prophecy in this tradition is not about the future; it is about telling the truth of what is happening now in our relationships, collectives, and the world in general. Telling and revealing the truth is perhaps one of the hardest roles for anyone because most of us don't want to hear the truth and can be especially antagonistic toward truth tellers, as their work creates a lot of discomfort. However, there can be no liberation without the truth. Matter of fact, liberation is only the truth.

Tenth, the work of the New Saint is sacred. Sacredness is both the realization and the embodiment of the essence of all phenomena. In a Tantric worldview, all of the phenomenal world is sacred because everything is already liberated, as the nature of all phenomena is the union of emptiness, space, and energy potential. The New Saint's work of liberation is realizing the essence of everything and helping all beings experience that essence for themselves. This view of sacredness isn't about what is right or wrong but whatever helps us to experience liberation and realize the essence.

The Magic of the New Saint

In traditional Buddhist mythology, the bodhisattva, or the Buddhist saint, can sound like a superhero, as if they are Wonder Woman, the Black Panther, Sailor Moon, or Steven Universe and the Crystal Gems. I believe that our modern understanding of superheroes is very much in line with the spirit of the Buddhist saint. However, the notion of superpowers is distracting because the ultimate spiritual weapon of the Buddhist saint is not supernatural ability. Rather, the real superpower of the Buddhist saint is giving a shit—giving a shit is an expression of their bodhicitta, or their deep desire to help free people from suffering.

I am not saying that some—or perhaps many—of the great spiritual saints of the past did not possess abilities or gifts that could be considered extraordinary, otherworldly, or beyond the bounds of ordinary human capacity. Yet it wasn't their extraordinary powers that made them special. It was their dedication to helping people that made them extraordinary. Even though a New Saint can develop magical abilities such as healing, clairvoyance, other psychic skills, or even flying, the real magic of the New Saint is in the welding of two practices.

The first practice is the expression of what I call awakened care: an expression of love and compassion for themselves and others, an expression of joy all grounded in clarity. The most profound care we and others can experience is to be free from suffering and all the causes and conditions of suffering.

The second practice is the development of the capacity to disrupt habitual reactivity to everything that arises for us by choosing to experience what arises for us, which helps us transition into a place of responsiveness. Experiencing and then choosing how to respond with care is an expression of liberation. The New Saint can choose the most beneficial way to respond to anything.

Together, these two practices offer the New Saint the most profound way to reduce harm and violence, while cultivating transformative care with the goal of helping all beings get free.

Moreover, this magic makes it possible for the New Saint to do four primary activities: give a shit (about everyone's liberation), figure out their work (what they are supposed to do), do that work, and return to that work, again and again.

The New Saint as Ordinary

Because we love and venerate the saints, because we pray to them for blessings, developing deep devotion to their embodiment of the Divine, because we tend to elevate them to a place of godhood, it is easy to believe that they didn't start out just like us: ordinary, struggling, and basically human. Many of us believe that we can never experience the Divine like the saints and so we stop trying.

There's a popular saying in the circles in which I travel that goes, "Try Jesus, don't try me." Translation: "Don't fuck with me because I will fuck with you right back. Take it to Jesus, someone who will love and forgive, maybe turn the other cheek, because I am only going to return violence." Though I laugh when people say this, there is some real truth behind how we elevate saints and believe that they have this natural capacity to practice peace and patience, while we don't. So we give up and pass the work on to the saints.

I believe so much of the violence that seems to come out of Christian communities is based in this separation between Jesus and his followers. This separation has become so wide that it has become infected with a disbelief that Jesus cannot be touched, or his practice embodied. This disbelief feeds both our grief of never being able to be like Jesus and the rigid, ever-present weight of original sin. The tension from all this is experienced as shame manifesting as self-hate. When self-hate goes uncared for, it is weaponized and projected onto others, especially those who don't seem to suffer from the shame of not being good enough to embody Jesus.

The New Saint must remain ordinary and human, grounded in a strong relatability that radiates the sense that they are doing something that any person could learn to do. If the New Saint doesn't do this, then it becomes difficult for others to believe that they can embody the same expression if they train and commit to the path of liberation.

The Four Yogas of the New Saint

The New Saint's path expresses itself in four categories that I call the Four Yogas of the New Saint. I have been training in and practicing various forms of yoga for over twenty years now, and what is important to understand is that yoga is more than the physical postures (called asanas) or an exercise—it's a complex system of study and practice designed to help the practitioner or yogi experience liberation through the dissolution of duality. The word *yoga* itself means "union" or "to yoke," referring to the union of body and mind but conveying more generally the work of uniting what seems separate and disparate into an experience of wholeness. Once wholeness is achieved, the experience of oneness dawns.

Nothing can be freed in fragments, especially beings. These Four Yogas of the New Saint are areas of practice that guide the work of liberation for the New Saint and the communities they are working with, but they must be practiced together for liberation to happen. The yogas are dream, clarity, work, and care.

— THE YOGA OF DREAM —

When we talk about freedom, we are also talking about freeing our minds. This is the primary focus of Buddhism. All phenomena are energy. Our minds are intelligent energy, which is to say energy that has the capacity to be aware. Because of this intelligent energy, our minds have agency to shape themselves and other energies. Our minds have gotten distracted by the phenomena they have created, like thoughts and emotions, and we find ourselves shaped and fixed into this reality, which seems real and rigid. Freedom is remembering that everything fixed and solid is only so in our minds and that we can free ourselves at any time, if we remember.

The movement of freedom is more than just *becoming* free. It is also remembering the state of oneness and piercing the illusion of ego, or self-existing, which historically functions to keep us distracted. Oneness is returning back to the nature of the mind, which, in the New Saint's path, can be equated with returning back to the experience of God as the Mother or Father, or returning back to the experience of energy itself.

The yoga of dream for the New Saint is the realization that this reality that we live and struggle through is not our true home. It is a dream, an illusion, or even a figment of our imaginations. It is the matrix, and like the groundbreaking film of the same name, we are wandering through an experience of delusion, trying to break out of it into the real world. However, unlike the film, we are not trying to break out of this matrix into an even harsher reality. We are breaking out into freedom. Our current reality is an experience that we are trying to understand in order to figure out what freedom really is.

It is important to understand that the New Saint is trying to free everything, even things considered unconscious. To free unconscious phenomena, such as unconscious biases or narratives that are not true, means disrupting our perception of what things are so that our experience of phenomenal reality becomes transparent, fluid, and, basically, less real. This is how we experience freedom from the realness of things; when things are less real, we begin to feel more spacious and, therefore, freer.

The path of the New Saint is a path of freedom, not of comfort or of happiness. Freedom is transcending the experience of comfort and happiness to a state where there is no such thing as comfort or happiness. Freedom is simply being in a state beyond the dualism of happiness or sadness and comfort or discomfort.

— THE YOGA OF CLARITY —

Dharma is a Buddhist word that is often translated as "teaching" or "wisdom." I tend to think of it more as wisdom, or as the truth of how things actually are. All Buddhist teaching should lead us back to the fundamental wisdom that all things and phenomena are expressions of emptiness itself. There is no fundamental existence, no "there there," as Gertrude Stein once declared. Dharma is wisdom, and wisdom is an articulation of oneness beyond the illusion of phenomenal reality. It is the experience of the mind itself, which is the experience of conscious, unbound energy permeating everything. In the New Saint's path, I call wisdom clarity, and it is this clarity that makes the magic of the New Saint possible. Clarity is the ocean or wide-open fertile earth from which liberation is possible. We are already free; we just need to remember through the training of getting clear. This is the basic truth of the Buddhist path as well as the New Saint's path.

Ethics arise out of our training in clarity. The ethics of liberation include more than just an understanding of what is right and wrong. This binary expression of ethics is too rigid and lacks the potential for creativity. It creates the conditions for universal prescriptions of what is right and wrong and leads people to dominate others with their view of what's right, which is seen in systems like imperialism and colonialism. What is right for one person may not be considered right for another. Instead, the New Saint chooses what is conducive to achieving the dream of liberation for themselves. For instance, I personally do not need to set boundaries around recreational drugs and alcohol. I consume these in moderation, and the consumption doesn't disrupt my liberation work. However, many people do have to refrain from substance use, as it does create obstacles to their liberation and overall wellness. What is OK for me may not be OK for others. That's fine. In this particular ethic we all can figure out what is conducive to our liberation.

— THE YOGA OF WORK —

The yoga of work is the training the New Saint undergoes to free themselves and others. It is the essential labor that Carrie Sealine spoke of. It is loving in a way that is generous and spacious, not controlling or rigid. Further, it is figuring out the nuances of the work of liberation, knowing that each saint's individual work will look different because we all are starting out in different places. The path of liberation asks us to surrender to our work and to internalize the discipline of liberation work so it becomes as natural as breathing or thinking. To become the work is to become the embodiment of freedom and a source of inspiration for others.

Because the New Saint is also training in getting clear about why we suffer, they will understand that all beings are trapped in experiences of suffering they can be freed from with help. The New Saint understands that beings will never be truly safe, well, and resourced until they are completely free from suffering. This intention begins to awaken the wish for everyone to be free. The more the New Saint yearns for freedom, the more they are compelled to work for freedom for all. This deep compassion evolves into awakened care when they realize, through the deepening of clarity, that the essence of everything is already free. From this realization, they develop a fierce love for beings and a wish for them to be happy and free. The union of compassion with clarity and love evolves into awakened care. Basically, the New Saint gives a shit about how they and others are suffering and vows to disrupt the causes and conditions of that suffering.

Awakened care guides the vision or dream of the New Saint. The dream of everything being liberated from delusion is the labor of remembering that everyone and everything is already free. The New Saint works to first liberate themselves from their own delusion through developing awakened concern and then to inspire others to do the same work. All phenomenal reality is liberated when we realize the nature of everything is an expression of a fundamental boundless spaciousness and emptiness imbued with energy.

— THE YOGA OF CARE —

Without care there can be no work. Getting free is like preparing for a long road trip through the country of our delusions. We must pack our provisions, service the vehicle we are traveling in, plan the route, and reflect on who can help us in our travels. When the journey is overwhelming or exhausting, how do we rest? We will never get free or have the capacity to free others if we are not well enough ourselves.

I have seen so many people who are drowning in trauma and despair but are trying, nevertheless, to help others out from that experience of being overwhelmed. What always ends up happening is that they pull others deeper into the experience of being overwhelmed, or otherwise become more work for the people they were trying to help, who realize that they must figure out a way to support the person they thought was coming to help them. How can we save others from drowning if we can't swim? The path of the New Saint is about training to experience freedom for ourselves and then using our experience as a source of expertise, which in turn supports others in their work to get free. In all this labor, we engage in care to fuel the work.

Self-care is a buzzword that carries a lot of self-indulgent classist baggage. But in the context of the New Saint, self-care is how I figure out how to sustain my individual liberation work in order to support collective liberation work. Self-care is also collective care because the more I can understand how to care for myself, the more care I can offer to the collective while also opening to the care the collective is offering me in return.

In the spirit of Mother Fannie Lou Hamer, the great organizer and freedom fighter, at some point we have to get sick and tired of being sick and tired. We need to get fed up with the nonsense, chaos, and intricate folds of suffering to generate the fundamental revolutionary aspiration of the New Saint, which is to finally get the hell out of here. But when this aspiration arises, we don't just go anywhere; we start divesting our energy of the dramas that perpetually trap and drain us and start reinvesting in awakening ethical care and clarity. We not only start caring about others, we start caring about ourselves and what we need to get free. When we start caring about ourselves, we can finally establish the boundaries that make it safer for us to start really caring for others and what they need to get free.

The New Saint's Levels of Change

The work of the New Saint happens on multiple levels of change that must be engaged with for liberation to happen. These levels include the outer, inner, secret, and the super-secret. They are also expressed as commitments because until all four levels of change are engaged, no liberation is possible.

The outer level of change is the recognition of the phenomenal world and the basic reality of suffering and delusion, which I call the carceral state. When the New Saint works on this level, they make a commitment to the liberation of beings from systems of harm. The outer level of change is the dream of people being free from violent domination, having access to the resources they need to be well, and experiencing a basic level of happiness.

The inner level of change is the recognition of the inner experience of mind and body. It is an understanding that real change doesn't happen until our minds change, becoming clearer and more spacious, which shifts the experience of our bodies. The inner level of change is what fuels and inspires the work of the New Saint to help liberate others.

The secret level of change is the acknowledgment of the unseen world: the world of spirits, deities, personified energies, and other configurations of different dimensions and energetic planes. When the New Saint allies with the unseen world, they open themselves up to working in solidarity with unseen beings who also want us to be free. The New Saint is in solidarity with the unseen beings, helping them to get free as well.

The super-secret level of change is understanding that the nature of all phenomena, both seen and unseen, is an expression of emptiness within boundless space imbued with energetic potential. This level is the heart of the New Saint's personal experience of liberation, and it is this very subtle level that must be embodied for liberation to evolve beyond a dream and into a lived experience.

The Seven Sorrows of the New Saint

When I first started studying bodhisattva literature as an early practitioner, I was deeply moved by the bodhisattva vow not to leave any
being behind and how they commit to ushering all beings through
the door of enlightenment before they themselves enter. At the
same time, the tradition explained that beings were numberless
and that as long as one being was not free, there would be a carceral
state, even if it existed for one being only. Even the Buddha is said
to have entered Nirvana, returning to the great consciousness or
essence, without having freed all beings.

The sorrow of the New Saint is the experience of realizing that
the work of self- and collective liberation is driven by uncomfortable, confusing contradictions that we must embody. The New
Saint metabolizes the grief of dealing with these contradictions
and realizes that liberation is complex. These contradictions must
be tended to by mourning them and offering the discomfort space
while experiencing and releasing the sadness. This grief is what
I call the sorrow of the New Saint.

There are seven great sorrows of the New Saint: (1) we will leave
people behind, (2) much of our labor will go unseen, (3) we will be
misunderstood, (4) we will have to figure out what we need, (5) we
will disappoint people, (6) we will always embody the potential for
violence, and (7) we will make mistakes. These are the contradictions that we must tend to in order to do the work of navigating the
illogic of liberation and actually getting ourselves and others free.

— WE WILL LEAVE PEOPLE BEHIND —

We will not get everyone free because not all of us are ready to be
free. When someone isn't ready to be free, forcing them to do the
labor of awakening becomes an act of violence. We can neither
drag people to freedom nor scare them, manipulate them, intimi-
date them, or use one of our favorite collective techniques—yell at

them on social media—to get them to freedom. We are not Mother Harriet using our rifle to keep people in check as we journey to freedom. Training in awakened care is training in love, compassion, and joy, which helps us to get clear about what it takes to get people free. We can't do work for others. Each of us must choose liberation on our own terms, and in doing so, commit to our individual labor.

— MUCH OF OUR LABOR WILL GO UNSEEN —

When we think of the spiritual saint, we tend to think of people who are super famous, who sparked and led massive freedom movements that helped millions of people get access to resources they needed—people like Gandhi, Mother Teresa, or Dr. King. However, an overwhelming majority of people who are committed to this labor will not be known or celebrated. These beings figured out what their work was—work that may look very different from the work we are called to do. I say much of our labor will go unseen because often people around us may not consider our labor important or even labor at all. For example, one powerful expression of labor is prayer. Prayer is imperative in liberation work but is not so public or tangible. But we are being helped by countless beings at this very moment, and we may never be able to understand their labor, just as we are helping others around us without them understanding. I do not expect applause or a parade. My only expectation is to do the work of liberation for myself and others.

— WE WILL BE MISUNDERSTOOD —

When we choose to get free and vow to help others to get free, we are embracing a life that sets us apart from most beings. To choose freedom is to choose clarity, love, compassion, and joy; their manifestation as awakened care will influence us to make decisions that other people who have not made the same vows will not understand. When I made the decision to enter a long retreat in order to embody my commitment to this path, I was misunderstood by a lot of people in my life, especially close friends and family. My activist friends accused me of running away from the real work of freedom. One family member accused me of being selfish. Another told me I was joining a cult. Someone even accused me of having a mental illness. Most people felt like I was making an extreme decision that made no sense.

None of this bothered me because I was sure that this was what I needed to do to get free—and it was. People who are not trying to get free will not understand what the work looks like and will try to disrupt that work because they will think you are making a mistake. Your work may remind them of the work they are not doing and that may be painful for them—they may attempt to sabotage you. As my elders say, keep your mind stayed on freedom and trust your choices and instincts.

— WE WILL HAVE TO FIGURE OUT WHAT WE NEED —

The bodhisattva tradition promotes selflessness as a virtue, which is often misunderstood to mean that what we need is not important. What we need is vital. If we don't get our needs met, not only will it be difficult to meet the needs of others, but we may also start manipulating those we have committed to help to get our unmet needs fulfilled in ways that are harmful and unethical. On the New Saint's path, we must figure out what we need and acknowledge that our unmet needs create distractions for us and impact the work of liberation for others. This is one of the most challenging aspects of the New Saint's work. We must love ourselves enough to care for ourselves and, in doing so, reduce the labor we force others to do for us.

— WE WILL DISAPPOINT PEOPLE —

I often say that if I have not disappointed anyone in this work, something is wrong. When we commit to the path of liberation as an expression of care, people start expecting a lot from us. They will be disappointed when you maintain boundaries in order to make sure you have the space to be well. People (including dead folks!) will want you to always be accessible because you may very well be one of the only sources of authentic care they have. The eighth-century Indian philosopher and scholar Shantideva wrote in *A Guide to the Bodhisattva's Way of Life*, one of the most important bodhisattva tradition texts, that we should become both the doctor and the medicine for beings. This doesn't mean that our physical bodies and energy are always accessible, but that through prayer, we can send positive energy to other beings. There are a lot of people—both living and dead—who reach out to me, and while I can't show up for everyone, I can pray and ask other beings who may be better resources than I am to help those I can't get to.

— WE WILL ALWAYS EMBODY THE POTENTIAL FOR VIOLENCE —

The New Saint is committed to the reduction of violence. It is not possible to completely disrupt the harm that we can create for beings; even the Buddha was said to have stepped on a few insects in his lifetime. If we love someone, we will always have the potential to express violence. For example, if you are a parent and someone comes along and tries to hurt your child, you will probably not just let your child be hurt without protecting them and fighting off the aggressor. We must consider how some forms of violence can sometimes only be disrupted by other forms of violence. Sometimes I have had to raise my voice and cuss people out because that is the only thing that can reduce the harm that I or others around me are experiencing from an aggressor. There have been times that I have had to physically protect myself from the harm of others because I care for my well-being as much as other people's well-being. The New Saint chooses violence only because they care for themselves and others and know that to protect people, including aggressors, we sometimes have to meet violence with violence. In other words, the New Saint can choose violence out of deep care for everyone, including an aggressor, while being clear that violence isn't meant as retaliation; it's meant to reduce harm.

— WE WILL MAKE MISTAKES —

We can't be afraid to make mistakes—we will inevitably make a lot of them. As one of my teachers Khenpo Tsultrim Gyamtso once taught, "Making mistake after mistake I walk the unmistaken path." This is not a path of perfection; it is a path of learning how to reduce harm and deepen care as a means of getting free. We learn from the mistakes we make. We have to understand that the carceral state is in perpetual chaos, and it takes tremendous effort to navigate this chaos. As we do so, we may not be fully aware of everything that's happening. We can only make choices with the information we have at the moment. Our meditation practice is important because it gradually deepens our awareness and clarity. Clarity arises out of learning from mistakes as well as not being afraid to make them. Holding the discomfort of mistakes can teach us deeper awareness and empathy on the path toward liberation.

The Profound Paths of Werk and Work

For the New Saint to commit to liberation, they have to get clear about the work it takes to even attempt a feat like this. The work is the labor we do to get free while helping others get free, which includes getting clear about what we are working for and making sure our work is full of care that makes the work sustainable.

I start by closing my eyes and feeling countless Black gay and queer men around me snapping their fingers, yelling for me to "Werk, Bitch!" I feel the snaps as swirls of quick jagged energy. I ask what the snapping means, and I am answered with rounds of "Bitch, don't act stupid! Yo ass knows." I do know.

In Buddhist Tantra, snapping can signal the ending of a practice or ritual or be used to ward off negative energies.

When the groundbreaking documentary *Tongues Untied*, directed by the ancestor Marlon T. Riggs, found me in my late teens, I learned that our snaps mean many things. Black gay and queer men celebrate and acknowledge each other through snapping. We set boundaries through snapping. We weaponize snapping as a warning when shit gets real. With a snap, we slay the shit that gets in the way of our joy. We channel our fierceness into the snap, letting all worlds and realms know that we ain't here for the bullshit of carceral logic. My ancestors and my community are showing up with me and around me to protect me and help me remember that I belong to beings that want me to be free—who are demanding nothing less than for me to meet the ugliness of this world and life with fierceness.

I think about the hit show *Pose* and its popularization of the slogan and mantra, "Live. Werk. Pose." The character Pray Tell, portrayed by the incomparable Billy Porter, proclaims it in the opening credits. This declaration is about more than ballroom culture, a rejoinder to the ways we have been traditionally restricted from full access to mainstream spaces; it is a commandment on how to thrive when a culture is trying to annihilate you. When we "live," we are choosing and offering our most authentic selves to the world despite the ways in which we are retaliated against. To "live" is to choose what pleases us, to choose our joy, and to link that joy to thriving and to how that thriving helps us get free.

The *werk* is the practice of choosing freedom. It is the labor and struggle of embodying joy that leads to the *pose*, which is the posture we take that radiates our choice to be free. It is the posture of resisting the violence of people and communities who would rather annihilate us than hold and care for their own pain of being trapped. It is the culmination of rigorous exercises of awakened care that becomes the embodiment of fierceness. Because of what we must do, we learn to live fiercely, werk fiercely, and pose fiercely.

Fierceness

In Tantric Buddhism, wrathful expressions have nothing to do with anger or rage but are instead the most powerful form of compassion because they name suffering regardless of how we feel about it. We spend a lot of time and energy hiding away from our suffering, so being the recipient of such potent compassion from someone feels uncomfortable. It can feel like the cruelest thing for someone to name an experience you don't want to deal with. But despite how it feels, we won't ever get free until we deal with it. Though it often feels like hell, it is a transformative offering of compassion from someone who wants us to be free.

In the path of the New Saint, the most powerful expression of awakened care is fierceness. Like compassion and wrath, fierceness is the true potency of awakened care because it tells a truth that we don't want to deal with. Fierceness is the expression of the deepest belief that everyone deserves to be free regardless of who they are or what they have done. It is a posture that says, *I deserve a right to exist, to take up space, and to embody my most authentic self, especially when this expression does not harm me or anyone else.* Fierceness refuses compromise or negotiation because it is responding to the suffering that comes from not being free. It is so precise and clear that it feels like getting cut by a razor. It says that everything deserves care, and everything deserves to be free, regardless of how you or anyone feels about it. The snap is the physical expression of fierceness that emphasizes the boundary we protect to ensure the survival of ourselves and our communities. But it also says, "If you are not trying to hurt me, you can practice your freedom as well, but if you are trying to erase me because you can't handle what my truth reflects to you about your pain, you will be disrupted or slayed." Snap! Thus, the snap is a gesture of slaying that releases the power of fierceness to disrupt the rigidity of the carceral state and begins to restore balance through boundaries.

Werk and Work

The carceral state is an expression of chaos and rigidity. This is to say that we don't have much control over the workings of the state. The only thing we have agency over is our reactivity to the chaos, which is the path of the New Saint. We manage and to some extent balance the chaos through developing clarity. Rigidity arises because we find ourselves trapped in the helplessness of the chaos. When I know this and can remember this, my relationship to the carceral state can be an experience of liberation because when I transition from reactivity to responsiveness, the state no longer dictates who I am, and I can start directing my energy toward liberation. When I forget this and start habitually reacting to the chaos, I am consumed by the chaos. This consumption means that the chaos, with this ambiguity and lack of order, begins to define me, resulting in my loss of agency and, therefore, freedom.

There is a difference between werk and work. Both are practices of choosing freedom; however, werk is the practice of choosing freedom by channeling fierceness into the chaos and restoring clarity and fluidity. When we are told to werk, we are being reminded that we have agency to change our relationship to the chaos, manifesting as any form of violence. For my ancestors and community, werk is how we named the chaos and the violence and chose to be in a responsive relationship to them. To know and name the chaos is to find the ground to stabilize ourselves. Once stabilized, we can move in the direction that we need to move in. When I werk, I am remembering that I am not the violence that is attempting to shape me. I then move into a responsive relationship where I can choose to meet and disrupt the violence.

Work, on the other hand, is the practice itself—the basic labor of developing awareness as well as awakened care to cultivate clarity and reduce harm, pointing us toward social and ultimate liberation. Work is how we develop the capacity to become aware of how we show up, how to hold space for and respond to our experiences, and how to be our most natural selves, all of which support the awakening of care and freedom from the carceral state.

I often say that if we don't do our work, we become work for others. If I don't do the labor of understanding how I am impacting relationships because of my lack of clarity, I force others to support me, often without their clear consent. I create more emotional labor for people because my lack of clarity and unwillingness to hold space for myself creates tension in relationships that others have to process and deal with.

Another way to think about the relationship between werk and work is to understand that for me to werk, or to have the capacity to transform the brutality of surviving into thriving through fierceness, I must have a solid foundation of work that has been the training in awareness and awakened care.

In the past, I have differentiated formal and informal practice, teaching that formal practice is intentional and takes place when we sit on our cushions, rehearsing practices in a workshop mentality, and informal practice is taking what we rehearse out to the main stage of life and putting it into use. Now I've changed my mind. I believe that informal practice is formal practice as well because the practice of surviving and thriving in the world is the formal work. Practice is practice. We are dealing with real shit on or off the meditation cushion.

On the outer level of practice, we are training in awareness, or developing the capacity to see and understand how we are showing up in the world and how that showing up impacts others. Once we have cultivated some awareness, we are able to sink into the inner level of practice, which is holding space for what we have become aware of while disrupting reactivity and shifting into responsiveness. Once we have agency in responding to what arises in our experience, we can rest in the secret level of practice, which is simply being.

My Practice

I began my formal practice in Buddhism with basic mindfulness meditation. I didn't like practicing; meditation was hard and the time I had to devote to it was time taken away from things I loved to do, like getting in trouble! I kept returning to my meditation practice because I noticed how much it was helping me hold space for the suffering in my experience.

Back then, what helped me to keep returning to practice that didn't seem fun was learning how to internalize discipline. Internalizing discipline meant that I disrupted thinking about how much I disliked practice and just practiced. I understood that the real issue was my thinking and not the practice itself. So, when it came time for a formal practice session, I noticed my aversive thoughts and then offered those thoughts space by not reacting to them. This space gave me the room to start my practice This method of internalizing discipline was itself practicing.

My primary ethic is to reduce harm against myself and others by learning how to get clear and develop care for all beings. My primary goal is to experience both social and ultimate liberation. My ethic and goal are my general work in this life and, frankly, all my lives. Beyond this general work, I have specific work to do that is perhaps unique to my situation and identities.

For instance, racism isn't my problem; therefore, it isn't my work. I know this sounds like a confusing statement. What I mean is that anti-Black racism, specifically, is expressed by white supremacy. This form of racism and racism in general is imposed on me even though the imposition has meant self-identifying with this violence as internalized anti-Blackness. Uprooting this internalized violence is definitely my work. Although all Black and Brown people deal with the violence of white supremacy, we do not have the capacity to turn it off. However, we do have the capacity to strategize against and disrupt the impact of most forms of white supremacist violence. By creating and practicing individual and collective forms of care and love that resist harmful narratives of inferiority, we can create boundaries limiting the impact of violence on our bodies as well as on our hearts and minds.

However, one problem that *is* mine to work on is patriarchy. As a cisgender man, I have been conditioned into a system that on the outside overprivileges my body and gender performance but at its core expresses a rigidity that makes it difficult for me to relate to my body as something that is fluid and organic. Some of the violence I have carried out in the past has been a conditioned reaction to the rigidity of patriarchy. To undo this conditioning, I choose fluidity over rigidity, emotional labor for myself and others over shutting down. This is my work and the work of all transgender and cisgender men.

When I werk, I am showing up against cultural and social pressure to hide or reduce myself because my authentic self does not fit into dominant standards of what is acceptable. In the past, I have often taught radical presence, the idea that I have a right to be my most authentic self as a spiritual teacher and as a person. I have a right to resist forces that seek to silence me, and I commit to receiving fair and reasonable feedback from my community if my showing up authentically creates harm for myself and others. If I am not creating harm, then I have a right to be unapologetically out and proud. Through fierceness, the hate and shame projected onto me are slayed. Awakened care is my weapon and armor, and my snap is how I cut through erasure and set my boundaries.

Werking and its expression of fierceness may seem aggressive, but there is a difference between aggression and confidence. Sometimes we read some behaviors as aggressive because they push against the shame that prevents us from living out loud. We also read aggression into confidence because we may not understand the energy it takes to survive in harmful contexts. If you do not experience harm for just being, then the context was created for your survival and comfort. Anyone who seems to challenge that comfort is labeled dangerous.

This is not to say that werking is not linked to trauma, because it is. Surviving systemic violence leaves scars, and the pain of these scars, if not tended to, can manifest as anger, which arises from the tension of being hurt and not knowing how or wanting to care for the hurt. So werking can become consumed by the reactivity to the pain, resulting in wanting others to hurt as much as we do instead of maintaining boundaries. In this case, our motivation is to get away from the pain instead of taking care of the pain and trying to establish the space to care for ourselves.

Struggle

Practice is not easy and often involves a fair amount of struggle. Many of us are not interested in struggling, but in my practice, I appreciate struggle because it is how I register the effort I invest into getting free. More than that, it is the process through which I get clear. Struggle is the experience of truth working its way into my body and mind, rubbing down the jagged, rough edges of my delusion. I believe that this is an experience that we all move through in practice and continue experiencing until complete liberation.

We each struggle individually to experience wellness. Living isn't easy. However, not all of us understand what it means to struggle as part of a community that has been disenfranchised from the necessary resources we need to survive. In collective struggle, we learn how to bridge our individual practice with collective practice. In that bridging, there can be tremendous mutual benefit. When we struggle, we develop a profound resiliency that helps us move through the discomfort of gathering resources and being free while focusing on cultivating values of collective care in the struggle. People who have not experienced collective struggle do not know collective resiliency, nor will they understand real solidarity. These folks are not suited to lead justice movements.

Nor do I trust spiritual leaders who have not experienced collective struggle. Even though their work and teaching may be authentic, offered straight out of their lineages, I do not trust that they have tested the durability of those teachings against the tension of collective struggle. I don't believe that anyone can claim the identity of a spiritual leader if they are not committed to the collective struggles of both social and ultimate liberation. If you understand collective struggle, then your teaching must be attuned to the collective as much as it is attuned to the individual.

A resilient teaching meets the complexities of the world, the trickery of the carceral state, and is focused on freedom. A resilient teaching is timeless and durable: it's good now, tomorrow, next year, in the next century, in the next life, and all the way up until final liberation. Resilient teaching is rooted in serious practice and is derived from a long lineage in which many others have practiced and gotten free. Although the dharma may embrace the cultural aesthetics of the times, it is still authentic. Good, clean water is still good whether it exists in an uncontaminated, pure spring or is bottled in hip packaging. The water will still tend to your need to be hydrated.

None of my work or teaching has come easy. It has emerged from decades of wrestling with these ideas, testing them out, getting pissed at them, cussing them out, and finally practicing patience to feel how this teaching has been integrated into my body and mind. When I share this teaching, I want you to feel the work that has gone into metabolizing it. I want you to get something that has been worn out and broken in, something that has worked its way through me. In this way, you trust that you are getting something that has at least worked for one other person.

In the past, I have been told that I may overvalue struggle. Struggle is the effort we put into getting somewhere or getting something. The energy of the word arises from the resistance we face when trying to make something happen that is being impeded by other forces. To achieve ultimate liberation, we must contend with the force of delusion, which makes it difficult for us to know what we are trying to make happen and disrupts our work to get free. Struggle isn't pleasant, but as long as our goal is freedom, it is generative.

Reflections on Exhaustion

When Mother Fannie Lou Hamer spoke about being sick and tired of being sick and tired, she was expressing a basic weariness from the trauma caused by years of sharecropping in Mississippi along with the violence she and others survived from White folks as they organized to get the right for Black folks to vote. From this core exhaustion she spoke of how the only solution for the suffering was change. I believe the change she spoke about was both disrupting white supremacy and Southern Jim Crow culture as well as centering the work of healing for Black folks. I think when those of us who are descended from oppressed people talk about being tired, we can easily be consumed by the experience of fatigue. But the labor Mother Fannie was doing for us was urging us to stop accepting the fatigue and start doing the work to change the shit that lay at the root of our depletion.

Sometimes I go through periods where the only mantra I have left to offer is "I'm so fuckin' tired." The mantra is a release and truth telling of what is happening for me at the moment. I am tired.

So fucking tired. I feel the exhaustion in my body, everything becomes heavy and uncooperative, and I am dragging myself around the house trying to do the basics of cleaning myself and eating. I know this fatigue comes from what I must do to get free, which is the depletion from all the emotional labor I am being called to do for many beings right now.

Most times I just want to stay in bed or lie on the couch in the stillness and quiet of my home, not bothering to answer calls and texts, ignoring knocks at the door, just lying and resting, dreaming of feeling energized. It is at these times when being around people scares me because of the emotional labor I am forced to do around them.

I don't even want to be writing right now. Having written this, I suddenly want to go to sleep. I notice this reaction of wanting to sleep when I am in the process of heavy emotional labor. Naming the reality of anything is emotional labor. We often avoid the truth of things because we know on some level that relating to the truth will take work. Coming back to truth means having to hold space for and metabolize uncomfortable energies and experiences.

Guidelines for Liberatory Work

In Matthew 13:33, Jesus teaches that heaven is like yeast that a woman is mixing into flour. Of course, yeast is a leavening agent that helps bread to rise. Yeast itself is a tiny microorganism that multiplies rapidly, feeding off sugar and giving off carbon dioxide. In bread making, as yeast gives off gas, it is caught in the gluten of the bread, which results in a light, fluffy texture in the finished product.

There is another story from Buddhist scripture about a sitar, or lute, player coming to the Buddha for advice on practice. The Buddha asks the musician what happens if the strings of his instrument are too tight, and the musician responds by saying that the strings will break. The Buddha then asks what happens if the strings are too loose, and the musician responds by saying that they will produce no sound. By the end of the conversation, the Buddha helps the musician understand that the strings, like practice, can't be too tight or too loose.

When I interpret these scriptures together, it helps me to understand that practice is something that gets kneaded into our lives and slowly saturates everything, yielding a life that is nurturing and sustaining. However, we must be concerned with balance, knowing how and when to practice in ways that are conducive to our well-being and freedom.

However, there are two considerations for practice that have taken me years to figure out. First, it is important to note that learning how to do something well isn't the same thing as mastery. There are so many certification courses that train people in everything from mindfulness to healing. Sometimes we think we can go to a few weeks of training, get certified, and be teachers or experts in these practices. But to be a teacher means acquiring mastery, and mastery can't be acquired in a few weeks. Mastery develops over years of dedicated study and practice. Mastery also requires that the practice be deeply embodied—we become the practice. In my professional life, I don't teach practice; I share the ways in which practice is shaping how I relate to myself and to the world around me.

Second, it can become easy to mistake collecting practices as the practice and work itself. As a young practitioner, it felt exciting to be exposed to all kinds of practices in Tibetan Buddhism. I loved attending teachings with different lamas, and I especially loved reading every book that I could get my hands on. As I have mentioned before, what I didn't love was doing the work of practice. Getting all these teachings, doing all the reading, and feeling deeply inspired were essential in helping me practice, but at some point, in order for these teachings to change us and point us toward freedom, we must do the work and engage in the struggle of getting clear. Once we start to get clear, this clarity becomes a gift that yields more clarity and deeper insight. I know a lot of brilliant thinkers in the contemplative traditions, but not all of them possess the clarity of practice, which might otherwise point them to freedom.

THE PRACTICE OF PRACTICE

Here, I offer a few guidelines from my practice. They are by no means comprehensive. I encourage you to use these guidelines and adapt them to support your personal and community practice.

Be Clear about Intentions

We should always start out with a clear sense of why we are practicing. My intention lines up with my overall ethic. So, my intention when doing any practice is to reduce harm against myself, cultivate awakened care, and get myself and all beings free from suffering, which is the intention of the New Saint. My intention is never to be happy or comfortable. Those experiences come as a result of the higher intention to achieve liberation.

Call in Support

I am a big believer in asking for help and relying on the support of both seen and unseen communities of beings who love and want me to be free. When I start practice, I first call in the earth, along with the beings of my unseen communities like my ancestors, teachers, elders, deities, and members of my spiritual lineages. Feeling their presence around me helps me feel held and guided. Sometimes, you can ask beings to practice with you. There are many beings around us who are still trying to get free through practice in the spirit world.

Choose the Appropriate Practice

It may take time to find the right practices or tradition for you. Start with practices that interest you and go deeper.

Find authentic teachers that hold the practice and lineage it comes from. It is also OK to shop around until something seems interesting to you as well. However, in the New Saint's tradition, we are looking for practices that link social and ultimate liberation, practices that incorporate freedom and agency of the body, practices that support collective work (and werk), and practices that emphasize freedom over happiness and comfort.

Commit to the Practice

We have to commit to the practice. It is easy to pick a practice, work with it for a short time, and feel like it isn't doing anything for us. However, the most important practices will require us to dedicate a lot of time to them in order for us to experience their impact. Coming from cultures that are focused on instant gratification and results makes this difficult. Real liberatory practice takes a substantial investment of effort and care. I practiced meditation for over ten years before I felt what is called meditative stability—a feeling that my awareness was steady enough to maintain focus and presentness at will.

Celebrate Progress

Pay attention to the fruits of practice or the positive results of doing the practice. Over time, positive things begin to happen. In my earlier meditation practice, I noticed that I was more aware of what I was feeling and experiencing in my body. After years of being unaware, I was thrilled to be experiencing this. I allowed myself to celebrate, and that celebration offered me more motivation to keep going deeper into the practice.

Release the Care

At the end of any practice, it is important to release all the positive energy we have cultivated and direct it to people and communities that could use this energy for their care and liberation work. This release is a way to close practice, as it helps us remember our intention as well. This release doesn't deplete the impact of our work for ourselves but rather intensifies it because it invites us into expansion rather than contraction. Freedom is never experienced in contraction.

What I know now is that our practice must evolve to meet the chaos of the time we are living in. What many of us may be realizing is that no matter how hard we thought we were practicing, we are being called to practice harder and deeper, to peel back these superficial layers of performativity and surrender into the struggle of real engagement with the complexity of our hearts, minds, and bodies. This kind of real authentic practice is messy and unruly. There will not be opportunities for social media postings or self-congratulatory moments. There will, however, be moments of subtle awakening and gratitude where we will be thankful for having the capacity to offer this work to ourselves, which will be the same work we offer to our communities. You will learn to hold on as I have held on, get fierce when needed, cry when it is called for, and keep moving further into the awakening that I call liberation.

Figuring Out Your Work

I am often asked about ways to figure out what our specific work is. My main strategies have been praying and asking for direction, leaning into what feels difficult, and getting feedback from people around me that love me. I have compiled other practices below:

- If it feels easy, it's probably not your work.
- Lean toward what feels hard.

- Listen to others around you and get feedback from people who know and love you.
- Hold space for the energy of urgency. Holding space lets us practice agency over urgency, which gives us space to make wiser, more appropriate decisions instead of being pushed into reacting.
- Take an inventory of your talents and try to align your work with your talents.
- Figure out what you love to do and see if your work can extend from what you love.
- Pray and ask for signs leading you to your work.
- Read the signs. What is the phenomenal world pointing you toward?
- Look around you. What do you think needs support?
- Look at where you've been put. Look around the spaces and places you naturally haunt. What is there to do around you?
- What work feels right? How does it feel in your body? In your mind? Do you feel like you have fallen into a groove?
- Does the work you've chosen feel as if it's natural? Can you envision expressions of the work into the future? Is there a sense of joy? Satisfaction? Gratitude?
- What is your basic ethic in life and does your work line up with this ethic?
- Look at the work others are doing. Which work resonates with you? If someone is doing something you vibe with, try to learn from them in formal or informal relationships.
- Does your work feel generative and restorative?

Loneliness of the Work

It seems that I am both lonely and alone. Being alone is a conscious choice. This choice is an expression of my agency. It is what I choose in order to create the space I need to take care of myself. It is a decision to have space to listen to myself, to take breaks from the constant caretaking and emotional labor that I am always doing for many beings, especially right now as I write this.

This aloneness is a boundary that I not only establish with the world and all beings but one that I establish with myself as well. It is the commitment to choose myself and to take care of my needs in ways no other being will ever be able to do. This is the labor of figuring out that I am not in relationship to other beings' needs or projections but in relationship to what I need. Choosing aloneness reminds me that though I belong to others, I still belong to myself, and because of this belonging to myself, I am accountable for my own healing.

Choosing aloneness doesn't mean that I disconnect from the experiences of others, especially their suffering. I don't think I will ever have the capacity to forget the suffering of others. But what it does mean is that I can notice and hold space for others' suffering without trying to absorb it into my experience.

Sometimes aloneness means that I am living outside of people's experience, which again is a risk because it intensifies the likelihood of people not doing the labor of getting curious and attempting some level of empathy to relate to others. Without that connection, I can be misunderstood and become an object of fear, and I am more likely to be annihilated.

Most people do not choose loneliness. Instead, loneliness chooses them, and their experience is one of being consumed by it. The suffering of loneliness is compounded when we believe we have no agency in relation to it. Choosing aloneness is more than just deciding to be alone. It is also the practice of choosing loneliness, of saying to it, *Since you are here, I might as well choose you.* It is a mind trick, really. It tricks us into believing that we want the experience, which in turn bolsters our belief in an inherent agency to choose what we are experiencing.

Sometimes I think that loneliness must be pain's longing for stillness—its longing to let go of needing to feel so raw, to rest in the essence of itself, the essence of holding on and letting go at the same time. Perhaps this is the subtle burn of loneliness: wanting more than is needed but knowing one has what is needed at the same time and being absolutely helpless in the peaceful reconciliation of the two. Finding balance between reaching and contentment can make the experience of loneliness exhausting.

Spiritual Loneliness

In the words of Dorothy Day, the great activist and cofounder of the Catholic Worker Movement, spiritual loneliness feels like a "long loneliness." This one phrase completely articulated an experience that had been with me for many years. It spoke to me of the distance I felt between myself and others as I chose a life of service. It was the loneliness I felt engaging in a lifestyle that was so radically countercultural and misunderstood.

When you start working to get free, you will experience the most intense loneliness because you will realize that most people around you will not understand what you are beginning to work toward. They, like you at one point, are self-identifying with the experience of incarceration, which is the experience of contraction. When you choose freedom, you choose spaciousness, which will make you look suspicious and make you dangerous because you remind everyone that they are complicit in their contraction into incarceration.

Spiritual loneliness means I am living within God, which means that I am touching into the formless expression of love taking me out of a linear timeline. I am living in the past, present, and future all at once but still trying to stay in relationships, get work done, have fun, and eat dinner and trying all the while not to alarm people around me as I struggle to communicate that though it seems like I am here, I am really not and that the complete truth is that there was never a "here" to be at. Spiritual loneliness is the work of living through the illusion of there not being a "here."

And the great loneliness is that others may not understand what freedom is because all they have ever known has been endless delusion, endless suffering, and endless shame. If you are not swallowed by suffering, you will be misunderstood, and that misunderstanding may mean violence, death, and erasure. Who can bear that kind of long loneliness?

This is the loneliness of the New Saint.

Getting Free

The New Saint's end goal is liberation for themselves, all beings, and all phenomena. Everything must be freed. The cultivation and unification of clarity, love, compassion, and joy point the New Saint toward freedom and unlock the cage that keeps us bound in the delusion called the carceral state. The work of freedom is the work of awakening from delusion.

When I say "freedom" or "liberation," I am talking about our fundamental capacity to choose responsiveness over reactivity. Experiencing the sensations of our minds and bodies reduces reactivity and allows us to experience fluidity. When there is more fluidity, there is more potential for care, and that care helps us to reduce violence against ourselves and others. Freedom is the agency to choose how we want to be in relationship with ourselves and the world around us. This project has been at the heart of my practice for over twenty years now.

Levels of Freedom

The experience of freedom is complex and multilayered. In my description of these layers, I tend to focus on individual experience, as there is no collective liberation without individual liberation. Understanding freedom for oneself makes it possible to understand and engage in liberatory work for the collective. How can we save others if we haven't learned how to save ourselves?

— OUTER FREEDOM —

On the individual level, outer freedom is social freedom. It is having access to all the resources I need to experience wellness, safety, community belonging, and happiness. It is possessing the agency to make choices about the care I need and how I wish those around me to relate to me. This level of freedom necessitates reducing harm to myself and others.

We can reduce harm and violence, but we cannot annihilate them. We form community by being in power with ourselves and others, while being sensitive to how we dominate others. We have agency to determine what we need with the support of the community, and the community helps us discern when we are harming others or are not adhering to an ethic of care for self and community.

On the community level, outer freedom means that the community has agency to determine what it needs and has access to what it needs. Individuals are held, loved, and given space to meet their needs within and with the support of the community. It means being able to live in harmony with other communities and not feeling dominant or feeling the need to dominate. There is room for cooperation and understanding. Resources are not only shared but also made appropriate for the needs of the community consuming them.

— INNER FREEDOM —

On the individual level, inner freedom means that I am in a responsive relationship with everything that arises. I can experience my mind. Everything is offered space and is cared for. Awakened care is the bridge that allows me to be gentle, and it is the bridge that connects me to the experience of others.

Inner freedom is choosing to abide in the space that arises between a stimulus and a reaction. Freedom from the carceral state means that we learn to use this space to migrate from reactivity to responsiveness. In that space, we have a chance to gain perspective about everything because we have the chance to decenter ourselves. We let go of focusing on one tree in order to get a sense of the whole forest.

Moreover, when we understand how that space points us to the ultimate nature of everything, we begin to experience ultimate freedom. Enlightenment is the realization that everything is an illusion, including the sense of a self. When the sense of self is realized to be an illusion, we are freed from our compulsory relationship with it.

On the community level, inner freedom is the capacity for communities to collectively understand how experiences arise for individuals and how those experiences collect and become collective experiences. When a community experiences inner freedom, it chooses how it responds to those collective experiences. The experiences of the individual are in conversation with the experiences of the community and promote reconciliation. There is space for change to happen, and it is from this same space that a community can choose revolution to bring about sweeping change.

— SECRET FREEDOM —

On the individual level, secret freedom means that I understand the nature of things beyond duality, binaries, or labeling. Not only do I know the nature of things, but I also begin to embody this realization. The world and all phenomena comprise an expansive ocean of emptiness, space, and energy potential. This fundamental expression is what has been called the nature of mind, buddha nature, or the essence, God, the Mother, the Father, and the sacred unarticulated Divine. Arriving here is a homecoming. We return to what we are and where we started.

The secret experience of freedom is the realization that I have always been free. I arose free as intelligent energy radiating from the essence of God, and my labor is to return back to that energy, which is a matter of remembering. On the community level, secret freedom is the collective realization that there was no individual to begin with, nor is there any such thing as a community.

In the end, we must understand that our feelings about freedom have nothing to do with freedom. Freedom isn't a feeling; it is as much a state of being and experiencing as joy. To be free is to remember that I have always been free. The real labor of liberation is acknowledging that there is always a choice, even though I must work to get back to that choice.

The Carceral State

Ever since I can remember, I have been trying to get free. My first anxiety was that the outer world—the world of things and beings—was caging me in. Life and living felt so full of suffering: murder, genocide, slavery, famine, war, hate, subjugation, and exploitation. I felt the terror, sadness, despair, and hopelessness of struggling in a world that made being happy, safe, and resourced an epic struggle. So, I started working toward something different.

It wasn't until I began practicing and studying Buddhism that I began to understand what samsara was. I find samsara to be a beautiful word. It drips off the tongue like honey, but it is, ironically, far from sweet. Strictly speaking, samsara is the endless cycle of birth, death, and rebirth that is fueled by craving, delusion, and hate, which are all derived from misunderstanding. I often define samsara as the expression of delusion, which codifies individual and collective trauma into a shared systemic reality. I use the term *systemic* because delusion creates an order that is predictable and rigid.

Over the years, as my practice of abolition has deepened into a practice of spiritual abolition, I have begun to relate to samsara as the carceral state. Typically, social and political abolition understands the carceral state as an extension of the prison industrial complex in which vulnerable communities are subjected to policies and practices of control, surveillance, and hyperpolicing. Samsara is similar; all beings struggle with incarceration, or lacking agency within a state of delusion that intensifies our suffering. Delusion polices our efforts to get free by instilling fear and distraction.

The carceral state is maintained and strengthened through the mind. The more we begin to believe in it, the more rigid it feels. When I begin to understand the nature of all phenomena by practicing meditation, the carceral state is disrupted. Its disruption is experienced as the capacity to feel the illusionary translucent quality of everything. Everything feels less real and more fluid, spacious, and malleable.

The fundamental violence of the state is rooted in our misunderstanding of the nature of the phenomenal world. We keep relating to everything as real and permanent, when in fact it is an expression of space, emptiness, and energy potential. We intuitively understand that we are free but have been distracted by illusion. Regardless of whether we are conscious of this or not, our deepest longing is to remember our liberation, but if we are not actively working to get free, then in a way we are consenting to the delusion of the state.

Trauma and the Carceral State

The carceral state is an expression of both individual and collective trauma. We have experienced a deep woundedness from forgetting that we are already free. Tension arises first from our deep unconscious longing to return to our liberated experience and, second, from the confusion of not knowing how to return to liberation. The reactivity to this tension is what has been normalized as reality. We have become trapped in this experience of incarceration.

But there is a second layer of incarceration as well. We are also reacting to tension arising from the contradictions and extremism of the phenomenal world. We unconsciously know this reality isn't happening, but it seems so real. We struggle to break our attachment and reactivity to the illusion of realness. When we have no awareness of the choices we are making, and all our agency is exhausted by wrestling with delusion, it is hard to understand freedom, let alone do the work to get free.

In spiritual abolitionism, samsara is the perpetual carceral state in which delusion feeds the trauma that drives the experience of captivity. Captivity is thus rendered and lived as "normal" or "how things are." Trauma is the cycle of choosing the delusion and confusing it for freedom. Or in other words, the carceral state is one reaction after another based on the belief that there is no other choice to make.

Complexity experienced as contradiction is an expression of the carceral state. We spend a lot of time struggling to understand what's happening and how it's impacting us and others. We believe that to know is to be free. However, freedom is more than knowledge. It is also understanding complexity and learning how to respond to it in a way that helps us get free. We won't figure out everything because not everything will make sense. Part of navigating the state is learning how to hold space for contradictions without being distracted by them while directing our work toward getting clear about our own experiences and who we are.

How We Get Free

The work of the New Saint is to realize that all phenomena are inherently empty. This realization is possible only when we begin to develop an authentic care for all phenomena. This care functions as acceptance, which dissolves our fixation on the belief that everything is real and solid, which helps us to relax and start connecting to the space that is holding everything. When we start experiencing spaciousness, we can respond to trauma rather than habitually react to it. For most of us, that can be enough to feel balanced, safe, and happy.

There are no shortcuts here. There is no all-powerful and omnipresent gatekeeping god to negotiate with. No one is going to save you. No one is going to save me. You are saved through your own labor with the support and inspiration of your community and other individuals who embody liberated living. We all must do the same labor to get free, regardless of what we have survived. This is the labor of the New Saint's liberation, and we must know that not everyone will consent to the work. However, when you step on this path, you are committing yourself to this labor and view. If this view does not win, you are not really interested in liberation.

You may have often said that life isn't fair. This is true; life isn't fair. The carceral state is not based on justice or virtue. It is a fundamental expression of delusion that has indoctrinated our minds, bodies, speech, actions, dreams, and imaginations. We must give up on the idea of justice and commit to liberation, as some of our ideas about justice are not about complete liberation but the illusion of universal comfort for all beings. Freedom and comfort are two different things. To aim for liberation is to transcend the limitations of comfort and return back to who we really are: expressions of the same great consciousness.

Reactivity and Violence

When we are lost in delusion, reactivity will often lead to violence. The carceral state is an expression of violence because to not know who we are is to live in perpetual harm against ourselves and others.

The great Tibetan saint and yogi Milarepa knew a little something about violence. Before his awakening he murdered many members of his extended family as an act of revenge. His father, a wealthy landowner, had died when Milarepa was young, and his father's wealth was transferred to his uncle and aunt on the condition that it would be handed over to Milarepa when he came of age. (As a woman, his mother could not inherit his father's wealth.) However, his aunt and uncle turned him, his sister, and his mother into servants and refused to transfer the estate to him after he came of age. Enraged, Milarepa's mother urged him to find a way to avenge the family. So, he went off and learned black magic and returned during a family wedding, casting the spell that resulted in the brutal death of his extended family. Feeling overwhelmed, he sought a way to purify the karma of this act and met his teacher, another great saint named Marpa. Milarepa trained diligently with

Marpa, releasing and healing the trauma of his actions as well as the trauma of childhood abuse. Eventually, he achieved complete enlightenment and had a profound impact on Tibetan Buddhism.

I think about Milarepa a lot not only because I have trained in his teaching and have been deeply inspired by his realization but because he has taught me why we choose violence over healing, and how we hurt others because we feel like we do not have the capacity to tend to our own suffering.

Violence means something is happening to me that I don't want to happen. Because I resist the happening, I am not prepared to tend to the woundedness that comes from the happening, and that woundedness stays in my body and mind as trauma, which begins to shape my relationship to myself, other individuals, communities, and the world in general.

Having my personal boundaries crossed without consent results in feeling unsafe and disrespected, which further leads to feeling othered. Surviving violence means that I do not know who I am anymore because the boundaries I created to help define who I am were disrupted by someone or something. Recovering means deep care work for myself, which includes reestablishing the belief that I deserve to be protected and cared for.

There is an old memory that will not quit me. I was thirteen and in Paris for the first time, visiting the famous Centre Pompidou. In the courtyard, I noticed two men begin to fight. Everything seemed like it was in slow motion. It wasn't a particularly physical altercation; it was just thirty seconds or so of wrestling until others came to pull them apart. But what I remember is feeling the energy between the men. They were being swept up in reactivity. What I felt then and can say clearly now is that they were deeply hurt over something, and instead of holding space for their anger and tending to their hurt, they attempted to annihilate each other.

We often only consider violence to be physical because we consider our physical bodies to be an important expression of who we are. Emotional violence is often invisible because so many of us have normalized emotional harm. We have been conditioned to believe that we do not deserve to feel safe or happy and that how we feel doesn't matter.

It is not possible for the carceral state to be completely nonviolent. Violence lies at its core, just as genocide, anti-Blackness, and capitalism lie at the heart of America. There is no America without these forms of violence, just as there is no carceral state without this fundamental violence. We are so disconnected from our true selves that we can't help but express violence against ourselves and others unless we develop the care and clarity to reduce this harm by returning to the experience of the essence.

I think about all the violence I endure, survive, and struggle to heal from, from personal violence to institutionalized and systemic violence. I also reflect on the ways I have been the agent of violence, both knowingly and unknowingly. I think about how violence was a second language for me—one that had been validated for me, particularly as a cisgender male benefiting from patriarchy.

Recently, someone grabbed my forearm in frustration when I forgot to perform a task. They did not intend to hurt me; the gesture was a habitual response that was informed by their cultural and ethnic identity. I was of a different cultural and ethnic background. There was something lost in translation. From that one touch, I experienced strong anxiety. I felt unsettled, off balance, fearful, and confused. Physically, I noticed a rapid heartbeat and a loss of energy and felt somewhat faint.

Sometime during or after this experience, I felt anger at the person who touched me. The anger seized my body and was concentrated in my chest and throat. Memories of other times my body was hurt by physical violence were triggered: times when physical violence was used to discipline me, to dominate me, or when violence occurred accidentally. Our bodies keep detailed records of how they have been hurt, while our minds maintain an emotional interpretation of the body's records. One touch opened up past experiences in such a way that I felt I was reliving these past experiences.

I wanted to leave the space immediately. There were many other people around, and I felt claustrophobic and unsafe. I felt both invisible and like everyone was watching me at the same time. There was not enough space for me, and there didn't seem to be enough air. When I saw the person who touched me, I felt a mix of strong fear and anger.

I also noticed a feeling of paranoia. I was anticipating that violence would happen again. In situations like this, it is very difficult to trust my body. When I am triggered, what I am experiencing is disembodiment. Disembodiment is when I struggle to be attentive to the sensations of my body. Sometimes, the hurt the body holds is too much to focus on, so I live outside of my body and lose contact with its sensations. Despite this loss of body contact, my body is still keeping record.

What does it mean to choose violence, to use force to meet force? Sometimes I have chosen violence not because I wanted others to hurt as much as I did, but because in the moment, violence was the only way to reduce the violence against me and others I cared about. I believe that violence can be chosen from a place of care. Sometimes, I know that I must say or do something that will be emotionally or physically harmful to others because I know that is the only means of neutralizing aggression. Sometimes cussing is the only language someone will understand, as it reflects the violence of being out of control back to them.

Freeing Our Minds

The first magic of the New Saint is understanding the mind. By moving from reacting to the thoughts and emotions—or the material—of the mind to experiencing this material, we can develop the agency to direct our work. This is the heart of the freedom we are trying to achieve. And this is what I call practicing agency in the mind.

Before his awakening, Siddhartha Gautama, the being who would later be called the Buddha, had it all. He was born a prince, with good looks, great hair, loads of money, a beautiful palace, and fantastic health. He had no worries except for a nagging feeling that he was supposed to be doing something else. He couldn't quite shake his intuition that he was being distracted from something important. So he escaped from the palace to see what was up in the real world and soon found the reality of suffering, which, while not exactly what he had been looking for, would confirm his long-felt urges around the need to get free. Getting free became the point of his life. So he renounced his privileges, including his wife and child, and journeyed into the world, becoming a wandering practitioner, trying to figure out what freedom was. Eventually, he found himself sitting under a Bodhi tree, and after several years of deep meditative practice he finally realized the illusion of the carceral state and achieved enlightenment.

The historical Buddha is said to have achieved enlightenment over twenty-five hundred years ago and in doing so initiated a cult of followers into his discipline of awakening, which would later become one of the most influential paths to complete liberation: Buddhism. *Buddha* means "awakened one." Much of what we know and understand about this state of liberation has been informed by Buddhism's detailed and precise philosophies and practices, which have been cultivated by masters and students for twenty-five hundred years. This tradition of enlightenment is the convergence of compassion and wisdom, meaning that enlightenment is the recognition of the illusion of all phenomena. When we realize the illusion, we are freed from reacting to the realness of everything and can experience the space from which we help others get free.

What Is Mind?

When I think about the mind, I feel the great Mother Yemoja. Anything I attempt to say about the mind must begin with praising her, the great mother who is said to have given birth to all the great orishas (the powerful deities of the Yoruba religion of West Africa), the mother who emanates from the ocean of oneness, the essence of all phenomena—vast, boundless. From her waters everything emerges, and into her waters everything submits. In my practice, her brother is the primordial Buddha Vajradhara, who first revealed himself to be the expression of mind but is blue like Mother Yemoja—and clear, fluid, and awakened like her as well. In other words, when I think about the mind, I think about a vast pure and clear ocean.

The mind is a boundless experience of consciousness, an energy that is knowing and intelligent. When I say "knowing," I mean that there is nothing that is not held in awareness. When I say "intelligent," I mean there is a clarity expressed as agency to make decisions.

Mind consciousness is not sensed through our sense faculties or the physical organs we rely on to process data about the phenomenal world. The truth is felt and experienced beyond these faculties. All phenomena radiate from the true nature, or essence, of everything. The essence is the simultaneous expression of emptiness, space, and energy potential. This essence is at the same time our experience of mind consciousness. The essence transcends suffering and dualism.

The historical Buddha is not the first being to achieve enlightenment in this world, nor will he be the last. However, what the Buddha showed was that we needed to figure out the illusion of self—the idea that we are autonomous, separate entities—in order to get free. To do that, we need to know what the mind is so that we can divest ourselves of the idea of the self and invest in the essence and mind consciousness. Mind consciousness is the simultaneous converging and arising of the three great and subtle qualities: emptiness, space, and energy potential.

— EMPTINESS —

Emptiness is a difficult concept to grasp. The truth is that everything is empty, which is to say that there is no inherent existence to anything that arises as phenomena, including our bodies, the earth, the material in our minds, and so forth. Everything is a dream. Enlightenment is like the relief we feel upon waking from a nightmare and realizing what we've experienced was just a dream. Just because we can sense phenomena doesn't mean things are real.

Even our sense faculties are empty. Things are only real because we think they are real. Recognizing emptiness means recognizing that when we stop believing in the realness of things, they become more fluid and translucent.

When we begin the process of realizing emptiness, we begin to experience wisdom, which I translate as clarity. When we get clear, we suffer less, experience more joy, and are near ultimate liberation. We finally begin to understand that we create suffering through the delusion of realness. There is no greater clarity than realizing emptiness. When we realize emptiness, we unshakably awaken care for all beings participating in something that is not quite happening.

Training in emptiness also opens us up to another great law of the phenomenal world: impermanence. Because there is no fixed realness, everything is being constructed through our own minds. This means that everything is constantly shifting because it's being created in the moment. We can learn to shift reality by thinking differently, which allows us to experience hope. Hope is a belief in change. By training our powers of hope, we train our capacity to change our minds. The only real experience is consciousness, which is the expression of the essence itself.

— SPACE —

When we transition from reactivity to responsiveness, we begin opening to the experience of spaciousness. Initially, space is experienced as relaxation. We feel more flexible, as if there is more potential to choose how we want to feel. All the material in our minds and bodies may still feel solid, but it will be more malleable. The realization of ultimate space becomes the doorway into emptiness.

Space offers the capacity to exercise agency. Agency is our capacity to choose responsiveness over reactivity, and in doing so we can choose how to respond to something. This is the most revolutionary ability in our practice of getting free. Suffering and the violence we survive and perpetuate are rooted in our habitual reactivity to everything, especially discomfort. Meditation is training in this agency, and without this training we will not have the skills to journey toward freedom. Liberation begins with deciding to get free and then training in liberatory practices like meditation. But we will never reduce harm or get free until we learn to move from reactivity to responsiveness.

— ENERGY POTENTIAL —

When the self, which is an expression of delusion, shapes energy, it leads to incarceration. When we forget that this shaping is illusory, we start believing that everything is real and thus too permanent to change. The energy of the mind makes anything possible, which is why training in meditation is crucial to getting free. We can begin to shape our liberation, just as we are constantly shaping our incarceration.

The energy potential of the mind reveals that it is both complex and simple. It is simple because everything arises out of the boundless ocean of emptiness, space, and potential. The complexity arises because we have gotten so involved with this shaping that we have forgotten how to let go of the shaping itself. We have become self-identified with the labor of shaping, orchestrated by the self, which is itself a shaped phenomenon.

What Is Meditation?

Meditation is the practice of developing a deeper awareness of our minds and the world around us. Meditation is the method that helps us release our fixation on the self and expand our attention into awareness and the expanse of consciousness.

Meditation is also the work of tending. Tending is how I care for my mind, which is how I can care for others as well as the phenomenal world. When I tend to my mind, I hold space for what is arising. I let my mind be. When I hold space for myself, I can hold space for others. When I tend to others, I am showing up, holding space, and staying open to what they may need. When I tend to all other phenomena, I am allowing everything to arise as an expression of tending. Tending is expressing gentleness and vulnerability as we care for ourselves and the world.

In meditation, we are strengthening our capacity to know and be aware. We are training to steady our stream of awareness, letting it flow evenly toward where we direct it.

While awareness is the energy of holding many things, attention is a more focused energy of holding one object or anchor at a time. Attention is also what gets called mindfulness and is driven by the subtle practice of concentration. Concentration expands into attention, attention expands into awareness, and awareness expands into consciousness itself.

Practicing Meditation

Meditation is the labor of becoming aware of the nature of our minds, the expressions of our minds, and the workings of the world around us. It is the work of noticing what's up and choosing how to respond to what's up. While meditation itself is not the first magic of the New Saint, which is transitioning from reactivity to responsiveness, it is how we train in the first magic of the New Saint. Below is an introduction to a meditation tool that can strengthen both our awareness and attention.

SNOELL

It is important to have a practice strategy when attempting to deepen our awareness. SNOELL is a mindfulness-based attention strategy that helps us to hold space for material in our minds. It is a method I developed based on the oldest ways of developing awareness and experiencing mental freedom from the Buddhist tradition.

SNOELL stands for:

See it: Begin the process of noticing material in our minds or physical sensations.
Name it: Name the material that helps us to get clear about what we are noticing.
Own it: See this material as arising in our body and mind.
Experience it: Get curious about how the material feels.
Let it go: Release the material back into the spaciousness of our minds.
Let it float: Let space take care of the material.

Below is an example of how I practice this method. In this case, I am focusing on emotions.

I begin by bringing my attention to the material of my mind and noticing thoughts and emotions like waves rising and falling. At this point, I'm just paying attention to what's happening in my mind. This is the first step of SNOELL: seeing.

Then I focus on noticing my emotions. I begin by asking myself how I feel. Sometimes I am feeling a lot at once; I go through each of my emotions and name them. I pick one emotion that feels pleasant for me, like happiness, joy, or gratitude. I name this emotion in my mind by saying, *This is _____.* This emotion becomes my anchor for the practice. This is the second step of SNOELL: naming.

Once I have named my anchor, I keep my attention on it for a few moments. Then I tell myself, *This emotion is happening now in my experience. This is my emotion.* This is the third step of SNOELL: owning.

I relax with this emotion and say to myself, *I am experiencing* _____. I notice how this emotion feels in my body and mind. I even notice some of the other thoughts that come up about this emotion. This is the fourth step of SNOELL: experiencing.

Now that I have owned and experienced this material, I let it go. While noticing the emotion, I try to relax and tell myself, *I am experiencing* _____. I try to let go of the emotion. Letting go of the emotion feels like staring up at clouds passing through the sky. They are there, but I can't touch them. I imagine that this emotion is a cloud passing through the sky of my mind and that I am gazing up at it not being able to do anything but watch it pass. This is the fifth step of SNOELL: letting go.

Now I just sit and let the emotion pass through my mind. I notice all the ways I attempt to touch it or grab onto it. Whenever I notice that, I just return to relaxing and watching. This is the final step of SNOELL: letting it float.

OCEAN-LIKE MIND

I begin this practice by shifting my attention to my mind and imagining that my mind is like an ocean: vast, clear, expansive. I allow my awareness to spread through this ocean. My mind is feeling fluid.

I begin to imagine waves rising and falling over the ocean. These waves are thoughts and emotions rising out of the stillness of my mind and eventually returning back to the stillness of my mind. I allow this movement to happen without interfering.

SKY-LIKE MIND

I begin this practice by shifting my attention to my mind and imagining that my mind is like the wide-open sky: vast, clear, bright, and expansive. The brightness represents the natural clarity of my mind.

I begin to imagine clouds moving across the sky of my mind. These clouds represent thoughts and emotions. I watch the clouds float through my sky-like mind without getting involved.

MOVING INTO THE ESSENCE

I begin this practice by choosing an anchor. I begin with the weight of my body making contact with the seat. I allow my attention to be held gently by that sensation.

Next, I allow my attention to expand into awareness by noticing other anchors around me: sounds, scents, light, and so on. I am holding multiple sensations in my awareness at once. I continue to let my awareness spread like an ocean—without limits.

Slowly, I imagine that the material in my awareness begins to dissolve in the energy of my awareness as my awareness expands even more into the emptiness of phenomena and is united back with my consciousness. I rest in consciousness for as long as I can.

Spiritual Abolition

When I began practicing community service and activism, I was trying to get free from the violence of systemic oppressions ranging from racism to queerphobia. It seemed that the best way to honor my life was to dedicate my life's labor to studying freedom, trying to get free, and helping others around me get free.

My first experiences of freedom came in church when I learned about Jesus and then about the Exodus. I was always moved by Jesus. I knew him as a divinely anointed spiritual teacher who turned water into wine, walked on water, resurrected people, cast demons from people, and who was said to have died for my sins. I was drawn to Jesus, who had figured out how to transcend the physical limitations of the world. I now see his divine magic as the work of an activist. While working as a reformist of an ancient religion and as a disruptor of the Roman occupation, he also manifested as a master alchemist and healer.

Along with the ministry of Jesus, the Exodus has also shaped my understanding of freedom. Moses gave up so much. He was raised as a member of the ruling Egyptian class until God reminded him that he was actually born a member of the enslaved Hebrew people. With the remembrance came an ethical responsibility called compassion, and he found himself thrust into epic spiritual warfare between God and the state of Egypt, headed by the pharaoh himself, a man who was once his brother. Moses knew the strength of the great Egyptian state, and he especially knew the will and stubbornness of his brother. But who can stand against the mighty will of God, channeled through an initially hesitant but soon quite confident sorcerer whom God had designated to free the Hebrews, the descendants of the father of Israel? Through Moses, God leveled ten plagues, culminating in the pharaoh conceding and freeing the Hebrews. Finally, Moses gathered at the Dead Sea with his people, and God worked through him to part this ancient sea to make the final escape: the Exodus.

The Exodus story helped shape my early relationship to freedom in the same way it shaped Black American culture and my ancestors' devotion to freedom. When slave owners were feeding my ancestors Christianity as a means of control, I don't think they realized that my folks would connect these stories and find in them an affirmation that they had a right to be free—that if they remained devoted, God would deliver them like he delivered the children of Israel from the tyranny of slavery and Egyptian authoritarianism.

On top of what I was learning and beginning to love about the stories of freedom in the Bible, I also consumed anything and everything fantasy and science-fiction related, from books to television shows. I was particularly drawn to *Transformers*, *Voltron*, *Captain Planet*, and anything else that was about transforming from one thing into another or different beings uniting to become one stronger being. These kinds of toys and media offered me an opportunity to imagine a different life outside of being poor and Black in the Deep South. How could I be this kid whose imagination felt free and rich, racing through galaxies and fantasy realms, while at the same time feeling stuck and limited? The outer world was placid and rigid, full of suffering and limitations, compared to the boundless, golden, rich experience of my mind. There came to be a bittersweet tension between my imagination and the world I was navigating.

I became obsessed with learning how to practice transforming my present conditions into something more fluid and rich. I intuitively knew that my imagination was more than just rich—it enabled me to experience things that other people weren't aware of. I never had doubts about the existence of the unseen world. I could feel weird things around me. When I slept, it seemed like someone was watching me. I never felt alone. Although I had heard my fair share of sermons about angels and demons, no one ever talked about ghosts. I didn't have the language back then to talk about energies and planes of existence, but what I did know was that there was much more happening than what I could see or touch.

I hold the story and mythology of the Exodus as sacred teachings and have been deeply shaped by liberation theology, which teaches us that if God delivered the Hebrew people who were positioned as the most oppressed, then God is on the side of those who are most oppressed. My practice of liberation theology has been informed by the liberation work of many thinkers, activists, and spiritual leaders like Gustavo Gutiérrez, James Cone, bell hooks, and Paulo Freire.

When I converted to Buddhism, I began to understand how social liberation and ultimate liberation related to each other. After I became a teacher, my passion for the liberation of everything joined the passions and vision of my comrades Rev. angel Kyodo williams and Dr. Jasmine Syedullah. Together, we coauthored the book *Radical Dharma*, which explores the integration of both social and ultimate liberation, arguing that there is no ultimate liberation without social liberation. The book has given way to a tradition of practice and study based on the union of social and ultimate liberation. Since then, my practice of radical dharma has opened to the lineage of spiritual abolition.

When I was growing up, I never called myself an abolitionist, but I knew that everyone deserved to be free, even if we needed to abolish systems and institutions that seemed to prevent liberation. The only thing that I have ever wanted was to be free. The question of freedom has driven all the important choices in my life. In small, southern Black communities, we were never confused about how our right to be free was heavily contested. We could see and feel otherness imposed on us by this country, its laws, its continued violence against our bodies and minds, and its blatant disregard for the ongoing impact of chattel slavery.

I believe Mother Harriet Tubman was the heart of the abolitionist movement. Her work, along with the tireless and dangerous work of many antislavery abolitionists, laid a practical foundation for abolition. Abolition was more than the work of ending slavery; it necessitated dreaming of liberation and then working to awaken that dream in the world. However, one of the most important lessons Mother Harriet teaches us is that abolition must involve the union of both social and ultimate liberation. As we work to free people from harm in the relative world, we must also be working to experience liberation from all suffering by remembering the nature of our minds and the nature of all phenomena. Mother Harriet, as an awakened bodhisattva, knew that real freedom is realizing the essence of everything, and to experience that realization, our abolition practice must also be a spiritual practice in which we ally with the unseen world of beings who are working alongside us to get us and everything free. I can hear Mother Harriet now saying that if we ain't praying, we ain't serious about getting free.

Spiritual abolitionism means that the entire ecology must be liberated, that we have to do the labor to get ourselves free, and that same labor we do for ourselves is the same labor we offer to our collectives, which include blood and chosen families, friends, communities, identity-based affinity groups, cities, and countries. This is the same labor we are doing for our entire unseen ecologies of ancestors and descendants.

Spiritual abolitionism is more than a critique of power and how social systems work to grant and deny people resources that they need to survive. It is more than just abolishing the material carceral state with its prisons, police, and surveillance. Spiritual abolition is dreaming and then beginning to live beyond the violent indoctrination of the binary that enables people to express dominance over others. Abolition is a fluid, ephemeral word that demands that I stop basing my dream of a liberated future on the preservation of the "good" qualities of present systems and enter the real struggle of imagining brand-new ways of being in relationship with myself and my communities. These relationships are not based on dominance, overconsumption, or trauma and despair. We abolish anything that prevents us from being in direct, honest, and compassionate relationships first with ourselves and then the communities we belong to.

Spiritual abolition also means that I always consider people within the context of their suffering. This means that I begin to understand that people do the things they do because of deep discomfort that they may or may not be aware of. Violence is often a reaction to discomfort. So many of the people that create the most harm for us are themselves suffering and do not know how to be in relationship to their suffering. I don't want people to be punished for the harm they cause me or others. I don't want people in prison, in jail, or executed. I want people to be free from the suffering they experience and the suffering they cause others. In the context of spiritual abolition, the best way to ensure this is through accountability based on an awakened care ethic. I want the nature of people's violence to be named so that they can start understanding the ways their reactivity to their suffering is creating harm.

Liberation Pessimism

Most of us are afraid of getting free because in freedom we have to do the labor of figuring out who we are. Being born into the world is like being born into a dark closet with four walls, a floor, and a ceiling. We are cramped in this closet, but we are comfortable here because we can reach out and touch everything. The closet offers us boundaries, and we feel less anxious. Everything is predictable. The ego functions best when its boundaries are defined for it. Imagine that someone comes along and opens the door to that closet and on the other side is a wide-open sunny pasture. This would be a shock to us—suddenly there's light and no more boundaries. We would basically freak the fuck out. We can't handle space and openness; we don't understand what they say about who we are.

Many of us will not be free anytime soon because we don't want to be free. It costs too much. We are too dependent on being defined by the closet. We have an overwhelming and seductive addiction to the material world, which does not offer us insight into the illusion of the world. We have become acclimated to the suffering of everything, and we tell ourselves this is how it is and must be.

And then something happens that offers an experience of what it is like not to suffer, and we find our acclimatization disrupted. This is a profound blessing. It is a divine intervention into the stagnancy of the material world. It has happened to me several times, and it has felt like being shoved out of the way of suffering for a split second so that I can feel what it's like to experience something other than suffering. Then I snap back into place. This disruption interjects an unbearable juxtaposition, which is the tension of experiencing ourselves beyond the suffering and then returning to that suffering, knowing that we are choosing it.

Karma

Almost no one understands karma. I often find myself grasping at straws. It is easy to reduce the workings of karma down to a fatalistic notion that doing bad things means bad things will happen to you and doing good things means good things will happen to you. I see this view expressed in pop culture. However, karma is more complex than a simple equation. It has everything to do with balance and what is conducive to liberation.

Karma is made up of cycles of energy that we rehearse so much that they become patterns, which morph into narratives, which solidify into realities. Those realities become boundaries that we intensify through habitual reactivity. This rehearsal is how the carceral state is maintained—or how it is disrupted. To put it another way, karma is the energy that drives the experience of reality as an experience of incarceration or as an experience of liberation.

Everything that we think, say, or do creates a kind of energy that eventually settles into a psychic reality. What is important about what we think, say, or do is the intention behind these acts. The intention can be good, bad, or neutral. If our intentions are positive, what we do will generate positive things. If our intentions are negative, what we do will generate negative things.

However, the phenomenal world is based on balance. Liberation is my primary goal in life, and I am training to align everything I do, say, and think with the goal of liberation. Therefore, I do what is conducive to getting free, while letting go of activity that is not conducive to freedom. This framework helps me to understand that what others have to do to get free is not necessarily what I have to do to get free and vice versa. This keeps me from judging other people's work.

Doing what is conducive to liberation and letting go of what isn't helps us to understand that balance is the key to liberation. We understand what is and is not conducive to liberation by figuring out our work and cultivating experiences of balance, fluidity, clarity, space, and joy. When we are doing things that are not aligned with liberation, we cause harm, violence, and rigidity.

Karma also shapes our relationship to pleasure and pain. Everything—including thoughts, emotions, and physical sensations—is energy. We perceive and thus experience energies or material that we label comfortable, uncomfortable, or neutral. This happens because we misunderstand energy and get wrapped up in reacting to it instead of caring for it by acknowledging, holding, experiencing, and releasing it.

Regardless of how close to liberation we are, we will experience discomfort in the form of pain. As long as we have a body, it will need care, and it will express that need through discomfort. When the body can no longer be cared for, we begin the dying process. Dying itself is not a result of bad karma—we all must die. How we die and our mental state at death is based on how thoroughly we have cultivated fluidity and care in our lives. Open, fluid minds embrace and lean into death, while rigid, closed minds fight against it, leading to a difficult transition. However, the cause of death—be it old age after a long life, illness in one's youth, or murder—is related to past karmic energy that needs to be ripened. The ripening of past karmic energy means that there is a complex plethora of energies embedded in our consciousness from past lives that need to be released and expressed like releasing steam from a pressure cooker. When that pressure is released, whatever is being cooked is impacted, the risk of the pot exploding lessens, and/or the risk of being burned by the released steam increases. Similarly, when karmic energy is released, it will impact our lives in different ways, sometimes for the best and other times for the worst. However, regardless of the difficulties we experience in life, no one deserves to suffer. We are all inherently free, and once we remember this, suffering dissipates.

My Personal Ethics of Liberation

I am trying to achieve complete personal liberation from suffering to help as many beings as possible get free. I am awakening the reality of freedom by getting clear about my work and the care it takes to do this work. As I shared in the introduction, my work is to give a shit (about everyone's liberation), figure out my work (what I am supposed to do), do that work, and keep returning to that work.

My ethics involve choosing to divest myself of conditions that perpetuate suffering for me and others and choosing the dream—the liberation from the domination of others—which is how I want others to experience freedom. My ethics are based on empathy, which is the sensitivity to my personal experience of discomfort and the expanded contemplation of how others are uncomfortable in the same ways. My intention then becomes an expression of awakened care, which is the need for all beings to be free from suffering. It is this intention that begins to guide the work of the New Saint. It is also intentions that begin to shape the reality of karma, creating the energetic causes and conditions of what I experience.

My ethics are also how I maintain my integrity. My integrity is my clarity as it pertains to the work I am doing in this life. My work is to get free and help as many others get free as possible. The intensity of this clarity is often read as arrogance from people who are not that clear about their work. Most people I meet have jobs and professions that they feel obligated to do to make money. A lot of people don't get joy from their work. It is hard for people to understand that my work is my life; it is what I have chosen as the best possible thing for me to do to benefit people. I am cared for in this work. I am joyful in this work. My needs are met in this work. I am fortunate to have the support I do in this work. This may sound like bragging, but this is what it feels like to find and do your work.

Heart Advice

When I sit and pray to Mother Harriet, letting my awareness mingle with the light of her consciousness, which is the purest and fiercest compassion, I am reminded that the most important thing that I can do with my life is to work for freedom and help others to get free. She reminds me of her last incarnation in this world and what it took to awaken to the level she did and what she did for my ancestors to free them. She reminds me that freedom is a process that begins with understanding what freedom means for me as a lived, embodied experience and that I don't need to wait for permission from the state to be free in my mind. Even though I may not have complete agency over my body, freedom means that I no longer believe that any state has agency over it.

After practicing dharma for twenty years and teaching for over ten years, I finally understand something important: the root of my practice and teaching has been grounded in the integration of both social and spiritual liberation. Over the years, in my teaching, I've been confused as to why so few people are committed to the hard work of liberation. I have wondered why my practice and choices—from entering a three-year retreat to studying in different traditions and allying with plant consciousness—have often seemed so extreme compared to others. I started practicing dharma because I wanted to be free from suffering, and then that initial motivation expanded into a need to achieve complete enlightenment. Although most practitioners of all identities are indeed reducing suffering, that reduction of suffering often has happiness and comfort as its end goal, and that is not liberation but rather getting cozy in the carceral state.

I don't teach people how to be happy or comfortable. I help people to remember the fluid, energetic, spacious, and empty nature of everything, including their own consciousness. Remembering the nature of everything, we are freed from the delusion of the carceral state that is fueled by our belief in the realness of ego and duality.

I am also speaking of the liberation of all phenomenal reality from the violence of forgetting the essence of what it is and is arising from. This freedom is not just for me but for all conscious beings in this world and all the worlds, both seen and unseen. Real freedom can only be fathomed when we can get a glimpse of who we are, which is our most natural state of being beyond the indoctrination of the carceral state.

When you are free from the conditioning of the state, you are also free from the experience of selfishness, which attempts to restrict resources to others. All liberatory work must also disrupt our tendencies to create mythologies that feel good and taste great because we are not interested in building the capacity to experience the discomfort of navigating the world of sensation.

Freedom is a process. No one is going to save you. No one is going to save me. You are saved through your own labor with the support and inspiration of community and other individuals who embody the expression of liberated living. Freedom isn't about you or me being special or good enough. It is about whether we are ready to choose clarity over bullshit and drama.

We can't figure out who we are beyond the trauma until we go back and figure out who we were before the trauma. To know ourselves before the trauma is to construct journeys back into history and time, back into old, forgotten narratives and even mythologies. Ultimately, we are trying to touch back into the primordial mind, the unborn essence of everything. As the ancient *Gate Gate* mantra proclaims, you must go beyond beyond, coming to the edge and stepping off the edge into the awakening of who you are beyond the boundaries set by the carceral state.

So, are you ready to get free or not? Because freedom isn't some willy-nilly shot in the dark with no intention or discernment. It's not something we randomly sign up for because we're bored, nor is it a hashtag we post to make us look woke. It's not a club we join because all the other cool kids are doing it. It's not a pickup line to impress lovers. And it's definitely not some hip existentialist intellectual pursuit that feels like the work but just shoves us deeper into the same old bullshit smugness that somehow confuses apathy with freedom.

If you choose freedom for real, you will lose shit and maybe never get anything back again. You will be misunderstood. You will not be invited to hang with the cool kids anymore. Your heart will break wide open, revealing the marriage of both sorrow and joy. You will fall into dark places. You will speak in tongues. People will avoid you. You will start to understand that what you thought the world was, it is not. You will start giving a shit, even for the people who hurt the most. This is not crazy, sexy, or cool. Nor is it glamorous. Your struggle will not be televised because people will not be interested in watching you fall apart outside of laughing at you.

Freedom is the shedding away of the skin this reality stuck on you and forced you to play in. And the freer you get of this skin, the more you will be blamed for the suffering of others because your labor will remind them of the labor they are not doing for themselves. And like many of our prophets in the past who were often just mirrors reflecting to people their labor, you will be stoned to death because erasing you is easier than doing the work to get free.

Awakened Care

There is no liberation without the profound practice of awakened care. The New Saint must learn to give a shit because if they don't, there is no way they will have the fuel to make this journey to freedom as they help others along. Awakened care is restorative and inspirational, and it doesn't give up on us if we trust it.

I don't like everyone. I gave up trying to like everyone when my teacher told me once that attempting to like everyone was a waste of time and that the real practice was loving people. This was the most important teaching I ever received from him, and it gave me permission to be concerned with people getting what they needed to be well and safe, regardless of who they were and whether or not I liked them.

It's hard being in the world right now, living, working, shopping, and going to school around people who consciously or unconsciously want you dead, enslaved, subjugated, silenced, back on a boat to Africa or wherever they believe you came from because it's obvious you don't belong near them. There are more people than I care to acknowledge who want me to suffer—not because I have hurt them, but because they don't know how to deal with their hurt. It can be hard to care about these folks. They don't even care about themselves. If they did, they would understand what being well, safe, and happy feels like, and they would want to extend that experience to everyone. Without the care of self, it becomes hard to tend to our suffering, making us more likely to weaponize it against others through acts of violence, thereby restricting the freedom and well-being of others.

There is an old story about the Buddha who, in a previous life before he awakened as the historical Buddha we all know and love, was a young prince. One day, he was out walking with some close disciples when he came upon a starving tigress with her newborn cubs. He felt, intuitively, that she was dangerously close to eating them. After sending his disciples off to gather food, the young prince became anxious that his people would not return soon enough. Out of great care for the mother and cubs and realizing the illusory nature of his own body, he offered his body to the tigress and cubs to eat. The extreme nature of the Buddha's choice, and the fact that someone might care so much for another being that they offer their body as sacrifice, might trouble some of us because of what we may be asked to offer if we engage in awakening our own caring potential.

And then there is Gloria Richardson, a civil rights movement leader who organized in Cambridge, Maryland, in the early 1960s. She and her followers were not proponents of Dr. King's nonviolent philosophy but rather believed force was sometimes necessary to advance freedom work. Most people, including myself, wouldn't know of her if not for the iconic photo of her pushing the rifle of a White National Guard soldier to the side. What strikes me is less the gesture and more what she is beaming back at him. Her face communicates a boundary, telling him and everyone that enough is enough—that she is sick of the bullshit and violence against Black folks and that a rifle and everything it represents will not hinder her struggle to get her and her people free. She is casting a warning against these soldiers who embody the totality of centuries of anti-Black violence. This photo haunts me because it reminds me of the audacity to choose freedom through care for others.

The Buddha and Gloria are talking to me right now. They speak of the ways in which authentic care calls us to do extraordinary things for others. For the Buddha, it was care to alleviate the hunger of a tigress and her cubs by offering his body. For Gloria, it was the expression of care needed to disrupt the threat of death and intimidation for herself and all Black folks. Yet it is more than just care that the Buddha and Gloria offered. I consider their offerings to be an expression of *awakened* care.

Bodhicitta to Awakened Care

Bodhicitta is central to much of contemporary Western Buddhist practice. As someone rooted in activism and care for community, it excited me during the early years of my practice and felt like the heartbeat of Buddhism's training in caring for all beings' wellness and freedom. To understand the bodhisattva as a spiritual warrior and their bodhicitta as magic was galvanizing because I wanted to be as powerful and helpful as a comic book hero.

Bodhicitta is traditionally defined as "the awakened mind," a mental state of clarity fueling a deep desire for all beings to be free, while emanating that desire from our own personal practice and experience of liberation. Bodhicitta is the audacious assertion that I am only trying to get free in order to get others free.

Over the years of my practice, I have often reflected on what bodhicitta has felt like for me. I know bodhicitta is only possible because of emptiness and space, which are accessible through the experience of clarity. I have experienced this clarity, but within this experience of clarity, there is also the experience of being in a vast ocean: warm and dynamic, clear and direct. The only word I had for it was *care*; not a basic care, concerned with helping people feel good, but an awakened care that was concerned with freeing beings from suffering by helping them to transcend the dualism of pleasure and pain. Emptiness and space are boundless, and therefore this ocean feels boundless as it expands out to be held by the emptiness.

But what was flowing into this ocean of awakened care? First, I felt love, which I experience as the need for beings to have all the resources to be free, happy, safe, and well. The energy of love is felt as nonjudgment, acceptance, and inclusivity. Second, I felt compassion, which I experience as the need for all beings to be free from suffering as well as the action of freeing all beings. Compassion is felt as an opening to freedom, fluidity, agency, and power to determine how we want to experience freedom. And third, I could feel joy, which is the experience of the natural mind in which we let go of the realness of everything and expand into space while noticing the inherent potential in the world. Joy is felt as the experience of encountering the world and all phenomena as spacious and fluid, not contracted or rigid. Gratitude opens us up to the experience of joy because it relaxes our minds, helping it expand back into its essence. I feel joy because I am grateful to be doing freedom work. I believe that this is the most important work I can be doing in this life. My joy springs from knowing I am aligned with my calling.

As love, compassion, and joy collect into the ocean of awakened care held by the spaciousness of clarity, the ocean becomes an inexhaustible source of energy that I drink from to nourish myself and offer others. I pour liberation out into the world from my flowing ocean of awakened care, which is maintained through practice. This is the magic of the New Saint.

Awakened Care and Irresistible Movement

Awakened care is an expression of all four yogas of the New Saint. It is the work (the yoga of work) we engage in when we get clear (the yoga of clarity) about what it takes to bring about the dream (the yoga of dream) of a liberated future where everyone is getting the care they need (the yoga of care).

Awakened care is the antidote to individual and collective narcissism. It is an expression of our natural state of being and a positionality that decenters our sense of self within the ecology. It is not just about me and my self-preservation anymore. It becomes about how we (me and all others) will survive. Awakened care is the realization that everything in my life can be aligned with not just my personal liberation but the liberation of all beings.

Awakened care is what the author, filmmaker, and activist Toni Cade Bambara wanted from her writing and cultural work; she wanted to make revolution irresistible. In this same spirit, when allowance, fluidity, agency, and a belief in space and potential unite in clarity, they give birth to a concern so sweet and yet disrupting that we lose a sense of agency and are swept up in the agenda of the liberation of all beings and things.

To be clear, the development of care always begins within our own experience. We become the first ones swept up in the irresistible struggle for liberation. If this movement does not begin in our own hearts and minds, it becomes an unsustainable and resistible movement.

The Four Activities of the New Saint

In the New Saint's tradition, the outer level of awakened care is the labor of freeing all beings from suffering. The inner level of care is the commitment to freeing ourselves. The secret level of care is the truth that we are already free to begin with, so everything we are doing is an act of remembering who we are and what the nature of everything is.

The New Saint experiences this ocean of awakened care in their body and mind and then pours this energy into the world and the lives of other people through the four activities: giving a shit, figuring out what the work of liberation is, doing the work, and returning to the work.

Giving a shit is rooted in the ways that awakened care helps us to empathize with others, a practice of considering and even feeling what others are going through. Empathy decenters but does not erase our experiences as it makes room for us to hold the experiences of others. When we know our own suffering alongside the suffering of others, we understand that no one wants to suffer, making it more likely for us to help to alleviate suffering all around

When we start giving a shit, we can then figure out the best way to help, which is figuring out our work. The work is the labor we give to creating liberation for ourselves and others, which in the New Saint's tradition is the labor of remembering we are already free. It can take some time to figure out our work because it doesn't necessarily look like what other folks are doing. We are all at different stages of the path toward liberation and embody different capacities along with our various identities.

When we give a shit and that profound and simple way of caring helps us to figure out what the work of self and collective liberation looks like for us, we then must do the work. This is the space we stay in for the longest period. The work is often not glamorous or sexy. It involves doing emotional labor, developing awakened care, and expressing that care.

In meditation, we often begin deepening our capacity to be aware by first training in the skill of returning our attention to an object or anchor repeatedly. This is how we strengthen our agency to direct the energy of our awareness. It is the same for the practice of the New Saint. Once we figure out what our work is, we do it repeatedly, regardless of how hard or boring it is. What has helped me return repeatedly to my own hard work of liberation is connecting to the joy aspect of awakened care, which helps me celebrate and feel inspired by doing work that matters in the world.

The Three Great Streams of Awakened Care

When I am practicing awakened care, I am experiencing the streams of love, compassion, and joy flowing together, collecting in my mind and body as a potent energy of vulnerability and truth, while also pulsating as the very nature of my mind. However, these three streams are also full of data and energy that must be practiced and embodied before releasing them into the ocean of awakened care.

— THE STREAM OF LOVE —

I have written about love so much in my work that I don't really know if there is anything useful or new to say about it. However, I do feel as though I have been overly romantic about it in the past. More plainly put, I find that my writing on the power of love has been more poetic and entertaining than practical. So, I am asking Jesus to take the wheel.

Like many people growing up in the Christian church, knowing John 3:16 by heart was, for me, standard practice. The verse says, "For God so loved the world, that he gave his only begotten Son, that whosoever believeth in him should not perish, but have everlasting life."

It bothered me that God as *the* Father and as *a* father would send his only son to earth, to struggle with a whole bunch of hard-headed people and to eventually be executed by them. I never understood the significance of Jesus consenting to be crucified and how he paid for it all by dying for our sins, especially since it seems like I am still paying for shit!

It was Buddhism and the practice of dharma that helped me to understand Christianity in a way that made sense for me. I began to relate to God in the same way I relate to my awakened mind, as a boundless expression of conscious energy that permeates everything. This conscious energy was like a great ocean that my mind was trying to remember to flow back into. And this great ocean is always trying to lure me back to oneness. If this great ocean of conscious energy is God, then Jesus was just an expression of this experience, whose only intention was to lead everyone back to the oneness, the great ocean, and God.

In Christianity, it is believed that Jesus was a physical expression of God who intentionally emanated here to liberate beings through his ministry. I believe that in his dying, Jesus became a kind of living effigy whose torture and eventual execution mirrored the violence of the Roman occupation for people to see firsthand. That mirroring became a way for collective trauma to be metabolized, helping people to understand the violence of the state and make choices to divest themselves of that violence and turn more strongly back to God's love. I also believe that because of Jesus's awakened nature, he had the capacity as a living effigy to absorb the violence directed toward him and release that energy back into emptiness and the nature of God.

It later dawned on me how much love it takes to choose to enter a situation knowing that trying to get people free will involve work and that the cost of that work doesn't matter because all you want is for people to be free. I don't believe that Jesus liked all the people he came to free but only that he believed, as the emanation of God, that all beings deserved to have access to the resources that allowed them to be safe, free, happy, and well.

There's a fierceness to the practice and embodiment of love. It does not let go. It leads to the needs of others but does not forget what we need. It considers everything and leaves out nothing. And the love we offer to the world is sourced from the love we cultivate for ourselves. Self-love is a spring of clear fresh water we offer to ourselves first, which makes it more possible for us to offer it to others who are also thirsty from the opposite of self-love, which is self-hate.

Our deepest wish is to be in love, to surrender to something that is not an old, familiar wave of grief, isolation, or fear. For me, love has involved a basic yet profound acceptance of who and what I am. It is the basic labor of allowing myself to be without judgment or policing. When I allow myself to be, then I can do the work of emotional labor, experiencing and metabolizing the pain to allow love to open back to space itself. Love is being myself and then wanting others to have the space to be themselves. When people have the space to be themselves, they can then gain access to the resources they need to be well, happy, and safe. The space of acceptance is the soil from which our resources are gathered, like a harvest in autumn.

Love means we touch the ground of reality as it is, not as we want it to be. It is the labor of telling the truth and allowing the truth to tell us. And none of this is supposed to be easy. Allowing ourselves to expand the pain into the space and then to start identifying with the space is how love frees us.

Often, I can feel the world pulsating with love, radiating this warm sensual energy that I register as an invitation for me to consent to being accepted and cared for. I want to fall into this experience of trusting the care, but this is challenging because it always reminds me that I am self-identified with the constriction of pain rather than the space that love is. Because we survive so much violence, pain is more familiar, and it feels much more like home than the freedom of connecting to love.

I have worked to allow my attention to return to recognizing that I am embodied, holding space for pleasure and pain while practicing gentleness. This is how I offer love to my body. Soon, happiness begins to arise as the feeling of being content and at ease with how my body is showing up in the moment. Tension melts away, and I am not engaging in an old, familiar judgment of my body. I feel safe to be in the moment with my sensations, and that is the experience of love.

— THE DEITY OF LOVE —

My first real training in love came with Chenrezig, the first Tantric deity I practiced with formally. I met Chenrezig when I began attending a small chanting group during the early days of my practice. Chenrezig is the embodiment of love and compassion. Though Chenrezig is often identified as a male deity in Tantric traditions, Chenrezig arises out of an expression of gender fluidity and is more venerated as a reflection of the feminine bodhisattva Quan Yin in Eastern Asian Buddhist traditions.

In Tibetan, Chenrezig means the "Great Gazing Eye." Chenrezig holds everything, both pain and joy, equally and without judgment, which is the most profound expression of love. Chenrezig's sacred speech or mantra is *Om Mani Padme Hung*, which translates into "behold the jewel in the lotus." The mantra promotes a union of the male and female principles with mani (jewel) representing the masculine phallus and padme (lotus) representing the female yoni. The mantra is pulsating with the erotic, which is the pleasure we experience in union. Essentially, what Chenrezig teaches us is that love is an expression of the erotic because love is the expression of the essence in union. In Tantra, pleasure becomes a doorway into the experience of the essence.

When I practice the mantra, I feel it as an incantation that gathers the most disparate, fragmented parts of me and reassembles them into the union so I can experience the essence. The recitation reminds me that when I am struggling to love, I am actually struggling to be in this state of union.

The carceral state is the perpetuation of the illusion of separation. This separation is yet another obstacle that keeps us from experiencing liberation. Our liberation struggle is about disrupting and remembering that there was never any separation to begin with. Love is the recognition that we can never be liberated until we are whole. Healing is understood to be a coming back together, a reassembly of our fragmentation through remembering and re-membering. Love is the basic state of union beyond the illusion of separation.

Unconditional loving is loving and experiencing love from the space that opens up from nonreactivity. Spaciousness helps us to feel relaxed and resourced enough to want others to feel the same way we do. We offer ourselves the grace to be, while offering others that same grace as well. Conditional love is an expression of love from a place of separation and contraction. People weaponize it against others. I consider conditional loving an act of both personal and interpersonal psychic terrorism that hurts both the person expressing conditional love as well as the recipient.

PRACTICING RECEIVING LOVE

My practice of love is informed by community. I know love because I have been loved by so many people and beings: family, friends, teachers, lovers, ancestors, deities, and the earth herself. The practice of love is really about opening oneself to the love that is always being expressed to us. However, for many of us, the work of opening to love means having to hold and experience the hurt we have received from surviving the psychic terrorism of conditional loving.

I have created several practices meant to help people experience love. They range from simple to complex.

The practice I offer here is a simple practice that gets us started on this path of receiving love.

When you are ready, come into a position that feels supportive and restful. Slowly begin reflecting on all the beings that love you, including people, deities, ancestors, and even pets. Imagine that they begin to appear around you. If it is difficult to think of a being, just open your mind and welcome any being that loves you, maintaining clarity that you are inviting loving energy only. Though you may not sense them or know who they are, they are gathering nonetheless. I call these beings benefactors.

Now, imagine that your benefactors begin to radiate the energy of love around you. You can imagine this energy as white light or warmth surrounding you, or whatever feels appropriate. Imagine this energy feels like the last time you experienced love, either from someone who often expresses love to you or the passing love of someone smiling at you or letting you cut in front of them in a line. Let these experiences of love spark the expression of loving energy from your benefactors.

Slowly begin to imagine your body absorbing this love. Imagine your skin, muscles, bones, tissues, and organs drinking deeply from this energy. Imagine this love saturating your cells and DNA. What does it feel like to allow yourself to float in this energy of love? Can you release any pain or suffering into this experience of being loved? What does it feel like to let yourself be loved and be held by your benefactors? Stay in this practice for as long as you can or need to.

When you finish, thank your benefactors for loving you and return your attention to the weight of your body contacting the seat. Do some simple movements to reawaken the body and to move energy through the body that may have gotten stuck. Take three deep breaths and imagine releasing any heaviness in the exhale. Hydrate well with water. Imagine that the water is love, nourishing and restoring you.

— THE STREAM OF COMPASSION —

Growing up, *compassion*, like *love*, was a word I couldn't define. I believed that compassion was synonymous with being nice or kind, or even having pity. I know now that being nice or kind are sometimes superficial expressions used to weaponize and manipulate others or to bypass conflict. Pity is just another way of perpetuating power imbalances. When we express pity, we sidestep our own discomfort to highlight the suffering of others, shaming and blaming them while establishing our own moral superiority in the face of their moral failure. When people practice this kind of compassion, they are practicing violence against themselves and others.

I didn't understand compassion until I met God expressed in the form of the Mother called Tara. *Tara* means "star" in Sanskrit. In the Tibetan language, she is called Dolma, which I translate as the "Mother Liberator." She is the embodiment of compassion. When compassion is deeply embodied, that energy shines bright like a star in a dark world full of weaponized niceness and pity. Tara is the North Star. For thousands of years, people have relied on her for safe passage, including my ancestors as they escaped chattel slavery and headed for the promised land of the northern states. She guides us from suffering to freedom.

When I began working with the formal chanting practice of Tara in 2005, I already had a strong practice of compassion, which began to evolve as she guided me into a deeper relationship with my discomfort. The practice of Tara helped to create in me the capacity to hold space for heartbreak.

By 2014, I wasn't practicing Tara as seriously as I had in previous years. However, that summer, Michael Brown was murdered by a Ferguson, Missouri, police officer, and the image of his body lying in the street reminded me of all the ways I was struggling to survive in a country that did not care for Black people. Tara, the Mother Liberator, began calling me back into practice, into the reawakening of compassion for myself, my communities, and all beings who disrupted people's access to the resources they needed.

— WHAT IS COMPASSION? —

My working understanding of compassion begins with the basic Buddhist definition, which is the wish for myself and others to be free from suffering. Compassion is the meeting point between deep empathy for our pain and the pain of others and the wish for us all to be liberated from this pain. The work that arises out of compassion is the strategic and informed intervention into the experience of pain. This understanding of compassion emphasizes action because compassion is useless if we are not actually doing something to get ourselves and others free. Reflecting on compassion and developing compassionate aspirations to liberate ourselves and others is not only the beginning of deepening compassion but also the actual work that begins to bring compassion to its fullest realization.

As I have gotten older, I've begun to feel compassion as an opening to freedom, fluidity, agency, and power to determine how we want to experience freedom. Compassion is not just about caring. It is not the obligatory "thoughts and prayers" after a tragedy. It is the work we engage in that begins to undo the root causes of the tragedy.

Compassion is more than just needing everyone to be free from suffering; it is needing everything to be free. When I say everything, I mean that phenomenal reality must be freed from our misconceptions about it. Freedom is remembering that all phenomena arise from the same essence and will eventually return to that same essence. Compassion frees us from making meaning that does not ultimately point us to freedom but links us deeper into materialism and rigidity.

Choosing compassion means that we must decenter, not completely erase, our sense of self to make room for considering the needs of others. This is an uncomfortable shift. I believe that we must choose discomfort because we will experience discomfort anyway, and by choosing it, we open more to it, reducing the tension we feel when trying to push suffering away.

Aspirational compassion is the basic interest in being free from suffering. This level of compassion feels good. It makes us feel like we are good people. And although aspirational compassion is important, it can be quite performative. We can disrupt performativity by allowing aspirational compassion to evolve into active compassion, which requires moving from wishing to end suffering to doing something to end suffering. This move involves risk; nothing is ever freed without risk.

Compassion is also heartbreaking because it asks us to name our suffering. Just as love is about acceptance of what is and telling the truth of how things are, compassion is the truth of how we suffer and that others are suffering with us even though we tend to forget and try to run away from everything. It is about learning to touch the things we habitually run away from—the brokenheartedness, the trauma, and the rage—and allowing them to be present as we choose to tend to them through practice.

Compassion is also dangerous because we will be compelled to empathize with others, to begin to acknowledge their pain. As a result, our hearts will soften toward people, especially those we dislike and hate. We will begin to humanize them, which is to say that we will no longer be able to label someone inherently evil and choose not to understand the complexities that have informed how they show up in relationships. Compassion restores the truth of complexity for us and others. It reveals that declaring something evil is often just another way we express our unwillingness to do the emotional labor of understanding that "difficult people" may be surviving the depletion of not getting what they need to be well.

So often the people who have hurt us the most do not understand how to get free from their own suffering. Our suffering turns into violence when we can't hold space for the discomfort it causes. We react to it in ways that erase or bypass the experience of who we believe is causing us to suffer. This reactivity replaces the labor of holding and experiencing, distracting us from tending to the primary suffering.

It's hard to get free from suffering when we are so self-identified with it. The years of struggling make it seem like all we are is suffering. We go around saying "I'm angry" or "I'm sad," when in fact we are lying to ourselves; our true nature, our essence, is free from suffering and even liberated from the duality of pain and pleasure itself. To be trapped in the carceral state is to identify with the state that cannot free us. However, when we remember that everything is an experience, we are freed back into a space of fluidity, where even suffering can change because we see it as an experience. It is not inherently who we are.

When I experience compassion, I notice my discomfort, and then I am slowly held warmly and gently in this discomfort. A thought arises, reminding me that in this moment of pain, I am not the only one going through this and that there are countless beings who are uncomfortable. I am not alone. There's something transformative about considering the experiences of others. That empathy offers us space to connect, letting go of the isolation that often comes with suffering as we move from a self-centered pity to belonging to a massive collective of beings. When I experience this spaciousness, I have the room to discern how to get free from suffering as well as to consider how I can be an agent of care for others. It is through this practice that I understand that my suffering as well as the suffering of all beings is asking to be tended to with awareness and space.

We learn to consume suffering by acknowledging it, holding space for it, experiencing it, and responding to it by making choices to reduce that suffering.

PRACTICING RECEIVING COMPASSION

This practice is based on moments when we have experienced compassion from someone that deeply moved us. Once, I was fired from a job that I really loved and had to pack up my things immediately. I was crying through the whole experience: first, because I felt I was unjustly let go, and second, because I felt like I was being thrown away from an organization to which I had offered a lot. As I was packing and crying (frankly, if you haven't found yourself in this situation, you haven't been living!), one of my supervisors (not the one who fired me) came into my office. Her eyes were full of tears. In that moment, I felt like someone understood my suffering. No words were exchanged, but my supervisor still met me in a vulnerable moment with her own vulnerability. This is what I call a spark experience: something I can use to generate the experience of receiving compassion.

When you are ready, come into a position that feels supportive and restful.

Reflect on a moment when you received compassion from someone or another being like a pet. What was that experience like? How had you been feeling before being offered this needed compassion?

Imagine that this experience of receiving compassion begins to awaken in your heart center as light, warmth, or anything that feels natural for you. As this energy grows, imagine you are breathing into the heart center, feeding the energy and allowing it to grow. As you exhale, imagine exhaling that energy throughout the body instead of directly out through the heart center.

Keep inhaling and exhaling like this until you feel as if your whole body is filled with compassion. Now imagine other experiences of receiving compassion from other beings and how that compassion is also filling up your body and mind. Let yourself sit in this energy. Allow it to saturate your body, all the way down into your DNA and even your atoms.

What does it feel like to allow yourself to float in this energy of compassion? Can you release any pain or suffering into this experience of being cared for? What does it feel like to let yourself be held by compassion? Stay in this practice for as long as you can or need to.

When you finish, thank your benefactor who offered this spark and return your attention to the weight of your body contacting the seat. Do some simple movements to reawaken the body and to move energy through the body that may have gotten stuck. Take three deep breaths and imagine releasing any heaviness on the outbreath.

— THE STREAM OF JOY —

For much of my life, I have felt distant from joy. The distance has been informed by a belief that I don't have a right to experience joy and that feeling joy is impossible given the weight of social oppression and transhistorical trauma.

Growing up Black in the South, I was always acutely aware of how Black folks lived at the intersection: we were constantly being excavated and mined for our labor, talent, and creativity by White dominant culture and other subcommunities of Brown folks, all while we were constantly struggling against annihilation from the same cultures that consumed what we produced. On one hand, we were loved. On the other hand, that love was choked by a deep, unnamed insecurity that wasn't held but was reacted to, resulting in various forms of violence against Black folks.

Surviving this intersection pressed us into another intersection: that of joy and sorrow. The collision of these opposite experiences created a tension that jolted us into a sober relationship with the world and how we were placed in it. Even as a child, I understood that so much of what it meant to be Black was an experience of having no choice but to live in the stark truth of how we were not cared for by dominant White culture.

Growing up in church, I sang, "This joy that I have the world didn't give to me / The world didn't give it to me and the world can't take it away." So much has been said and written about Black folks' resilience and strength. We have survived centuries of chattel slavery and systematic annihilation from anti-Black racism. Yet I believe our survival has depended less on our inherent strength and more on our capacity to choose joy, to claim it and embody it as a strategy to disrupt the heavy rigidity of a hostile world.

Joy is an expression of our natural mind and is felt as fluidity and potential. It is the experience of realizing that there are always alternatives, always different paths to take. It is the letting go of the inherent belief in the realness of the phenomenal world and letting the world, which is only energy in space, move instead of staying fixed in place.

Felt in the body, joy is the experience of release, a letting go that feels like putting down a heavy package. At other times joy is the experience of the body as a blooming flower. Joy makes us expand outward to connect to all phenomena. We are no longer afraid of everything around us.

None of these experiences mean that the discomfort of the moment disappears. It doesn't even mean that we are attempting to bypass it. When we choose joy, turning our awareness into the reality of this energy, we notice and feel how all phenomenal reality is buzzing with joy. The potential awakens, and things become malleable, workable, and much less rigid. Though the discomfort doesn't disappear, it becomes more translucent and lighter.

It is also important to understand that happiness and joy are not synonymous. From my experience, happiness is a fleeting emotion, while joy is a permanent state of mind. Further, while joy and bliss are similar energies, they are also radically different experiences.

To explore the relationship of these three energies, let's think about the sun. Bliss is like the sun, which represents the pure, unfiltered, energetic experience of the mind. It is too much for us, as embodied beings, to experience. It would annihilate the body in the same way getting too close to the sun would annihilate our planet. It is an experience of the mind; the body cannot hold it.

Happiness is the heat and light we experience from the sun as earth-bound creatures. However, we can't always feel the full light and warmth of the sun. There are cloudy days and cold, wintery days during which we feel disconnected from the sun. Joy, on the other hand, is not only about feeling the warmth and light from the sun but also remembering that the sun is always there, even when the day is cloudy and cold. Joy is the consistent state of believing in the sun and having that belief constantly sustain us when we choose it.

It can seem impossible to experience and hold joy when the world around us is so overwhelming and dangerous. And for some of us, even if we can experience joy, we feel guilty and repress it because so many others around us are struggling to feel well.

A colleague once told me of their work within a particular country experiencing political unrest. Several militias were engaged in direct combat against a totalitarian regime. My colleague spoke of how members of the militias would celebrate before a day of fighting. They would dance, sing, and laugh, knowing that some or many of them would not survive. My colleague invited me to come and dance with them, these freedom fighters who were so committed to their liberation that they were willing to take up arms and put their lives on the line. And though going into an area of open conflict felt unsettling, I was moved by the display of anger, fear, and death held together by joy and celebration. It reflected the lives of my culture and ancestors, who despite the impossibility of the moment, chose joy as a vehicle to remember the blessing of life and the promise that through work, things could change.

I also think about being queer and about how the queer community has used absurdity and camp to cultivate joy in the face of repression, disrupting rigidity, blurring lines, saying what we have been taught not to say, wearing what makes us happy, laughing at what we take seriously for no reason to release tension and experience spaciousness, loving how we need to love, kissing whom we want to kiss. Choosing joy often means that we choose what is ridiculous because we need to be disrupted to surrender to joy.

Choosing joy is a radical act because it is choosing to see what is often unseen. It is the choice not to absorb the detrimental but to embody what is full of potential. When the anarchist and activist Emma Goldman declared, "If I can't dance to it, it's not my revolution," I felt that she was telling me that if I can't bring joy to the struggle in the same way my ancestors did, then it ain't my struggle. And indeed, so many contemporary freedom movements struggle because there is no room for joy, only a serious intensity that fights against fluidity and potential, sucking up the air and causing creativity and innovation to die.

— EXPERIENCING JOY —

To access joy, we must first learn to choose joy. This practice always proves to be difficult at the beginning because of all the ways we self-identify with suffering. When we find ourselves consumed and overwhelmed by despair or grief, with feeling heavy, rigid, and finite, imagine choosing joy. We won't instantly feel joy, but the energy of our awareness will shift into fluidity and space, shaking loose our identification with and fixation on discomfort.

GRATITUDE PRACTICE

Once we have chosen joy, gratitude practice becomes important because gratitude can easily open the door to the experience of joy.

Gratitude is first realizing that we are the recipients of care from many beings around us and then allowing that experience of being cared for to awaken vulnerability. Once we allow ourselves to be moved, to experience a tenderness and softening where there was once hardness and rigidity, room is made for the experience of joy.

To begin the practice, I invite you to shift your attention down to your heart center. Imagine that you're breathing in and out of the heart center. When you're ready to continue, reflect on something or someone that you're grateful for. After reflecting on this specific experience of gratitude, begin reflecting on all the ways that you've been the recipient of care from countless beings and what all this care has meant for your well-being. Allow this energy of gratitude to awaken within the heart center. What does this energy feel like?

As you breathe into the heart center, imagine that you're breathing into an awakening flame of gratitude. Just like oxygen being fed into a fire, let that flame of gratitude grow and circulate through your whole body. You are beginning to awaken your body and your mind with this profound energy of gratitude.

SHIFTING FROM GRATITUDE INTO JOY

As this energy of gratitude grows, can you allow it to really take care of you, to hold you? What does it mean to surrender to gratitude in this moment? What does it feel like to be cared for by gratitude?

When you are ready, imagine that this experience of gratitude expands into an ocean and allow yourself to float on this ocean, experiencing fluidity and spaciousness. Let yourself experience the pleasure of floating without obstacles or fear. This pleasure is joy. At this point tell yourself that you are experiencing joy. You can stay in this experience as long as you need, letting the experience of joy take care of you.

When you finish, thank your benefactors for caring for you and return your attention to the weight of your body contacting the seat. Do some simple movements to reawaken the body and to move energy through the body that may have gotten stuck. Take three deep breaths and imagine releasing any heaviness in the outbreath.

The Practice of Merging the Streams into Awakened Care

The practice of awakening care is the practice of allowing the streams of love, compassion, and joy to merge and begin awakening our hearts and bodies to start getting ourselves and others free. If you take time working with this practice, you will eventually experience a tender but profound spaciousness that will hold a fierce need to help others get free because you are beginning to experience freedom for yourself.

There are two parts to the practice of awakened care. Part one consists of six stages. First, we begin by developing our intention of getting free by practicing awakened care. Second, our intention leads us to acknowledging the state of clarity and emptiness. Third, after connecting to that clarity, we have the space to awaken our streams of love, compassion, and joy. Letting those streams flow together in our minds forms a vast ocean of awakening care. Fourth, we imagine that this ocean of awakened care flows down into our heart center, filling it up with this energy. Fifth, we imagine this energy circling throughout the body, awakening it. Sixth, we can reflect on how to be of benefit to others from this state.

In part two, we take the energy of awakened care and move through a deeper engagement with the practice in six stages: self-empathy, self-sympathizing, empathy for others, self-care, awakened care for others, and awakened care in action. These stages, described below, help us to deepen the practice in preparation to take action to free beings.

— SELF-EMPATHY —

Awakened care begins with the astonishing act of self-empathy. Awakened care is animated when we connect with our own reality of deep discomfort. By doing this, we are giving ourselves a life that is more realistic and truthful about the basic struggle that we are in. Self-empathy is an act of kindness toward ourselves; we are no longer interested in bullshitting ourselves. For instance, I am no longer interested in bullshitting myself about the fact that I am wounded and traumatized by systemic racism, patriarchy, queerphobia, and capitalism. These systems carve wounds that live deep inside of me. Self-empathy is the first act of kindness in my practice, and it helps me to start noticing these wounds. In the context of SNOELL, self-empathy is the work of seeing and naming our discomfort.

— SELF-SYMPATHIZING —

After we connect with our discomfort, we want to spend time sympathizing with that discomfort. Sympathizing means developing an affinity with the discomfort, which helps us to abide the discomfort. Sympathizing also means we are practicing being gentle and kind with ourselves. We can tell ourselves that it's OK to feel what we are feeling, that every other being in the world has felt this before, and that there are many beings feeling it at this same moment. While empathizing is seeing and naming our discomfort, sympathizing is owning and experiencing it. Sympathizing supports us in sticking with our discomfort long enough to accept it.

Sympathizing also offers us the space to learn that pain is a common and naturally occurring human experience. When I experience pain, I no longer believe that this experience is a special punishment for me. When I am connecting to my pain, I know that there are countless beings experiencing pain at this very moment and that I am not alone.

— EMPATHY FOR OTHERS —

While we can develop sensitivity to our pain through self-empathy and stay in relationship to it through self-sympathy, we extend that knowingness of our discomfort to developing a knowingness of others' discomfort. We begin to understand that there is a community that is shared by all beings, with pain as a part of our experience.

When I am sympathizing with my discomfort, I begin to wonder if there is anyone else who may feel the same way I am feeling. I believe that there are countless people who are having experiences of discomfort, even the person or people around me. This is my transition from self-empathy to empathy for others. It is the transition from "I am experiencing discomfort" to "others are experiencing discomfort, too."

— SELF-CARE —

Awakened care for ourselves begins when we turn our awareness back to our experience of discomfort and decide that we want to experience something besides that discomfort, that perhaps we want to be free from that discomfort. Awakened care for self can only arise when we begin to want a different experience than discomfort for ourselves and for others. It is when we don't want this discomfort for ourselves that we give birth to self-compassion, or the aspiration to be free from suffering. The aspiration to be free is fine. However, wanting to do something to get free is the mark of real, authentic compassion for self.

— AWAKENED CARE FOR OTHERS —

Having generated this wish to be free from our discomfort, we more naturally want others to be free from their discomfort as well. We think that if we don't want to experience this discomfort, then others may not want to experience their discomfort either. When we want others to be free from their suffering in the same way we want to be free from suffering, compassion for others arises. This basic experience motivates us to engage in action to help free all beings, including ourselves, from suffering.

Awakened care for ourselves is so critical because it is through the experience of generating this wish for ourselves that we have insight into generating this wish for others. Compassion for ourselves is the energy that we draw upon to offer compassion to others. As I am wishing and working for others to be happy, I am being guided by the same work I am doing for myself. When we are not drawing from our own self-compassion, the care we offer others will be limited because we will not have the energy to keep extending ourselves. Compassion is like sharing money with people while having enough left over to take care of our needs.

At this point in the SNOELL strategy, compassion is something that I can let go of and let float. This feels like letting go of needing or trying to be compassionate and resting within the experience of compassion itself. The experience is for both me and others. This is the edge where we can understand what it feels like to *be* compassion itself.

AWAKENED CARE IN ACTION

It is easy to interpret the traditional teaching on compassion as developing a specific attitude that says suffering is not an experience that any being prefers, which leads to us just wanting all beings to be free from suffering without taking the risk of getting involved with helping to free beings from suffering. The cause of suffering is ignorance, which in Buddhist philosophy is the opposite of wisdom or clarity. Thus, suffering arises from our lack of understanding the true nature of our minds and phenomenal reality. However, in my teaching and practice of compassion, I have given myself no choice but to see compassion not just as an attitude or even an aspiration but as the fuel that drives my action to liberate people. The practice of awakened care can help us transition from the safety of aspirations into the risk-taking of liberation.

Part One: Beginning the Practice

To start, allow yourself to come into a position that feels good and supportive for your body. When you are ready, begin reflecting on your intention for the practice. An intention is not a goal or an agenda. It is the answer to the question of why you are doing this at this moment. In the New Saint's tradition, we are practicing to free ourselves and everyone and everything around us. Imagine that this intention is beginning to guide your session.

Now shift into your basic clarity practice, moving through SNOELL and connecting to emptiness.

Turn your attention to awakening the three streams. Begin with love and imagine that energy beginning to fill your mind. Do this with the other two streams as well. Imagine that these three streams are flowing together in your mind, creating a vast, boundless ocean that is forming the experience of awakened care.

Now imagine that this ocean of awakened care flows down into your heart center. Imagine that your heart center begins to awaken as it drinks deeply from this ocean of care. Fill the heart center up.

Next, imagine that you are breathing in and out of the heart center. Slowly imagine inhaling into the heart center and then exhaling into the body, carrying the energy of awakened care throughout the body. Keep doing this until you feel like the body is full of awakened care. What does it feel like to fill the body with this energy?

Finally, from this state, reflect on the ways you can be of benefit to others and even imagine that this energy is flowing out of your body (without your body being depleted) into situations in the world that need this energy.

Part Two: Going Deeper

Take a short break to readjust yourself and settle again into a position that seems appropriate. Reconnect to the energy of awakened care in your mind and body.

Now, turn your attention to the first of the six stages, which is self-empathy.

Using the first two stages of SNOELL, I invite you to see and name any experience of discomfort. Once you have named this experience, direct the energy of awakened care into the experience. Imagine that the ocean of awakened care begins to hold this experience for you.

Next, allow yourself to sympathize with the experience (stage two). Continue to notice and experience it. As you experience the discomfort, allow the energy of awakened care to support you and the discomfort itself.

Now shift your attention toward developing empathy for others (stage three). Remaining grounded in awakened care, begin to wonder about the experiences of others and how they suffer just like you do. You are not trying to take on the suffering of others, but you are noticing it and feeling how other people's discomfort mirrors yours.

Shift your attention back to yourself and offer yourself awakened care (stage four). At the same time, wonder what it would be like to be free from this discomfort and anything that keeps you from the resources you need to experience happiness and safety. Anchored in awakened care, spend as much time as possible imagining what freedom would feel like.

Now turn your attention back to others. Imagine what it would be like for others to be free and have all the resources they need to experience happiness and safety (stage five). Imagine radiating the energy of awakened care out to all beings while not depleting your own awakened care in your body and mind.

TAKING THE PRACTICE TO THE STREETS

It has been so important for me to take the practice of awakened care and radiate it outward as I move through my day. Like you, I must interact with people most days, and some of those interactions can be frustrating. Anytime I have conflict with someone, I use contemplations like these to open my heart and deepen my empathy for people, putting awakened care into action (stage six).

Contemplations

How much do you know about the person in front of you? You may think that you know their gender or race or ethnicity. This person may identify in various ways across gender and sexuality spectrums. Maybe they identify in ways that you do not understand. Maybe you judge the ways in which they identify. Maybe you assume that they are as well educated as you. You may think that they have the same spiritual beliefs because you are here together. What else do you assume about this person? How do you think they suffer because of the assumptions that others make about them? Are you really seeing this person or are you seeing your own assumptions projected onto them?

At some point, the person in front of you may have survived significant trauma, sexual assault, or other forms of physical violence. They may be a survivor of emotional or other kinds of psychological abuse, or they may be in an abusive relationship right now. This person may be in recovery from substance abuse, or they may be struggling with addiction in some way. They may be struggling now to be present. At some point, this person has been afraid. Fear may have been and may continue to be crippling for them. Maybe they are afraid now. Maybe they are afraid of you. Maybe you are afraid of them.

The person in front of you has at some point been sad. They may have cried. Maybe they have cried a lot. Maybe they have cried recently. Maybe they have felt alone and lonely. Maybe they feel alone now. This person may be a survivor of depression or be struggling with or managing depression or other mental illnesses. Maybe they have a hard time trusting the world and do not feel safe in many places. Maybe they have gotten used to never feeling OK in a space. When you first saw this person, did you wonder why they were here? Did you think that they did not belong?

The person in front of you has at some point been misunderstood. Maybe they have a hard time expressing themselves. Maybe they have often been in spaces or situations where their ideas have not been valued or taken seriously. Maybe they don't feel safe enough to express themselves. Maybe they have something to say but can't find the words to say it or feel like no one will care. Maybe being misunderstood has been a large part of their suffering in the world. Maybe this person wants, above all, to be understood, heard, and seen. Maybe you want to be heard and seen as well.

The person in front of you is just like you. They, too, want to avoid suffering and be happy. They love someone or something. They want to be happy and perhaps they want the people they love to be happy as well. And maybe just like you, it is difficult for them to do that.

Maybe it's hard for them to know how to make better choices. Perhaps they have significantly hurt other people before, intentionally and/or unintentionally. Maybe they seek to reconcile with those they have hurt. Maybe you are the person they have hurt. Or perhaps you have hurt them in some way.

How can you hold the complexity of what has risen for you in your experience?

Practicing Self-Care

Like you, I have been really exhausted. Though I now enjoy my life, it has required intense labor to get to where I can experience this level of mental and physical wellness. I am grateful for the labor, but it has cost a lot. The past couple of COVID pandemic years have invited me to reevaluate how I spend my time and direct my energy. I have come to understand more deeply that I must protect my energy, especially in a culture where we are encouraged to ignore the preciousness of our energy and often find ourselves spending it recklessly, resulting in imbalance.

Protecting my energy is one of the ways I have learned to practice care for myself. The care we offer ourselves is crucial in the New Saint's tradition because care is how we fuel our labor to get free, and it is what we use to fuel the work of collective care. I am intentionally focusing on individual care because it is often bypassed in discussions of collective care. Collective care becomes much more difficult when we, as individuals, haven't first done the work to understand what we need.

My goal is to care for myself in order to care for my collectives. I have not been called to be a martyr in this life, and you have probably not been either. I am called to survive to help bring about the new world that I believe we are giving birth to.

Mother Audre Lorde has been shaping my understanding of self-care for years. When she wrote in the *Cancer Journals*, "Caring for myself is not self-indulgence, it is self-preservation, and that is an act of political warfare," she taught me and many of us that self-care wasn't only about feeling good; it was about understanding how to survive systems of violence that attempt to annihilate us. Our survival through self-care was how we helped our communities survive.

Self-care means that we begin to develop a sensitivity to our emotional, physical, and mental well-being, and we offer ourselves permission to gather and receive the resources needed to reestablish that well-being. Experiencing well-being means that I am experiencing balance. Balance doesn't just mean feeling good. It also means that I have the capacity to hold both comfort and discomfort in awareness. When I think of care, I return to the work of tending. Tending expresses tenderness, gentleness, love, and compassion. The softness of tending feels warm and expansive.

Being resourced means that I have the energy to do the work that is needed to care for myself, loved ones, and my community. I often imagine this energy of resourcefulness being like a fire offering warmth and light that must be tended to by feeding it with wood. The wood is the actual self-care we are doing to feed the fire of being resourced. When I am not feeding the fire, I am going cold and shutting down.

Self-care has too often been aligned with overconsumption and materialism. When we hear about self-care, we tend to think about self-indulgence. This understanding of self-care is pleasure-based and highly isolating. In the New Saint's tradition, we practice self-care to experience enough resourcefulness to return to the work of supporting others. This is liberatory self-care: it is care we rely on to get free and to help others get free. The difference between liberatory self-care and self-indulgent care is intention. Whenever I do something to care for myself—from resting to watching TV—I am clear that I do these things to feel well enough to help others feel well.

— DESERVING CARE —

Even liberatory self-care remains difficult for many of us because we don't believe that we deserve care to begin with. I often say that the world is trying to care for us, but we keep sabotaging that care. I frequently sabotaged care from others because I believed that I wasn't good enough to be cared for. I also believed that I didn't deserve care because there were so many other people in the world going without it. I felt that if I received care, then that would take care away from others. It helped me to reflect on my personal ethics related to liberation and how I could never offer the help I wanted to offer to others if I wasn't receiving and opening to the care that was being offered to me. If I am not getting the care I need, then I am likely entering into relationships depleted and taking resources from others instead of offering needed resources back. So, my current ethics related to self-care are one, as a human I deserve care to experience well-being and two, if I can't get the care I need, then I will not have the resources to help others.

— EXPLORING NEEDS —

Sometimes I struggle with care simply because I don't even know what I need. The question of what we need may be hard for many of us because we have never thought about what we need. It may also be challenging because we have never been encouraged to understand our needs, let alone have those needs met. Or maybe this question is challenging because we confuse needs with wants. In my personal practice as well as in my practice supporting others, I have often found this question to be triggering because it forces us to not just understand what we need but to name the hurt we feel from not having our needs met. So, in other words, to explore our needs is to also explore the woundedness from having those needs unmet.

A need is something that is imperative for our physical and emotional well-being. I need food, clothing, medicine, healthy relationships, and rest. These things help maintain my health, and when I get these things, I feel well enough to help others. Sometimes I get confused about my needs and wants. Though I think it's wonderful to get what we want, our needs are primary resources we must focus on gathering. Needs provide a more lasting nourishment. They leave us feeling connected, balanced, and resilient.

A want is something that feels good to have and experience. Wants fulfill basic desires for pleasure and fun. Though pleasure and fun are wonderful and can also be needs, when we lack an awareness of how to use pleasure as an experience of liberation, it can become self-indulgent, leading to overconsumption. Overconsumption means I bypass what is needed in favor of accumulation. Often I use consumption to cover up or numb discomfort.

In our practice, we can merge our needs and wants. This happens when we get clear about our needs and experience the restorative effect of having them met. That feeling of restoration makes us want more of it so what we want becomes also what we need.

— EXPANSIVE AND CONTRACTING HABITS —

My self-care is about understanding how to balance contracting activity with expansive activity. In general, self-care should feel fluid, as it opens space for us to move and understand what is possible. Expansive activity opens us up, as we are remembering and leaning into the space in and around everything. Contracting activity is what shuts us down and prompts a tightening around discomfort. We are naturally hovering between these two extremes because we are constantly negotiating work we don't want to do, prompting constriction, along with work we do want to do, prompting openness. The goal is to train ourselves to balance these two experiences. This is the teaching of the middle way of Buddhism, which is the embodiment of balance.

There are a lot of things in my life that I don't want to do. This list includes answering emails and texts, dealing with suffering, dealing with difficult people, paying taxes, and the list goes on and on! Because I don't derive pleasure from them, I have an aversion to doing them. This experience of aversion is also the experience of contraction or shutting down, which is the disconnection from the inherent space in and around everything. Although I think I am avoiding these things, I find myself fixated on not wanting to do them, which is very similar to being fixated on the things themselves.

When I talk about expansive self-care habits, I am speaking of how we engage in activities that promote experiences of spaciousness. These are the things that I want to do because of the pleasure I get from experiencing them. Whatever is expansive is what inspires and excites me. This kind of stimulus helps us to open and relax, to have the space to settle more instead of residing in tension. Therefore, it's important to balance contracting work with expansive work. Knowing that I am not excited about emails, I try to balance that contraction with the expansive activity of listening to music.

— GETTING CLEAR ABOUT OUTPUT AND INPUT —

I put a lot of energy out into my work, relationships, and communities through spiritual and emotional labor. When thinking about times I have experienced overdepletion, I have invested more energy out than was returned or reinvested in me. There must be a balance between what we put out and what is returned to us, even if the resources that should be returning to us are resources that we must gather and offer back to ourselves. My teacher, Ma Jaya Sati Bhagavat, taught that we must drink as we pour, meaning that a huge part of our spiritual and community work is getting sensitive about how we are pouring too much into the world, which may leave us depleted.

Over the past few years, I have gotten much clearer about how I pour energy into the world and how boundaries have helped protect my energy. This has pushed me to think of relationships in terms of skillful transactions. It is easy to reduce work into transactional terms that mimic capitalist models. Yet when I say "skillful transactions," I mean to highlight and name what I need to do the work of caring for others. Without resources, I offer my labor from a place of depletion, which will end up harming me as well as those I am in relationship with. Reaction to depletion manifests as resentment and passive aggressiveness toward others.

Boundary work has helped me to understand the importance of skillful transactions in all my relationships. I enter relationships because there is something important I can get out of them, which contributes to my experience of feeling resourced, and at the same time I try to be clear about what I am offering back into the relationship that helps others experience being resourced. It is OK to have some sensitivity to what you are getting out of a relationship if you are clear about what you are offering in return.

And then there are relationships that I enter into solely as an agent of support where I must be careful about understanding that having boundaries helps me to take breaks from the relationship to gather resources instead of expecting the people or communities to offer something back.

In my professional life as a teacher, there have been many cases where I have felt that my desire to be of help has been taken advantage of. I want to be cared for and respected by others as I offer important labor, but so often I have felt the opposite of care. After years of feeling frustrated, I started setting protective boundaries. At first I tried to accept all invitations and opportunities I was offered, but now I am careful about making sure appropriate resources are offered to me—things like financial compensation (so I can have a resource to gather other resources like food, housing, etc.) or the feeling of being cared for and appreciated for my work.

We must practice intentional selfishness when we are attempting to take care of ourselves. We must know what we need and what we want in order to support the collective in a way that is not reproducing harm and violence. When I know what I need and want, I'll also understand the things that I can't do for myself. And so when I lean on the collective, knowing what I am asking those around me to help me with, I also understand what I can offer back to the collective. The path of liberatory self-care isn't about bypassing what I need in order to perform a kind of selflessness that makes me look good. Liberatory self-care is about understanding what I need and then understanding how to get what I need while offering others what they need. Ultimately, what we all need is to get free.

The Four Sweet Liberations

This chapter is about, dedicated to, and in celebration of Black queer, trans, and gender-expansive folks—a community that refuses to keep silent when told to shut up, that dances when told to be still, and that sings even though we know our music will be stolen for other people's profit. We sing because we are happy, we sing because our hearts are full of sorrow, and we sing because those who wish us dead need to hear what real beauty sounds like so that they, too, can remember their beauty and their preciousness.

As a child, I never felt like I had a right to beauty. There was something ugly and incomprehensible about being a little boy in a house full of extended family. Our neighborhood, on the east side of town, wore the marks of decades of redlining. Some Black people had just managed to achieve the dream of homeownership in the shadow of Jim Crow by getting jobs at the mill or factory or by collecting life insurance payouts from departed loved ones. We fought off the brutality of poverty by banding together, living collectively, contributing something to the bills and mortgages, and surviving on land our ancestors had been laboring on for hundreds of years.

As I grew older, I longed for ways to reshape the ugliness around me, from the worn-down appearance of homes and streets in my neighborhood to the sadness and anger I felt in the people around me. When my mother and I moved to the projects, I began watching the few cooking and home improvement shows on TV back then. I was desperate for something beautiful, and I was willing to learn how to create it. From then on, I struggled to understand my relationship to beauty and wanting nice things, especially as I made a more formal entrance into activism and developed insight into the harm of consumerism. Entering the spiritual life on top of activism resulted in a good deal of anxiety over my attachment to beauty, as I was being taught to strive for simplicity and to let go of craving for the riches of the material world.

Liberation Through Style

For most of my life, I was aware of André Leon Talley but never knew who he really was outside of the fashion magazines like *Vogue* I glimpsed him in. However, several years ago, I felt a sudden urge to learn more about him and found myself studying his life.

He mirrored so much of me—Black, gay, southern born and raised, larger bodied, educated, excelling in communities where Black folks are severely underrepresented, and generally devoted to some form of fabulousness. He became a teacher for me; he embodied an ethic that was often dismissed but for me held joy and clarity.

He challenged me to claim my right to beauty. In the opening of his documentary *The Gospel According to André*, he reflects the following:

I don't live for fashion. I live for beauty and style. Fashion is fleeting. Style remains. I think that beauty comes in many forms. It can be a flower. It can be a gesture. It can be so many things . . . But you must also cultivate your own aesthetic in your own universe. Create your own universe and share it with people that you respect and love.

Talley has taught me to dream of liberation and to invite others into that dream. From his teaching I understand that although liberation is the hardest work, it is also the most beautiful work. To notice how the mundane world arises, simple and uncomplicated, points us back to the essence. Style is the form in which we do the work of liberation. This book is an expression of my style of liberation work, which is rich, multifaceted, complex, and joyful. One of my dear friends taught me that when we choose a style, we must own it—owning it makes it meaningful for us. Others may not understand our style but will appreciate our commitment to it.

Talley also taught me that clothes have meaning and that they reflect something vital about our own inner beauty. My style reflects the communities I belong to and how I want people to relate to me. People often imagine that a spiritual teacher needs to be draped in earth tones and flowing garments. Frankly, these are not my colors, and I don't need a lot of extra fabric hanging off me. My style is urban, street, hip, contemporary—what I like to call "spiritual fabulous." This style has helped me teach better because I am comfortable with what I am wearing, and it tells the truth of where I come from and belong.

Nevertheless, I wrestled with the question of how to offer this clarity as a spiritual practice while simultaneously disrupting over-consumption, capitalism, and escapism. My answer? The Four Sweet Liberations: leisure, beauty, opulence, and pleasure.

The Four Sweet Liberations

The Four Sweet Liberations are the practices that I had to reclaim for myself to experience care and freedom in a world that too often frames beauty as an aesthetic of material consumption. The practice of the liberations isn't about showing loyalty to capitalism. Neither is it about having fun to bypass our deep insecurities.

The liberations are a means for me to think about the many energies in and around me. In this framework leisure, beauty, opulence, and pleasure are only energies that take on the drag of material things. These materials are trying to take care of us but because we misunderstand their worldly appearance or abuse and manipulate them to bypass pain, we are not living in a balanced relationship with them.

For example, I would like a BMW. I don't need a BMW but getting one would make me feel really special. Having worked with this desire for years now, I can finally understand that a BMW is just an expression of energy that helps me to feel valued, especially after growing up and having to continually survive systemic anti-Blackness, queerphobia, and antifatness. I don't want to just experience the energy of something valuable; I want to embody that energy to restore my constantly attacked self-worth. It was the ancestor Octavia St. Laurent, a daughter of the House of St. Laurent featured in the groundbreaking documentary *Paris Is Burning*, who said it best: "I wanna be somebody. I mean, I am somebody. I just wanna be a rich somebody." The ballroom culture explored in *Paris Is Burning* and shows like *Pose* was created as a container to simulate conditions for my community to experience being valued and seen. To echo and extend what Octavia shared, I am somebody as well, but I want to feel the richness of somebody who belongs in the world and who doesn't have to fight every day to be seen and appreciated. I want to be that kind of rich.

We overconsume resources not only because we are attempting to use the pleasure of consumption to bypass our suffering but also because we have yet to understand that it is not the things we want but rather the feeling of being wanted and appreciated. It is the longing to be the recipients of the same love our favorite clothes or jewelry get. It's the yearning to feel like we are wanted and loved.

The phenomenal world is just a swirl of energy that our consciousness is constantly shaping into phenomena. What the Sweet Liberation practices are attempting to do is help us connect to the energy itself, to let go of this exhaustive shaping and just experience the liberation of these energies without the overconsumption and intense materialism.

When we let ourselves drink deeply from the richness of the phenomenal world through meditation, we can begin to relax, expanding and offering space to this sense of self, and in that spaciousness, we feel satisfied.

When you think of leisure, you probably imagine people lounging on the beach, having a cocktail. All of this is in line with the spirit of leisure because leisure is about being at ease, which is an experience we can have anywhere, not just when we are at the beach.

In Western-convert Buddhist circles, you often hear the phrase "May you be at ease." It is a form of loving-kindness that wishes for people to have the grounding to hold space for whatever arises for them instead of feeling overwhelmed and swept away. Being at ease is an expression of leisure. Practicing leisure means that we have the agency to choose how to hold space for what arises and to choose a response.

Practicing leisure also means resting. Sleeping is not the same thing as resting. Resting is an intentional act of letting things go and letting everything float within the wide-open space of our minds, just as we do in the last two stages of the SNOELL practice. In letting go, we can enter a powerful restoration period. Our energy shifts away from producing anxiety to settling back into our bodies to help with healing.

Leisure is a practice of moving in your own time. Moving and acting in your own time means that you are moving at the speed of your body while training your mind to stay with your physical body in the present moment. The mind can be anywhere at any time, but the physical body is in the present and its movement is bound by the relative world.

Leisure is also a boundary that helps us protect our space to rest and be at ease. Leisure is hardest for those of us who are disembodied because leisure is dictated by the needs of our physical body. The most powerful tool in the service of our leisure is the word *no* because no is the ultimate boundary setter, offering our bodies the space to rest.

Leisure is the experience of slowing down. I notice fatigue in my body, and that fatigue asks me to tend to it. I want to allow my body to settle in a position that feels restorative. I want to offer the concerns of the moment to the space I encounter. When I experience leisure, I imagine offering this energy out to all beings so that they can experience what I'm experiencing now.

— BEAUTY —

Growing up Black, fat, and queer in the South, the world taught me that I didn't deserve to survive. It taught me that I wasn't beautiful and that I didn't have a right to beauty. When I talk about this in my work, some people get confused or think that I am overexaggerating because they haven't had to survive being called too fat, a faggot, or ugly or having to survive otherness as a Black person in a white supremacist culture. These words are spells casting doubt over your right to experience happiness or to simply exist.

André Leon Talley's proclamation that he lived for beauty and style may sound like a superficial statement if you believe that beauty and style are only about material consumption. But beauty is a personal experience of being drawn into something. It is an invitation to drop the barricade. It is an intimate alignment that prompts us to open and yield to something that triggers emotional vulnerability.

When I say something is beautiful, what I'm really trying to express is that I am encountering something that moves me, or something that has broken my heart open because it has invited me to transcend what is ordinary and expand into the extraordinary. Beauty helps me to experience myself in the moment, which includes longing for the beauty that has moved me. In this way, beauty makes me feel alive. Style, in this sense, is not so much how I do the work of liberation but how I embody and perform my experience of beauty. Style is also how I am changed by my experience of beauty.

A mundane, outward expression of beauty is the experience of attraction and pleasure. What I consider beautiful makes me feel good. When I allow myself to really experience what feeling good feels like, I notice myself surrendering—I may feel a loss of agency. I am doing nothing but letting go and resting in this surrender, which is laden with pleasure.

Beauty also feels familiar. When I think someone is attractive, I feel like I know them and trust them. They seem so familiar to me that I spend time trying to figure out where I know them from. I usually don't know them, but I let my guard down. This is one of the expressions of the politics of beauty: how we overvalue and trust attractive people.

In this state of rest, my awareness is expanding out into the spaciousness of pleasure and into the experience of the sublime. The sublime is the awakened state of beauty, which is an expression of the absolute, or God. The sublime is our direct experience of the absolute. To remain in the sublime is to allow the sublime to be without clinging to it or wanting anything from it. The more we let it be, the more we dwell in this awakened state.

Eventually, we fall back into the mundane experience of beauty. But as we come back, we will be changed because the awakened experience has helped us to experience beauty in its liberated state, and we will naturally want to incorporate that wisdom into how we move through the world. This incorporation is what I call style.

I have grieved more for the passing of André Leon Talley than I have for the passing of most of my lineage spiritual teachers. The grieving is so intense because I am missing someone who had been reflecting to me my right to choose something different for myself. I am missing someone who was telling me I have a right to be seen, to fuck up systematic erasure and choose the good stuff for myself. I am missing someone who helped me to understand that beauty is restorative, and my claiming of beauty and even elegance is transhistorical emotional labor that I am doing not just for myself but for all my ancestors whose land and forced labor were stolen to make White people and America beautiful and revered.

I share whatever beauty I experience out to all beings so that they, too, may experience the healing of beauty.

— OPULENCE —

To begin this discussion, I evoke the legendary ballroom emcee Junior LaBeija when he proclaimed in *Paris Is Burning*, "O-P-U-L-E-N-C-E! Opulence. You own everything! Everything is yours!"

Opulence is autumn, when the harvest is ready to be gathered and trees blossom in fiery oranges, yellows, and reds. Autumn reminds me that the land and plant life have labored to care for all of us and that this display is the final pageant before the rest that comes with winter. The autumn is always asking me to drink in this abundance, to feel restored and nourished.

Opulence is perhaps the hardest of the liberations because it challenges us to deal with abundance. It has been challenging for me because I have learned to be comfortable with depletion to such an extent that I experience it as normal. When you grow up in and around poverty, you get used to not having what you need, and you function out of that acclimation. So much of the work of justice is redistributing resources—channeling material and financial wealth from people and communities that are overconsuming or hoarding these resources to communities that desperately need them. Some of us vehemently reject richness because we feel it jeopardizes our solidarity with those who struggle to get basic resources.

Connecting to richness means that I am tuning in to the resources that are mine to consume. These resources include material things, but the resources I need most are love, kindness, compassion, intimacy, and belonging.

What opulence helps us understand is that we are out of balance. We are overconsuming what is detrimental and underconsuming what is imperative. And what is imperative is for us to consume anything that helps us experience wellness, love, compassion, and belonging to community.

Throughout my life, I have been invited into a deeper relationship with richness because I was stuck in malnourishment. This malnourishment felt like a lack of creativity and connectedness. It felt dull and boring. It was hard to open to richness because I felt like I didn't deserve or need anything. Once, I really wanted a pair of red shoes. I was hesitant to buy them because I had never owned red shoes. I didn't know how to incorporate them into my style. When I gave in and bought a pair, wearing them inspired me to try different things and eventually opened a door to a new creative side of me.

In a way, most of us are energetically constipated, which is to say that energies are stuck and blocked all throughout our bodies. A major part of Tantric traditions is learning how to use the breath to unlock and move energies around, which allows us to come into a manageable equilibrium. When we struggle to hold space for strong, energetic experiences like emotions or trauma, our energy is blocked. As a collective on this planet, we are severely blocked, which explains so much of the violence we are all forced to endure.

The outward, mundane experience of opulence is richness, abundance, and seeing the world as full of resources, both material and energetic, even though we feel as if we do not have access to these resources. When I start opening to the richness around me, I allow my mind and body to start absorbing this richness, guiding this energy into parts of my experience that need to be nourished. In nourishment I feel less anxious and can relax and expand my awareness into the space opening in and around me. When I can just be in this expansion without clinging or shutting down, I enter the state of repletion, in which I transcend both craving and aversion.

I dedicate the most and best of everything out to all beings so that they experience opulence and the healing that comes with having what they need.

— PLEASURE —

As I begin to write this, I am having a chocolate chip cookie made by a friend. Pleasure is as simple as relishing the flavor combination of butter, brown sugar, vanilla, and chocolate. I enjoy eating this cookie.

I relax my body and settle even deeper into my seat. This feels good. In this pleasure, the world doesn't seem so antagonistic.

Pleasure is related to enjoyment. Enjoyment, in this case, is the experience of holding space for everything that arises without reacting to it. When we feel enjoyment, we enter a fluid space where we can shift awareness to what feels good in our minds and bodies. This shifting of awareness to what feels good is desire. When I am doing the emotional labor of holding space, desire is something I can choose to enjoy.

There are many ways we can experience pleasure. The phenomenal world is full of it. Pleasure is at the heart of all the sweet liberations. I enjoy beauty, opulence, and leisure. These experiences usher me into space, and it is in spaciousness I can experience the essence.

I haven't always been able to allow myself to experience pleasure like this. I struggle with pleasure, just as I struggle with all the other sweet liberations, because I feel like I don't have a right to feel good. So much of my ancestors' pleasure was policed and surveilled. Their physical bodies were never their own, so pleasure as sensation felt distant for them. I used to distrust pleasure because I distrusted my body.

Desire as attachment is considered one of the three poisons in Buddhism that keeps samsara, or the carceral state, going. However, at the same time, desire is important because we have to want things. We have to want to get free, to reduce violence, and to benefit others. Desire can be tended to by awareness and care, offering it lots of space while we guide it toward things that are helpful for us. Desire is crucial to the very last second of ultimate liberation—or enlightenment—because wanting to get free takes us all the way to the threshold. To move beyond the threshold, we must let go of everything we are holding on to. It's like diving into a pool. We have to let go and fall in completely. This is the same idea for enlightenment. At the threshold, we let go of all desire for freedom, and at that moment, we achieve freedom.

This may come as a shock, but I enjoy a good strip club. For the few years leading up to my twenty-first birthday, I dreamed about finally being able to get into a strip club. There was an infamous male strip club in Atlanta that my gay friends would go to, and they would return with glorious stories of naked men, cocktails, and other activities I probably shouldn't mention. On the day I finally turned twenty-one, I made my first of many pilgrimages to the club with a few other friends. There was one dancer I nearly fell in love with. Everything about him was arousing. I had never felt that activated before. But after the club, shame started setting in, like a sunny day slowly being smothered by storm clouds. In the club, I felt so alive and free, but once I had left, I felt like I had done something bad and would be punished for it.

Erotic pleasure always felt tainted because queer desire has historically been treated as perverse and unnatural. This desire could and can get me killed. I am still risking so much by choosing to express desire and seek erotic pleasure with other men.

Like the other liberations, pleasure is something we can experience on behalf of other beings who may not have access to pleasure for some reason. So, I offer what pleasure I experience out to all beings.

THE PRACTICES OF THE FOUR SWEET LIBERATIONS

The practices of the Four Sweet Liberations can be done individually or all together, as offered here.

To begin with, shift your attention to the energy of leisure. Start reflecting on things that you find relaxing and restorative. As you reflect, imagine that the energy of leisure begins to awaken in your heart center as white light. As you inhale, imagine breathing into the heart center the energy of leisure, feeling that the breath is intensifying this energy. As you exhale, imagine exhaling the energy of leisure as white light throughout the body—an internal exhale.

Keep breathing like this until you experience your whole body full of the energy of leisure. What does it feel like to be filled with the essence of leisure? How does your body want to respond to this energy? Can you allow your body to respond?

Next, shift your attention to the energy of beauty. Start reflecting on things that you find beautiful. As you reflect, imagine that the energy of beauty begins to awaken in your heart center as white light. As you inhale, imagine breathing into the heart center the energy of beauty, feeling that the breath is intensifying this energy. As you exhale, imagine exhaling the energy of beauty as white light throughout the body—an internal exhale. Keep breathing like this until your whole body is full of the energy of beauty. What does it feel like to be filled with the essence of beauty? How does your body want to respond to this energy? Can you allow your body to respond?

Next, shift your attention to the energy of opulence. Start reflecting on things that you feel are abundant and opulent. As you reflect, imagine that the energy of opulence begins to awaken in your heart center as white light. As you inhale, imagine breathing into the heart center the energy of opulence, feeling that the breath is intensifying this energy. As you exhale, imagine exhaling the energy of opulence as white light throughout the body—an internal exhale. Keep breathing like this until you experience your whole body full of the energy of opulence. What does it feel like to be filled with the essence of opulence? How does your body want to respond to this energy? Can you allow your body to respond?

Now, shift your attention to the energy of pleasure. Start reflecting on things that you enjoy. As you reflect, imagine that the energy of pleasure begins to awaken in your heart center as white light. As you inhale, imagine breathing into the heart center the energy of pleasure, feeling that the breath is intensifying this energy. As you exhale, imagine exhaling the energy of pleasure as white light throughout the body—an internal exhale. Keep breathing like this until you experience your whole body full of the energy of pleasure. What does it feel like to be filled with the essence of pleasure? How does your body want to respond to this energy? Can you allow your body to respond?

Now imagine that all these awakened energies begin to merge together within your body, beginning to radiate with the radiance of these liberations. Like a star, let yourself radiate clear, pure light out into the darkness of depletion. Imagine that your light begins to illuminate others in your life who need to experience this restoration. Imagine that everyone your light touches begins to experience replenishment. At the same time, continue to drink in this energy all the way down to your DNA and atoms. Do this for as long as it feels appropriate before shifting out of the practice and gently moving your body.

The Care of Home

Ever since I was little, *The Wiz* has been one of my favorite movies. I loved how it revised the original *Wizard of Oz* story using the complexities of Black life, including the bonds we form in our families. I was drawn to one of the movie's central themes, which was understanding the power and importance of home. Dorothy, portrayed by Diana Ross, is transported to this alternative land called Oz, where she and her friends journey to meet the Wizard, or Wiz, of the hip and ultrachic Emerald City.

When I think of home, I think of being in a place where I am wanted. I think of being in a place where people notice me and see me. It is a place where I can say my name without fear of being judged or being afraid of hurting someone's feelings. Home means belonging not just to a physical location or a group of people, but to myself. When I say "home," I mean that I am resting in my own experience. I am resting within the recognition of who I am, not within the projections of those around me telling me who I am. This kind of belonging is restorative care we can offer to ourselves.

Home has also been a central theme in my life because it has represented safety, comfort, and the experience of being loved. When I was born, my mother and I lived with my grandmother and a few uncles. I remember the fierce love of my mother and grandmother. Later, my mother and I moved out into the projects, which became another kind of home as I lived closely with other kids my age, creating strong friendships and an experience of community outside of familial bonds.

We all need places to be and belong. One form of suffering is not having anywhere to go. I am most unsafe in an anti-Black environment when I do not have a place to go to experience safety and care. I struggle with looking idle in public places because of how anti-Blackness renders me dangerous. I feel most policed when White people glance or stare, wondering if I am looking to rob them or sell drugs or just believe that I don't belong because anti-Blackness means I don't belong anywhere.

I want to be surrounded by the things that I care about. When I offer that care to things in my home, they return that care to me. When I sweep, mop, or vacuum the floors of my home, I am extending care, and care is returned by having clean floors to walk on. When I clean my bathroom, I am creating an environment where I feel confident engaging in needed rituals of cleanliness. When I declutter my home, moving out things that I don't use or care for, there is a sense that my living space is breathing, and energy is flowing and supporting me in experiencing rest and safety.

Caring for my home is an extension of the ways that I care for myself. When I care for myself, it becomes natural to care for others and other things because I know how special and restorative it can feel to be cared for, and I want everything around me to experience restoration. At this point, I know that I struggle to care for other things when I am not feeling cared for—I feel as if I don't have enough energy, space, or inspiration to extend to other things. I can look around my home and it will tell me how well I am caring for myself by reflecting to me how well I'm caring for it, evidenced by a sink full of dirty dishes, piles of unwashed laundry, a dirty bathroom, or a disheveled workspace. I know that living and working in a home that feels chaotic is not restorative, so taking care to clean up and organize is how I can care for both my home and myself at the same time.

When a home is cared for, it returns that care back to you. When I am in my home, I am feeling my home radiate joy. I feel its pleasure. It knows that I am dedicated to its care because it knows that I am dependent on it for my well-being, just as I know that it is dependent on me for its well-being. When I am feeling exhausted or overwhelmed, I feel my home drawing close to me and reminding me that I am safe and being cared for. Because of this relationship, my home keeps me warm, dry, and comfortable—not because it must or because it is a natural function of its structure and purpose but because it wants to. My home cares for itself by extending care to me, making it possible for me to further care for it.

My home is conscious. To say that my home is conscious is to say that it possesses awareness. My current home is a home that I lease, which has also been blessed and lived in by friends in one of my spiritual communities. When the home was offered to me, I was excited to accept the offer, knowing how it had been cared for. After my friends who had been living here moved out, the house was empty for a few weeks as the owners did repairs before I moved in. In the evenings, I would come and sit on the porch and make smoke offerings to it. I felt that the house was mourning my friends leaving and trying to look forward to me moving in. I wanted the house and land to get to know me. I wanted to communicate my intention for moving in: I would do all I could to continue caring for it.

I believe that homes can experience emotions as well. Once, I lived in an apartment that simply felt depressed from not being cared for enough in the past. I have been in homes that have felt joyful and full of light. I have also been in homes that have felt angry and even vengeful.

My home is also an extension of the earth. My home is created from the earth itself, and when I am at home, I feel as if I am also being held by the earth. My home grounds, stabilizes, and nourishes me like the earth does. It has become important for me to relate to my home as I would the earth, as something sacred that demands to be seen and experienced as a vital part of my well-being.

My home is also an extension of my body, just as it is an extension of the earth. The earth, my home, and my body are a holy trinity forming an important foundation in how I am cared for. When I experience disconnection from one, I experience disconnection from the others. In this state there is no care for me if there is no relationship with the earth, home, or my body. So, when I return home, I am returning to my body, and when I am returning to my body, I am returning to the earth. It has been important for me to bind these three expressions together because care for my body has opened the doors to being cared for and caring for my home and the earth.

Caring for my home also means that when I leave for extended time away, I tell it that I am leaving for a while and ask the local deities and land protectors to guard and care for my home. I always thank my home as I am leaving and offer gratitude when I return. When I am away, I am praying for its safety and that it is being protected.

My home is part of spiritual ecology, which is to say that I share my home with other beings. Formless beings make their home here as well. They are the spirits of people who lived here before me, who still call this home's body home. I feel them faintly moving through the house, maybe noticing some of the other living residents of the home like the ants scavenging for food on the kitchen counter during the summer or the giant cockroach that sometimes makes an occasional appearance. Before moving into the home, I invited any energies or unseen beings who had a problem with me or who might be disruptive to journey on. Too many people move into homes with no care of the consciousness of the home or even the land the home rests on, let alone the unseen beings who may or may not be benevolent.

Prayer

It is early in the morning as I write this. My home and land are still except for the slight shifts of spirits moving about. Somebody is praying for me right now. I feel the energy of care surrounding me, fed by the earnest concerns and deep love of those who want to see me survive and thrive. The transmission of their love through prayer shifts the space around me. It caresses my heart and soothes my breath. My shoulders relax and my jaw releases. I feel myself surrendering. As the elders would say, somebody is "praying me over," and I am grateful.

My friend texts, calling me corazón, and says that I have been in her heart for three days. She sends me light and love to ease my restlessness. My heart breaks not from sorrow but from the love of this woman, this healer and daughter of the earth, a mother who also hears the suffering of so many and responds with the deepest care. I feel her prayers radiating from the awakened care of her heart. It is energy that supports me in this writing.

Once, when I was little, my great aunt Louise, whom we called Ease, told me that we could talk directly to Jesus over the phone. First, we needed to pray to him, and then we needed to pick up the phone and wait for the dial tone to die. She explained that Jesus was present in the silence. At that point, we could just start telling Jesus what we needed. It was overwhelming to think that I could talk to Jesus by picking up the phone. *How amazing*, I thought, *to have Jesus so accessible!*

Beyond the awe and respect for prayer that was instilled in me by my devout elders, I wouldn't say that I understood prayer as a young person. This isn't to say that I didn't experience moments of transcendence. At church, during the altar call, the main prayer of the service, we were invited to stand down at the altar, which wrapped around the pulpit and choir stand. As people gathered, the choir would softly sing "Pray for Me" to the tune of the old traditional gospel song "Precious Memories." Most often, it was not the pastor who offered the prayer but one of the elders. The prayer would usually begin with "Dear Heavenly Father."

I could sometimes feel the movement of prayer, as if the elder was transporting us from the world of suffering to someplace where the suffering could be muted for even just a few minutes. And in that muting, space opened for joy, and it was this same joy that sustained my praying ancestors, making it possible for them to live while pushing through and holding mountains of sorrow and fatigue. Prayer made joy and rejoicing possible because this joy was an expression of God and the Divine.

What my people taught me about prayer was that it could tend to the hurt we experienced in the world. Matter of fact, prayer could take us to meet God. God was waiting for us up there; if we could just close our eyes and open our hearts to God's grace, we would receive divine awakened care.

Prayer was also pleading with, needing, and mourning our condition of pain. We lifted everything we struggled to carry—all the trauma and brokenheartedness, the hopelessness and despair, everything that was represented by the cross of Jesus—and we heaved all this up to God, pleading for him to take the pain away. And when we came to pass from this, he would take us into his kingdom to live forever beyond pain.

Unfortunately, as I grew older, I lost my awe of prayer. As I became more aware of Black people's struggle to be well, safe, and happy in a social and political context that was created to erase us, I began to doubt the validity and effectiveness of praying to a God that didn't seem to like Black people very much at all. It seemed like after centuries of laborious supplication, we should be completely free by now. Our prayers began to sound like theatrical begging. It seemed like God was a sadist.

I was filled with anger, and beneath the anger was a deeper hurt: historical trauma, which I experienced as despair. I didn't need to transcend shit anymore. I needed the people who created so much violence against my community to be eliminated. I could feel my prayers turning vengeful. This didn't scare me. It felt good. Looking back, I can recognize this experience as a longing for balance. We suffered so much because we lived in an intense imbalance where the pain was overwhelming but was mediated a great deal by the joy we found and embodied.

I broke up with God in college, having convinced myself that theology was a sophisticated spiritual gymnastic that justified all the suffering and evil in the world through a set of principles that basically said that we would never know why bad shit happened and that if we trusted God, things would work out. But as I struggled to carry the burden of being Black and queer, I lost trust in God. So I left prayer altogether and wandered through the social activism scene, where prayer was replaced with action.

It wasn't until almost two years after college that I returned to prayer. My struggle to be well, coupled with my longing to understand freedom and be free, led me to convert to Tibetan Buddhism, and I was swept up in a culture of prayer that felt both exhaustive and poignant. Tibetan Buddhism is driven by devotion, or perpetual prayer expressed as profound love for the nature of reality. When that love is reflected back to us, it offers us the confidence to long for the liberation of everything from suffering. Though the traditional prayers were powerful and offered a more deeply focused training in supplication, they still felt foreign to me. Although I didn't know it then, I longed to embody the way my ancestors prayed.

Over the past few years, I have been called back to prayer, remembering the prayer practice of my ancestors and elders, like my great aunt Ease. I have learned how to tend to my brokenheartedness and trauma, which has opened space for more gratitude and joy in my life, even amid social struggle. I understand the complexities of freedom work, and I now know what prayer *really* is. I would not be here without the prayers of my ancestors and elders, and my descendants will not be able to transition into this world without the support of my prayers.

As my ancestor practice deepens, I experience their devotion to prayer. Even in their spirit form, they are still praying, and when I listen closely enough, I hear their prayers for me and the world we are surviving. I understand that there cannot be the change I need to see without prayer.

As I find myself sailing through my middle-aged years, it seems that I am becoming like the old church elders, always praying and fasting, watching and fighting. I used to rebel against becoming an old, praying Black man, but this expression is native to my flesh and bones, buried deep in my DNA. My ancestors have called me into the world; I consent to being a reflection of them.

What Is Prayer?

Prayer is an expression of meditation, an avenue for tuning our awareness to the frequency of the essence, connecting to the Divine. This connection is a channel that helps us to remember and trust our true nature as well as hold space for the suffering of all beings as we offer our longing for the alleviation of all suffering.

As we tune in to the Divine, our minds and bodies are being shaped by the clarity and care of the essence. When we pray, we are filled with awakened care as an expression of the Divine, and that experience is how we become calibrated to the frequency of ultimate freedom.

Prayer is our capacity to shape the phenomenal world around our deepest desires. My consciousness is intelligent energy permeating all phenomena, and as we train our awareness to expand into the boundless expression of our consciousness, we are connecting to everything and thus have this channel to impact or influence other energies.

My practice of prayer is also a form of extending my awareness into higher frequencies of energy to communicate with beings abiding in those frequencies. I can supplicate these beings to ally with me, helping to bring about what I desire as well. Prayer is also my way of simply being and of being open and authentic in the world. Physically, it is how I open my heart center to the world by lifting my shoulders and rolling them down my back while lengthening my spine and slightly lifting my chin. My heart center, the energetic location associated with empathy and care, has room to engage the world in honesty and directness.

Unfortunately, prayer doesn't just evoke goodness or benefit. Praying for others to be harmed is as much a prayer as praying for goodness. In other words, prayer is neither good nor bad. Prayer is simply prayer. It is our awakened care that shapes our prayers into benefit, while it is our delusion that shapes our prayers into harm.

How I Pray

During prayer, Mother Harriet has often reminded me that if we are not praying, we are not getting free. On the New Saint's path, prayer is how we not only tune in to the essence for guidance and clarity but how we begin to shape the phenomenal world around our deepest desires for all beings to be free from incarceration.

Prayer is now a staple of my spiritual practice. I pray as much as I can. Any endeavor I start begins with prayer. When I start a journey, it begins with prayer. I pray over my food and water. I pray for my house and land, and I make prayers anytime I am staying somewhere new or moving on land that is unfamiliar to me. I pray for people and beings of the unseen world. I pray for all beings to be free. No matter how hopeless something seems, I pray and offer my hopelessness or the hopelessness of the situation to the Divine. I have worked to make prayer as natural and unconscious as breathing or taking a shit.

With the support of my ancestors as well as the guidance of my teachers from the various spiritual paths I train in, I have developed a personal method of prayer that I engage in as much as possible. Prayer doesn't have to be formal or terribly complex. I believe that the practice should be simple, direct, and natural. The method

I offer below may seem a little complex, but these stages are ones we can learn to move through quickly and without much effort. The point is to establish a solid foundation that can hold the labor of attuning to the Divine and offering our needs for people to be free.

My prayer practice emerges in three stages. The outer stage is how I experience being called into prayer. The inner stage is how I experience dwelling in and interacting with the Divine. The secret stage is how I allow myself to rest within the open boundlessness of the Divine.

The Outer Stage: Approaching Prayer

I don't have a set schedule for prayer. I pray when I feel I need to. Sometimes I feel something in my experience that needs tending, or I am called to offer prayer for someone connected to me who needs support. Other times I feel the suffering of others in the world, and I am moved to offer prayer on their behalf, to disrupt their experience of suffering. Or sometimes I wake up in the morning and find myself slipping right into prayer. If someone asks me to pray for them, I start moving into this process right at that very moment.

— INTENTION —

When I am called into prayer, I start by naming why I am beginning to pray and my intention for prayer. My intention for prayer is always to help reduce suffering for myself and others. This is the awakening of awakened care, when I begin to understand that to care for beings, I must develop an intention for them to be free from suffering.

— LOCATING AND CALLING MYSELF IN —

Next, I locate myself. I notice where my mind is wandering, and I call my awareness back into the moment. I must be present to start the journey of attuning to the Divine.

— TOUCHING THE EARTH —

After I have called myself in, I anchor to the earth. I do this by noticing the weight of my body contacting my seat or the floor under me and slowly shifting my attention down to the earth, grounding myself, and taking a few moments to experience the earth's care. I begin all of my ceremonies and rituals by touching the earth, recognizing it as the anchor, ally, and primary support of the work I'm doing.

— RELEASING —

Once I feel anchored, I shift my attention toward the uncomfortable experiences that motivate me into prayer, such as fear, concern, and anxiety. I release as much of this energy as possible by inhaling deeply into every pore and opening my body into these energies before dissolving them and then releasing them with an exhale.

— TOUCHING THE BODY —

After touching the earth, I like to touch my body gently, reminding myself that I am moving into prayer embodied, while also asking the earth and my seat to keep me grounded as I open to higher frequency energies. I focus on neutral parts of my body. I like to gently touch my thighs, knees, and forearms, and to massage my hands. I also use this space to acknowledge that my body is an extension of the earth, and like the earth, it is a primary support—there can be no work without my body.

The Inner Stage: Touching the Divine
— YEARNING —

Once I feel grounded, I turn my attention to yearning. Yearning is the energy that drives me into prayer. I often feel it as an intense desire for beings to be elevated from personal suffering and collective suffering. This yearning is an expression of my awakened care, and it is this care that centers my prayer in deep care for myself and others.

I imagine the energy of this yearning filling my body and mind with warm white light. I take a few minutes to sit in this light and warmth; it begins to open into my experience of the Divine.

— OPENING TO THE SACRED AND DIVINE —

When I am connecting to the present and resting in the expression of this yearning and awakened care in my body and mind, I begin to slowly allow the experience to open into the stillness of the essence. That essence becomes my experience of the Divine. I try to dwell in this space for as long as possible. I'll allow the essence to take shape into whatever form that is most appropriate for me, be it an image, vision, or other experiences of God—the Mother, a Buddha, or any spirit or deity that is an expression of awakened care. I let this figure spring from my yearning to disrupt suffering.

— ARTICULATING WHAT I NEED —

Often at this point my experience of the Divine is being held in this ocean of awakened care, and I feel its emerging intelligence as God or even a wisdom deity. When I feel this expression of divinity, I begin offering my wants and needs into this energy like flowers offered to the ocean. Sometimes this is a mental offering, and at other times it is a verbal one. I pray for what is immediate, urgent, and close to me as well as what seems more abstract and far away. This allows me to dwell in the experience of care for myself and others and is also a form of self-care. I give myself permission to imagine the end of suffering without doubting that this ending will happen.

This is when we can offer formal prayers as well. This a prayer that I sometimes offer in this space:

I evoke all those beings and sources of refuge who have ever loved me to come sit with me because it is now that I feel most alone. I evoke the Blessed Mother, the Sacred Father, the Spirits of Light, the essence of wisdom, my teachers and elders, the communities who have always caught me when I have fallen, the ancestors who have never stopped holding me, all the elements including the sacred earth who help me to stand, and silence that wraps me in the space to be with my heart, and I call upon my own innate compassion.

To all those I have evoked, I offer my grief and what seems like my perpetual mourning in this body. I offer my fear, my numbness, and my inability to dream beyond my shutting down. Most of all, I offer my fatigue. I am tired.

Today, precious earth, let me lie upon you and be reminded of my body and my heart. I want many things, but I need only one thing now: to give up to you what I cannot hold. I pray that I evolve past my belief that my pain is mine alone to carry. To my sources of refuge who have been evoked, you have taught me repeatedly that this is not the truth. You have taught me that it is not my pain but our pain. You remind me that my worship of isolation is not conducive to my liberation. I want to be free, and so I offer to you what I struggle to hold right now knowing that you are only here to share this heaviness with me and to love me.

I am afraid of the world. I am afraid of people. I am afraid of what I must do to survive in the world. Even these fears, I offer to my sources of refuge. Today my precious sources of refuge, in your love, offer me rest. In your love, never abandon me. In your love, haunt all others who feel lonely and tired. Please continue to haunt me in this life, in death, and into all my lives to come until one day I become a source of refuge for other beings. Yet it is also my prayer to become a source of refuge for beings right now in this life. May I and all others in this realm and beyond be blessed forever. I dedicate this labor to my descendants who will one day lead me into my ancestorhood.

——————

— OFFERING EVERYTHING —

When I feel I have offered all my needs, I offer everything else into the Divine: my joy, sorrow, fear, and gratitude; everything I hide away from; everything I am too attached to; everything I'm ashamed of. This often feels like a final expression of vulnerability. I add fuel to my prayer, energizing it as things begin to shift around me. By opening wide into transparency and letting the Divine and other intelligent energies begin acting on my behalf, I get out of my own way.

The Secret Stage: Resting in the Divine
— RESTING THE MIND IN THE DIVINE AND EMPTINESS —

At this point, I slowly let go of doing anything and rest my awareness within the expansive ocean of emptiness as the Divine expression. I consider this a period of integration. I allow energy to settle, and I relax any tension that has arisen while moving through prayer.

— DEDICATING MERIT —

I usually end with a simple final prayer that any beneficial positive energy arising out of this practice be dedicated to all beings for the final liberation from suffering.

Working with
the Ancestors

Ancestor practice is imperative in the New Saint's tradition. The presence of ancestors is intricately tied to our well-being and safety in the material world. Ancestor acknowledgment and practice lie at the heart of a liberatory practice as well. If you are not working with ancestors, you are not doing real liberation work.

One such ancestor for me was my great aunt Louise, called Aunt Ease—the same aunt who told me to call Jesus. She was the sister of my great-grandmother Joy who lived to be a century old. Aunt Ease was the vocalist of my family and her signature song in the church's senior choir was "Whatever It Is." I can still hear her singing it. Her worn and delicate semiproper soprano lifting itself up to heaven, channeling that rock-hard will of countless elder Black women of faith, who, like mountains, could only be moved by God himself. She would ease into the bluesy, medium strut singing, "Whatever it is, it won't let me hold my peace." And not one person who heard her could hold their peace. Even now, when I close my eyes and think of her, she visits me, reminding me of that great mystery of whatever it is, and that above all, it will not let me hold my peace. I know that in her voice and deepest conviction, God dwelled. It was in her voice I would learn my first lessons of surrender.

I hear my Aunt Ease's music circling around me along with the rest of my ancestors who have chosen to accompany me through this life. They are men, women, children, and gender expansive. Some are powerful like deities in their energetic spirit form—others, not so much. They are reflections of who they were in their most recent life. Their personalities are the same. The ancestors I knew in life are the same beings I know and love as ancestors. I don't know who they all are, but they know and love me, and because of that love, they want me to be free as much as I want them to be free.

There are beings in the unseen world who want us to be free as much as they want to be free. Liberation work is expanded and deepened when we choose to ally with these beings, especially our ancestors. What will always surprise us is how narrowly we have defined ancestors. I now understand that ancestors are more than blood family that have passed on before me; they are unseen communities of beings that are connected to me through their deep care for me.

Who Are the Ancestors?

I was not raised with any practice of ancestor remembrance and veneration, but I always felt beings around me. It wasn't until after I became a lama that a dear friend practicing in the Yoruba tradition would reach out to me periodically with messages from the ancestors. I started getting curious about the ways in which ancestors were so central to their practice, and it later dawned on me that my ancestors were coming through my friend to encourage me to open to them so that we could start communicating directly. I intuitively knew that to connect with my ancestors; I needed to start talking to them. This became a path through which my belief in ancestors deepened, and over time I began to discern the many ways they were in conversation with me. They were speaking through dreams, visions, feelings, and even through physical sensations. They were connecting with me through scents and odors that triggered certain memories and images, and they sent audible messages transmitted through songs or random noises. Other times, they spoke directly to me, like someone leaning over and whispering into my ear. Sometimes I know that my grandmother Betty is close to me because I begin to crave sweet, creamy coffee—when I was a child, that's what she would have, and she would let me sip some of it. Other times I am drawn to old photos of different relatives who have passed on. Sometimes I can feel the energy of them willing me to make certain decisions.

My ancestor practice is grounded primarily in my own explorations of connecting to the spirit world, framed in my training of Buddhist Tantra and Indigenous shamanic practice.

Buddhism has helped me to train my awareness and to learn to relax more into the expansiveness and fluidity of my consciousness. This training has been key to noticing and tuning in to experiences of different energies in and around me without being too distracted.

Indigenous practices and philosophies have helped me to understand that ancestors are more than members of our families that have passed on into the spirit world. Allying with and surrendering to the care of plant medicines like ayahuasca, psilocybin, tobacco, and cannabis have taught me how to journey into the spirit world to connect to my ancestors. The journey is my consciousness intensifying its vibrational frequency to experience other intelligent consciousnesses and communicate with them.

My ancestors do not walk with me as much as they are embedded within an energetic orbit around me. I call and pull them close to me. In a way, I am the sun holding the attention of orbiting planets who need my light, expressed as intention, compassion, joy, clarity, and will. I offer this body and mind as a vehicle through which they can touch this world, continue important work, and, most importantly, support me in fulfilling the work of getting people free. Through me they continue living and loving, and they continue dreaming something better for a world they are still trying to figure out.

Moses Is with You

"Moses is protecting you," she explained somewhat quizzically. "He's with you."

This was all a little confusing for me. I was a twenty-two-year-old senior in college playing hooky from class with my friend who convinced me to ride with him down to Atlanta to visit a magic store.

After arriving, we discovered a medium was offering readings that day. My friend encouraged me to sign up. I had never done anything like this before and felt excited and somewhat apprehensive. However, I signed up anyway and found myself sitting in front of a middle-aged White woman who was giving me a lot of *Designing Women* vibes, meaning she was a very confident southern lady with big hair who had something important to say. Needless to say, I felt comfortable. After a casual conversation, she seemed to stare off into the distance, as if the confinement of the space around us gave way to wide-open distance that I couldn't sense.

When she explained that Moses was with me, I instantly thought of the biblical Moses leading the children of Israel out of Egypt. But that didn't seem to make any sense. Then something more familiar came to me. My grandfather was called Moses. It was his middle name.

"It's my grandfather," I disclosed. As I would start realizing over the next twenty years, discoveries like this started with mild surprise and quickly evolved into acceptance, like something I had always known but had recently forgotten.

"Yes. He's right beside you and has been with you since his transition." My dad's father had been a local Baptist preacher pastoring a small Black congregation. He passed a year after I was born, but I had always felt like I knew him as I was growing up.

"I see him dressed in a suit," she continued, "And feel that he has a lot of love and pride for you. But I get this vision of him being nervous about you being gay."

When we begin to contact our ancestors or any beings around us, we channel their feelings and desires. This is an experience of intimacy that links our consciousness with theirs. I experienced this in the moment with my grandfather and knew that his anxiety wasn't due to homophobia but simply to the fact that this was an aspect of me that was outside of his experience from his previous physical life. Because of this, he didn't feel like he could help me navigate this part of my life.

Sometimes, people struggle with the thought (or the basic truth) that we are surrounded by beings that are with us every second of our lives, including in situations where perhaps we want some privacy. We may ask if they need to be present while we are doing our business on the toilet or doing some real good business in the bedroom. I struggled some with this but slowly began to understand that being human and doing human things like shitting and fucking was nothing to be ashamed of. More than that, I don't get the sense that my folks are interested in everything that I'm doing. I am not as ashamed of my life and body as I once was. I trust my ancestors to have my best interests at heart, and I have never felt judgmental energies around me except for those coming from my own thoughts of shame. I have learned that my ancestors love me, and they want me to be safe, happy, healthy, and free. I am not doing anything that they didn't do in their own lives.

Over the years, I have learned to work in collaboration with my ancestors. They are part of my personal, spiritual ecological system. We do not have to know who our ancestors are because they know us and are wanting us to open our minds and touch them so that they can fully touch us back, helping us to navigate the labor of this life.

Not all ancestors are here to help. There are ancestors who are trying to hurt us. In my practice, it is important to set boundaries so the only ancestors around me are those here to help. Also, there are ancestors coming to us for help, and it is important to discern if we can offer the help that they need. I've come to understand that in this collaboration with ancestors and other spirits, we are helping each other, but when I feel underresourced, I ask for space until I can connect in a beneficial way again.

Pound Cakes and Collard Greens

I love making pound cake. For a year, I have been creating a recipe that I like, becoming one of those Black folks who have their way of making things from collard greens to sweet potato pie, so that anyone who tastes their food knows it's their food. It's not that our food tastes like us but rather that the taste is an energetic expression of all those who have come before us. Be it cake or fried chicken, the food we prepare is a culmination of the struggle, wishes, sacrifices, and deepest love of people who ensured each other's survival by doing what they could to nourish bodies. I want my pound cake to taste like generations of unconditional love embodied against the violence of genocide and erasure. When I am making pound cake, I am remembering my grandmothers and their mothers. When I am mixing butter, sugar, salt, eggs, vanilla, flour, and buttermilk, I am remembering how my ancestors would grow and collect these ingredients from the land and animals. My hands are the hands of Black folks who have always known how to shape the phenomenal world into beautiful expressions and continue to do so even when we are told our bodies don't belong to us. Making and sharing pound cake is how I practice the love of my ancestors.

Making pound cake or any of our traditional food, or even doing things my ancestors loved to do, is a way that I honor my ancestral line. Remembering their joy, I awaken their joy and in return they share that joy back with me. This is what I call a joyful collaboration, and I experience a deepening of my relationship with the phenomenal world. Things get more vivid and bright. Much more of the world shifts from being an antagonist to becoming a friend all because of this profound vulnerability with beings, my family, who love me and only want to see me thrive.

The Middle Passage

To experience the Middle Passage is to understand a fundamental experience that has shaped the lives of those of us descended from African slaves. To touch the Middle Passage is to touch a fundamental part of who I am because this experience has shaped everything—my words, thoughts, actions, dreams, desires.

I have known for a few years that as a descendent of enslaved people I would have to return, somehow, to the experience of the Middle Passage because, as Mother Alice Walker has taught, healing begins where the wound was made. Healing from my personal trauma has often meant returning in time and space to experiences that must be liberated. The Middle Passage is gigantic, trapped energy howling in our bodies and our thoughts and even sabotaging our dreams of a freer future.

This returning is necessary for those of us descended from people and communities that have experienced collective trauma. It will take a lot of us doing our part to metabolize not just our individual trauma but the collective trauma we all share.

During an ayahuasca ceremony, the medicine blessed me and opened the door back to this pulsating wound. It was not easy work, and I consider the experience to be the worst night of my life, but it helped me understand what my ancestors survived, and it taught me what liberation actually felt like.

My first journey into the experience happened in 2019. I was supported by my dear friend Spring Washam. I am reflecting on the teaching offered to her from Mother Harriet herself, recorded in her book *The Spirit of Harriet Tubman*. This particular teaching helps us as we move into these reflections.

Mother Harriet said,

Yes, Child, I understand. This is a door so many are afraid to open, but we must. As you work with this chapter, it's important to take slow, deep breaths. You and everyone else reading this may want to pause and offer prayers of love and compassion to our African grandmothers and grandfathers. You best believe they can hear you; they can see you, and they can feel your caring heart.

— FIRST JOURNEY —

I knew I had to journey to the bottom of that ship. An hour after taking the medicine, I sat cross-legged, peering down into my puke bucket and into a portal that led into the guts of what I have understood my whole life to be hell. There were the sounds of moaning and puking on top of the creaking of a ship hurtling itself across an ocean. I could feel the color crimson as both an experience of heat and an experience of something that was evil. I felt sharp anxiety rise in my experience, and I began to resist. *No, no, no,* I thought to myself. *Not tonight.* However, by then, the shaman was sitting in front of me and singing to the medicine, activating its consciousness to do the work it needed to do for me. I lost my agency. Even though I felt myself resisting, I was already there.

In the ship, I was an adolescent girl, lying on a platform next to other bodies. I remember the heat of the space saturated with both the bitter tanginess of vomit and the earthy nauseating stench of shit and piss. There was a subtle metallic hint of blood. People were dead and dying. I thought I was lying next to someone who had died. Around me I heard the moaning, sometimes a scream. Somehow, the medicine was keeping me from fully falling into the brutality of this experience. What I was experiencing was enough and at the same time it was too much.

I did not know what to do. Somehow, I was holding all the people, my ancestors, in my mind, and I confessed to them that I had no idea what to do. So I did the only thing I knew how to do, which was to take on all the suffering in that dark, sick place. I told my ancestors to give their pain to me. Slowly, I began to feel the energy of intense suffering and pain collect in my stomach, filling it up as if I were pregnant. I imagined myself sitting up in a pool of blood, piss, shit, and sweat, grasping my big swollen stomach, taking in more and more of this suffering. In the moment, I kept thinking that this wasn't enough, but it was all I knew how to do.

Later, with Spring's help and after other experiences, I was able to lift out of the ship to continue metabolizing the trauma for the next few days.

— SECOND JOURNEY —

After the year of COVID quarantine, I returned back into ceremony, heading back down into the ship, believing there was more work to be done.

At the beginning of my second set of ceremonies, I returned to the guts of that slave ship.

"You don't belong here anymore," I heard.

The ship was quiet and still. Light permeated the space, and I could see that everything was clean—the platform shelves once holding black bodies dripping with shit, vomit, blood, and saliva were all clean. The chains hung gleaming as if newly polished. It was comfortably warm, not overbearingly smoldering. It seemed like I was on some movie set after the film had finished production. I was confused and wondered if my time in the guts of this ship with my ancestors had been a dream. Did I imagine all of this?

"Why are you here?" She appeared ten feet in front of me, a Black woman that I seemed to physically tower over, whose age seemed ambiguous—as if she were all ages at once. She was both a youth and an elder. Her strength never faltered. She was both a mountain and running water, hurricane and gentle breath.

"I thought I was supposed to be here. I don't know where else to go. I don't know anything else," I said. I understood without any verbal or cognitive articulation that I was doing what I tended to often do, which was going back to the site of trauma and expecting to relive it. The stillness and light in the space slowly began to dispel the memories of the passage two years earlier, and I finally began to understand what was being said.

"Your work is done here. There is no more work for us here," she said. I began to recognize this short, powerful woman. It was in her body and mind that I relived the Middle Passage. She was the young girl I had been trying to keep from being consumed by the darkness of the Middle Passage and its evil. We were the ones lifting our human-fluid-drenched bodies out of the chaos, vowing that we would survive. We were the ones wishing for our people to be free.

We were the ones trying to rip through the belly of this monster so none of us could be fed to the demon of chattel slavery.

She had a handsome face, both soft and on the verge of erupting. That face offered no choice. There was so much that seemed familiar, as if I was looking into a mirror. In the back of my mind, I could hear my teacher Lama Norlha Rinpoche softly chuckling, "No choice. No choice."

"But who are you? What is your name?"

"They named me Emma. I am the first of our line. I am the reason you are here."

At that moment, I knew that I had always felt her around me, gently pushing me in directions that I couldn't understand. She was the voice that would form in my mind at a vital impasse, telling me exactly what needed to be done. She held the ancestral line together through her immense magic and will. And now she was here not telling me but teaching me the lesson of healing—when the wound is healed, you must move forward into the potential that the healing has opened. Lay the fear down, finally, dream forward, and be free.

None of this work is easy. When we commit to working on our healing, we are also committing to the healing of our collective. This is the greatest and most important way to offer healing to our loved ones, especially our ancestors. There is no liberation without the labor or the deep care.

Help Is on the Way

I cannot count the times the ancestors have shown up for me in a crisis. Once, I was suffering from what was quickly becoming severe dehydration because I couldn't keep any fluids down. I knew I needed to get to the hospital but was experiencing a lot of fear. I found myself on the toilet stiff with anxiety. One of my recent ancestors, who normally isn't with me, came to remind me of a time when she was dying but still held strength that kept the rest of the family supported as we began to mourn her eventual transition. Her mind became my mind, and with that merging, the warmth and expansion of her courage filled me. Her courage was nothing but love reminding me that I was never alone or separate from the beings who love me, even as we occupied the span of different energetic frequencies. It was enough to see me through that day, especially when another dear sister friend offered prayers to Mother Oshun on my behalf.

This is just one example of how the ancestors show up to lift me through times that seem difficult and impossible to manage.

Holding On

We translate the values of abolition into the unseen world while the abolitionist values of the unseen world are being translated to this world. The unseen world is also trying to get us free as well. What does it mean to connect to the powerful intentions of the unseen beings?

During 2020, at the beginning of the COVID quarantine, I had a vision of a few ancestors holding my feet and legs and then saw that there were ancestors holding their feet and legs, and that there were even more ancestors holding their feet and legs, and this pattern continued on and on. It seemed as if I was rooted at the beginning of a vast chain of beings holding and anchoring each other, stretching to the beginning of linear time. The teaching they offered was, *We're holding on.*

It wasn't just my ancestors holding me. All our ancestors were holding us, anchoring us to the earth, and grounding us to this world because this world needed us rooted to hold space for the transition of the apocalypse. Our bodies had to be presented as conduits for the movement and release of ancient traumas that the apocalypse was shaking loose through the tragic spark of a global pandemic. I was holding on while allowing myself to be held. To hold and allow yourself to be held is the heart of this prophecy.

STARTING AN ANCESTOR PRACTICE

I am often asked how to begin working with ancestors, and I offer the same practices that I developed to start my relationship.

First, begin by thinking about them, considering their existence and influence in your life. Wonder about their lives, what they survived, what they hoped for. As you do that, make sure to notice any physical sensations, emotions, or mental images that are triggered. These experiences become signs of how the ancestors respond to us. I can receive messages from my ancestors in multiple ways, from body chills to visions, but I only figured this out because of this early experimentation. However, when my ancestors want to express their support and solidarity (as they are doing now as I write this), I feel intense energy moving through my body like cold chills.

Second, create an altar in your home where the energy of your ancestors can be concentrated. I am a huge fan of altars and have lost count of how many I have in my home. However, an ancestor altar can deepen energetic bonds with our line. Making offerings of food, water, incense, and basically anything we feel they would like is a powerful gesture of care for them, which makes it easier for them to help us.

Third, pray to them. Tell them what's going on in your life and ask for help and support. Many of our ancestors will be resourced enough to help gather what we need. They are a source of support that can be relied on if we trust them enough to help.

Fourth, try to figure out what their lives were like. This can be difficult but not impossible. If you have a good sense of the people you descend from, you can easily imagine what their lives were like. Sometimes we will be able to receive messages from them about their lives through mental impressions, visions, and dreams. When you begin receiving this data, record it and find ways to tell their stories. This is perhaps the most powerful way to take care of our ancestors. Much of the literature we love to read includes stories of an author's ancestors.

And finally, try to trust them. Let them take care of you as you learn how to take care of them. I consider my ancestors cofacilitators in my life, so I am always listening for their guidance. I am not saying that they are always right, but they do possess insight that is valuable. Developing practices like this will make it easier to prepare for our transition from this life. The connections we make with the ancestors we know are pathways they will travel to hold us as we navigate dying.

Offering and Remembering

Tonight, I am sitting on my porch smoking tobacco. I am offering the smoke as a ransom offering. We are all surrounded by formless beings to whom we owe debts for different reasons. Often these are debts that we had no idea had accumulated. Sometimes these debts are grievances we have with beings from past lives. We move through the world, crossing all kinds of boundaries that we are not capable of sensing. We move into homes that are themselves conscious and harbor other conscious, formless beings without asking for consent beforehand or even developing an energetic relationship with the needs of this formless ecological system.

This system also includes the land and its consciousness, as well as the conscious formless beings.

I offer this smoke to those that have grievances with me. I offer it to my ancestors as well as to my descendants. I offer it to the beings roaming my street. I close my eyes and settle my awareness into the arising phenomena. I even take a few moments to listen to the wind as it gently brushes my exposed skin. In this moment, the wind is the gentle sighing of the world—one that is trying to get its inhabitants' attention. When I can allow the world to be, I find myself being. This being is floating within limitless spaciousness, which in turn offers me the capacity to open and drink in the enlightened consciousness of my teachers, gurus, guides, deities, and especially the ancestors.

Touching the Earth

So much of my practice for the past few years has been the work of touching the earth and learning how to extend my awareness into the awareness of the earth itself. I've learned to talk to the land and trees, tuning in to their secret language and allowing them to tell me what I need to be doing in this period of rapid climate change. I am not someone who imagined I would enjoy talking to trees and land, but the earth, as the Mother, has so much healing to offer us if we learn to pay attention.

My birth mother and I spent the first eight years of my life with my grandmother, my mother's mother. There was a pecan tree in her backyard, and there were always pecans all over the house. Back then, having a pecan tree on your property was like having a gold mine. Nuts, especially pecans, were expensive to buy at the grocery store. The tree always seemed like it belonged to the community, as neighbors would come through asking us if they could gather a handful or two.

As long as I can remember, I have felt that pecans are linked to Black people's lives. The shell reflected my skin tone and that of my family and everyone in the neighborhood. The shell was our shell, the hardness we needed to develop to survive anti-Black violence. When I bite into a pecan, I imagine tasting the brown nutrition of the earth, which holds the love of Black folks and the richness of what we have had to scrape together to survive the systems people have created to dominate the land.

Then, there was my great-grandmother, who we called Big Mama. She was a quiet but strong-minded woman. Every summer we traveled to her house for a family reunion, making our way from northwest Georgia, past the sprawling capital of Atlanta, where the Owens had been rooted perhaps for several generations. I felt like we were driving back in time. Even back then, I could feel the heavy residual traces of slavery in that land. It felt like depression and hopelessness in my body.

Big Mama lived at the end of a little road that gave up and collapsed into rolling hills of kudzu that stretched toward the horizon. The thick, tangled green vines covered the land like a patchwork quilt. It was a sight to behold. I would gaze out over the rising and falling hills, making up all kinds of stories about the creatures that lived in them, how the vines got there, and even what it would be like to clear the vines completely, revealing the earth's secrets underneath.

In the back of Big Mama's house was a small plum tree that never looked well-tended to but still yielded sweet, purple fruit. There are two full plum trees in my front yard, and as I gather the fruit in early summer, I remember Big Mama's tree. The land yields and provides in ways that most of us aren't even aware of.

All of these are memories of how I relate to the earth. The earth has always reminded me of family and food. As I slide my hands into it, to hold and pray to it, I lose any idea of where the earth stops and I begin.

During my long retreat one spring and summer, I attempted to grow a garden after finding a few packets of seeds for various plants. There wasn't much free time in the daily practice schedule to do much of anything besides the necessities of eating, cleaning, and resting, but I decided it would be worthwhile and grounding to engage in garden therapy. I decided to grow a few types of wildflowers, basil, sage, turnips, and mustard greens. Everything survived except the turnips, which were devoured by groundhogs. I was able to harvest a small bushel of mustard greens, which I cooked and offered to my teacher.

As I grew older and eventually settled into serious spiritual practice, I began to understand that the earth was alive and aware. So much of what is important is offered from the earth. The earth is conscious, which is to say that the earth possesses a mind that knows, that is expansive, that can feel. We call the earth Mother because without her, there would be no life. So, when I attune to the earth, I am establishing a psychic connection to the earth. We are in perpetual communication, sharing our needs together, which guides how we choose to develop ritual with each other.

When I say that I am an extension of the earth, and the earth is an extension of me, I mean that everything from my Ayurvedic dosha (mind-body type) to my astrological chart puts me deep into the earth. My body has always felt like a mountain with roots. When others are in crisis, I am in stability. When there is darkness, I am the light. When people are malnourished, I offer my practice, work, and care for their nourishment.

Like the earth, I hold a lot. Sometimes, I imagine that a lot of people are relying on me. I am attuned to the collective experience of suffering as well as joy. But it is the suffering that I am called to hold. I do not run away. I can't hide.

Surrendering to the Earth and Air

More and more, I am coming to understand that healing and liberation are completely bound up with the land. When the Buddha touched the earth during his awakening, he did so not as a symbolic gesture, but as a sign of solidarity. Touching the earth reminds me that I am a living extension of it. The ground feels like my own body. The water is my blood. The wind is my breath. The rain is my tears. The thunder is my anger.

The earth is our primary ally in liberation work not only because it offers the scaffolding that can be used to get us free. No one can get free without being guided and cared for by agents that are already free, or who are at least committed to our freedom. To touch the earth is to remember that the earth is alive, free, awakened, and feeling—that it remembers and mourns, that it loves and has no animosity toward us, that it can support us in getting free.

Yet as we touch the earth, we also began to touch into wind, water, and fire, which also rely on the earth for support. These elements along with the earth open a profound door to healing and liberation through the natural world.

To start this journey, I offer the most precious thing I have to give: my body. I come to lie on the earth, praying to decay back into it. As ashes return to ashes, and earth returns to earth, my body longs to return back to its most fundamental being, back to the fields of dark soil growing food, to the red Georgia clay my ancestors tell me they would eat when they were starving, to the soil at the bottom of the ocean, even to the molten rock lava that initially formed this land.

Roots begin to grow from the bottom of my body and extend down deep into the earth, into the soil of its precious body. I become a child, sinking into the Mother, becoming one with her again.

I summon the streams of love, compassion, and joy and let them flow together into awakened care and down through my root system, extending from my body to nourish the earth. The earth begins to awaken, to become conscious, and I feel its living energy and consciousness awakening under me. I take time to experience this awakening.

Now I shift attention to my experience of grief. I breathe into it and exhale it down into the earth, asking the earth to hold and stabilize it. The earth accepts my grief and brokenheartedness as they dissolve into the brilliance of the earth's awakened consciousness.

Now I offer my trauma to the earth, the lived record of surviving the carceral state. The earth does not know what the carceral state is, but to return to the earth in this moment is to know what it means to be free because I will know what it means to be held and cared for. The earth asks me to surrender this suffering. It teaches me to let go as it shows me that there is no energy too strong for it to hold and tend to.

The earth asks me what else I need, and I allow my body to answer in sensation. What my body needs now is to be held by the earth. And as the earth holds me, it radiates the energy of its awakened care back up through my roots and directly into my body. I am being filled with this energy of care, flooded and saturated, healed and freed all the way down to my DNA and through my line of ancestors.

I am slowly dissolving into this profound care.

Slowly, I arise as wind, as energy in movement, as air swirling and expanding. My breath is the wind. When I am breathing, I am feeling the pulsating passion of wind in my body, gathering the vital resources of oxygen and awareness, depositing precious elements in my cells and molecules. In the exhale the earth takes what I no longer need, like carbon, and makes it an offering to plant siblings. In this state, the wind can teach us how to listen to it.

LISTENING TO THE WIND

I enjoy listening to the wind. Not only can the wind transmit data, it can also be deeply relaxing.

To begin, on a windy day, go outside and sit or lie down on the ground or sit in a chair with your feet touching the ground. You must touch the earth and notice it beneath you. Feel the Mother under you rising to hold you and allow her to stabilize you.

Then shift your attention to the wind, its movement of twisting and dancing, its fluid flow and forceful gait. Let the wind touch you. Feel the wind caress your exposed skin and ruffle your clothing. Let the rising of the earth and the sensation of wind touching you fill your attention until your attention collapses and spills out into awareness. Allow your awareness to consume the wind, and allow the wind to consume your awareness.

What is arising in your awareness? What is being asked? What is being offered? Pay attention.

When transmission feels complete, offer prayers into
the wind as you would cast flowers out onto the ocean.
Let the wind catch and lift this energy of aspiration up
into itself.

Now offer your own needs to the wind. Pray to the wind.
What do you need? What must happen? When your
transmission is complete, offer gratitude and feel the
wind swell with your care for it.

Allying with Fire

The fire prayer ceremony is one of my favorite ceremonies and one
of the most powerful ceremonies I perform. My practice of the fire
prayer ceremony is based on ancient Indian Vedic ceremonies and
Tibetan fire ceremonies. I have adapted these influences to create
a ceremony that is innovative and fluid. I never do a ceremony the
same way twice because I am interested in allowing the ceremony
to adjust to my needs at the moment.

The fire prayer ceremony has two purposes in the New Saint's
tradition. First, it is a way to connect and ally with the fire element
and the deities connected to fire. Allyship means that we are open
to the consciousness of fire and its role in maintaining the spiritual
ecology, and from that openness, we can learn how it is helping us
get free.

Second, we practice a fire ceremony to transmute or change
substances from one thing to another. In this case, substances like
food or herbs are offered to the fire. As the fire is burning the food,
the essential energy of the substance is released from its material
form, and our prayers can then direct that energy toward helping
ourselves and other beings.

HOLDING A FIRE CEREMONY

A fire ceremony can be done with a large outdoor fire or a burning stick of incense or anything in between. The important elements of the practice are fire, substances that can be burned, and prayers. Below, I offer general instructions for a larger ceremony offered outside.

First, gather up the items that you would like to offer. If you're unsure, you can make a simple offering of a small bowl of grains, candy, and incense. Then set up a fire that is manageable for you, like a small campfire, and light it.

Second, when the fire is going, bless the fire by dipping a finger into a cup of water and flicking water on the fire three times. This gesture acknowledges that the fire is now being used to benefit beings. The gesture also helps to invite the water element into the ceremony, which encourages the fluidity and movement of the energy we will begin releasing.

Third, imagine that all the fire in the universe begins to collect in your third chakra, the energy center located in your solar plexus, around your naval, which holds a lot of fire energy already. As you collect and hold the fire, recite the prayer below:

The heat of my body is the heat that drives the universe. Precious fire, you change and transform, transmute and demolish, light and warm, release and relax. My heat is the fire of lava erupting from the earth's core to forest fires, the light of stars, the sun, all the way back to the warmth in my gut. My anger is fire raging, springing from my broken heart and ready to ignite the world in flames. When I listen to you, I am listening to the heartbeat of life and death itself, the constant burning away and emerging of what needs to emerge. I am the phoenix rising from the ashes of my own heartbreak. I pray to the precious fire element and all the deities connected to it to support this ceremony as I make offerings and pray for the benefit of all beings.

Now, imagine releasing the fire collected in your third chakra into the fire itself. Imagine that the fire is now ready for the ceremony.

Fourth, invite your ancestors and all benevolent beings, including deities, to join the space around you so that they can enjoy these offerings as well.

Fifth, hold the offering bowl and reflect on why you are making the offering and who or what you hope it benefits.

Sixth, offer the material into the fire. As the material begins to burn, imagine that its essential energy is being released into the world. Begin offering prayers as you imagine this energy being directed into the situations you are praying for. You can even imagine that the smoke from the fire permeates the land you are on, blessing all beings with what they need to be well and experience liberation.

Finally, when you feel complete, thank the fire for its kindness and all the beings for supporting the ceremony. To complete the ceremony, imagine that all beings are experiencing liberation from this ceremony and rest in the joy that may arise from that thought.

Muhheakunnuk and the Divine Clarity of Water

A river is nothing more than a dancing ribbon of water flowing from one extremity of birth to a final extremity of refuge. It is a natural and perfect kind of dance—one that mimics the cosmic dance of the Hindu god Vishnu, sweeping up existence in a graceful arch of arms and legs, tending to that creation through the joyful rotations of the hips, and finally bringing about the desolation of things with a knowing wink—then it all begins again.

The Lenape and Algonquin people taught that Muhheakunnuk is the river that flows both ways. Muhheakunnuk is one of many ways that God as Creator is expressed in the natural world, and this expression is a radically compassionate one because the Creator in this form is able to be seen, touched, worshipped, and relied on as an element to sustain our bodies and minds. Muhheakunnuk is also an expression of the Creator known as the Great Binder. If colonization had not burned the ability to feel from many of us, we could feel that this river is as sacred as the holy Ganges in India who, as an expression of the Mother, is worshipped as Mother Ganga and flows between the world of the living and the dead, binding these worlds together.

This binding is partially why Muhheakunnuk is known as the river that flows both ways. If you were really attuned to this reality, you would know that to touch this water is to touch the divinity of life and spirit together. If we could remember, we would know that Muhheakunnuk can float in and out of countless worlds.

The quality of energy churned from the tension of this binding of the worlds feeds and sustains formless beings. Some deities and spirits are expressions of the sacred water itself, while others are bound to it. The sacred river freely sustains both form and formless beings in this sacred ecology as long as all beings honor and vow to maintain this harmony.

I spent five years living along this river, with over three of those years in a long retreat in a room looking out over the river. At the time it was just a river, as I had not opened to the consciousness of the natural world. There was a marina across the river, and when the weather was warm, I could hear the music and laughter of parties drifting into my room as if the Ghost of Christmas Present himself was taunting me with memories of better times before I was trapped in a monk's dress, meditating through every trauma and bad mistake I had ever made. I longed to be wading in its waters, away from the painstaking and meticulous labor of experiencing my own mind and body while reaching tentatively to touch deities from a culture so distant from my own that I doubted if they were even listening. Yet even then I could feel this water calling in a language that would take me a little longer to become fluent in.

Henry Hudson was not interested in sacred ecologies or how the Creator was blessing this fragile world with precious energies and pure waters or even how Muhheakunnuk was inviting him to remember a part of himself that was less violent. When Hudson touched Muhheakunnuk in the early 1600s, he went only to where men like him go—into fantasies of wings that work because like many colonizers, his dream was to fly and soar beyond where ordinary people are.

What a man like Hudson meant by flying was to discover something that did not need discovering, causing it to be renamed after him and forcing us to memorialize a man who should have been forgotten for his own good. The Creator did not need to be found. Regardless, so much of the physical world is named after men (especially White men) who are desperate to enter immortality, to outrun the limitations of human life because, if it is nothing else, whiteness is the false promise of immortality fueled by conquering and naming. What is left are legacies of violence we must mourn because these "great" men could not fathom that their naming was actually cursing all of us far into the future. Though the trauma of the naming and the genocide of the communities that followed have been ours to bear, the burden is even greater for the men who initiated the violence that continues to spin out of control through climate destabilization and continued erasure of Indigenous communities.

Though Hudson is dead, he is not gone, and the trauma of his expression of insecurity haunts him even into the spirit bardo. In 1611, for recognition of his labor as a colonizer, his crew mutinied during an expedition on *his* river, casting himself, his teenage son, and several crewmen adrift on a small boat never to be seen again in human form. Thus is the nature of karma for him and for us. Karma is not fair or unfair; it just is.

I want to apologize here and explain that I don't want to sound angry. But I am, and beneath this anger is the bare heartbreak I experienced one afternoon sailing down Muhheakunnuk on a riverboat cruise, gazing out over its waters, its banks now dotted with the mansions of Hudson's descendants. Come with me now as I relive what I felt that day . . .

Standing on deck, I close my eyes and let tears fall, mourning the loss, again, of people and communities, rituals and ceremonies, beauty and kindness, all consumed by men's wish for wings that worked.

I turn my attention to my breath, allowing it to slow down and deepen, becoming more and more intentional about the deep inhalation of oxygen and the slow, methodical exhalation of carbon. Soon my breath catches the swirling wind, racing up and down Muhheakunnuk's back. My breath begins to move with the wind as I begin to listen. Listening to the wind always begins with breathing with the wind, allowing the spirit of the wind to move in and out of the body. This is how my early ancestors caught the wind and rode it up into the sky.

I am not trying to catch and ride the wind. I am listening, letting the wind tell me stories and news of the world. Today, the wind is only pointing me back to myself, my thoughts, the rising and falling of my chest, the sensation of my feet on the metal deck of the laboring ship. In that moment the ship whispers *tired* and *home* to me. And I mentally respond thinking, *Yes, I'm tired and want to return home as well.*

Turning my attention away from the ship, I choose to lose myself in the breath. Now, river and breath ride together and it seems as if I am beginning to fall into the tension radiating from the river's binding of the worlds.

In the radiance, I meet the formless beings arising out of Muhheakunnuk and those others that are bound to it. Many of them are worldly beings, still in relationship to some form of ego. Touching into the collective consciousness of these beings, I sense nothing but anger and sadness—their brokenheartedness reflects back to me my own brokenheartedness. The balance has been lost. There are not enough people supporting the ecology, not enough worshipping and offering through ancient ceremonies and rituals, not enough saying fire prayers, fasting, or honoring the full and new moon. More and more are forgetting that the world is a dream and that the communities working through the dream to liberation are disappearing. Everything has been replaced by the aggression of Hudson's descendants and their disbelief in the worlds, deities, and the dream of it all.

I am still crying and breathing, and I let my tears meld with the tears of the unseen beings. In our collective sobbing, we are crying through the heart of the Great Binder.

In my offering, I evoke the Mother and open my mind and heart even wider, expanding my awareness to touch as many worlds as possible. I imagine becoming a container, allowing all beings to pour their sorrow and anger into me while laying it all at the feet of the Mother. When we are consenting to take on the anger and sorrow of others, we must always have a way to offer this energy out of our minds and bodies to something that can hold and care for this suffering, be it the earth or the Mother.

I begin to radiate what joy I can find back out to all beings and throughout all the worlds. I especially offer this joy back to Muhheakunnuk. I feel the Great Binder flow through me, up and down my spine. On the banks, I feel the people gather, the women and men, the children, elders, healers, leaders, the two-spirit people, all coming to the river to witness the remembering. And this is all I can do now: remember. In this moment we see each other, hold each other's sadness, and realize that we have never needed wings because our freedom has always meant belonging to others, to the earth, and to Muhheakunnuk.

Later that night, some of the local deities visit. They resemble the early inhabitants of the region—brown skinned, wearing animal hides, their heads adorned with elaborate headpieces twisting in and out beautiful locks and braids of hair. They are both tangible and translucent at the same time, dancing in and out of time and sight as if this realm is barely keeping them here.

They tell me that there is one greater than them. I do not understand who that is initially. They offer a vision of them submitting to this greater one, returning from this submission with their heads completely bald. Again, they say that there is one greater than them. I do not know who that greater one is until I wake, understanding that this greater one was Muhheakunnuk.

The Body

So often when we talk about freedom, we think that we just need to want to get free, and it starts happening. We tend to underestimate the importance of our bodies in this labor. The body is an integral part of liberation in many spiritual traditions, including the New Saint's. The body is the vehicle that we ride into the experience of liberation, and it must have the resources it needs to partner with us to do liberation work. The body must be invited into the liberation work, and we must figure out how to care for and relate to the body in the process.

Before his enlightenment, the Buddha believed that the body was inconsequential to the pursuit of liberation. In fact, the body seemed to be a hindrance. Great yogis before him had revealed the importance of the body in experiencing higher states of consciousness. But the Buddha was hurling himself toward freedom, denying his body sustenance for years, opting instead to dwell deep in one-pointed concentration as his body became emaciated.

Eventually, the Buddha noticed that his enlightenment wasn't progressing, and he plateaued in practice. Coming out of a deep meditation, he must have been shocked to notice the withered state of his body. And like many awakened ones before him, he understood that everything must be cared for to get free, especially the body. Accepting a meal of milk and rice porridge from a local woman concerned for his health, he was able to regain his physical strength, which offered him the space to open wider to the essence of all phenomena, achieving complete enlightenment.

The Liberated Body

My earliest memories of suffering were related to my body, to the physical pain I felt, to all the unmet cravings of hunger, thirst, and pleasure my body craved. I felt indentured to my body. In other words, my first experience of the carceral state was the experience of my body.

Early on, I lacked agency and consented to my body being shaped by insecurities, fears, and other people's imaginations. We tend to project onto other people's bodies all our insecurities and unmet needs, and we attempt to subjugate people's bodies so that they fit into our narrowly conceived notions of what is acceptable or interesting. We manipulate other people's bodies to feed our appetites for pleasure. I had let myself internalize these projections, shoving aside my deepest needs to be free and happy. It's difficult to free ourselves from other people's imaginations when we have allowed those imaginations to colonize our own.

I have always avoided looking at my naked body. It has often not been possible to hold the disappointment that has greeted me in the mirror. Sometimes, it has been even harder to hold the affection of past lovers who have found my body attractive. I have often wondered what the fuck is wrong with them. I'm fat, and even if I wasn't fat, I am strangely shaped. I wasn't able to fathom how I could be sexy. Sexy was for fit guys with chiseled, muscled bodies, straight teeth, clear skin, round asses—like all the guys I used to like in porn.

Eventually, avoiding my body became too exhausting, and I realized that to get free, I had to return to what the Buddha had to learn: the body is integral to the project of liberation. If my ethic is to reduce harm, I must restore care to my body by telling the truth, holding both the pain and joy of that truth, and releasing and restoring that space with care. I am not trying to liberate myself from my body but to liberate my body from my judgment of it and my resistance to its clarity. To free my body from the violence of this judgment is to free myself from the violence of how everyone is shaping my body to meet their needs.

What Is the Body?

My body is nothing and everything at the same time. My body is more than just biology or flesh and bone or the intricate workings of atoms and cells. My body is more than just lumps of meat stitched together, stumbling about the earth, colliding with other masses of stumbling, stitched-together flesh.

My body is an expression of my mind, an expression of my awakened nature, an emanation arising from the great boundless ocean of emptiness, space, and energy potential that can either liberate or incarcerate. My body is a thought rising from this emptiness like waves rising from the ocean. When the wave of a thought rises, it takes form and wraps itself in earth to form my body's structure and weight, with wind becoming its breath, fire becoming its warm energy, water giving it moisture, blood, and fluidity, and consciousness filling it with intelligence and awareness.

My body is a loving extension of the earth. Stillness, stability, and a capacity for nurturing and growth are qualities that the earth and my body share. When I die, I will be returned to the earth through burial or fire. My ashes will be scattered back to the earth, my Mother. When I walk on the earth, I am walking on my body. When I lie on the earth, I am lying on my body. When the earth is in trauma, I am in trauma. When the earth is colonized, I am colonized.

My body is not here to be tamed or ordered. It is my awareness that needs to be tamed through training so that it may be invited back into resting in the great ocean of my consciousness. I don't see my body as being me but rather a partner with whom I am collaborating for the duration of this life. What my body seeks is to be, to exist without judgment. When did we stop asking our bodies what they need? When did we begin to assume that we know better than our bodies?

My body is ancient. Not ancient as in old but ancient as in my body holds countless lifetimes of data in the form of DNA traced all the way back to the earliest organisms and even further back to the stars all organic beings descend from. My body is more ancient than any system of violence created to tame it. How do I trust my body's ancient intuitive wisdom?

I pray to my ancestors, as well as the sacred earth called the Mother and the sacred sky called the Father to hold me as I make this journey back into my body to excavate the care and to free my body from imaginations of violence.

Awakened Care for the Body

I lie on the earth, feeling the Mother rise to hold me. I allow myself to connect to this simple act of kindness, this gesture. I surrender to the Mother, allowing my body to root deep in her, feeling planted and anchored. Above me, Father Sky opens my awareness, and I am feeling space from above and groundedness from below. I spark the streams of love, compassion, and joy and feel them flow into my heart center, braiding into awakened care, then slowly notice awakened care flooding my body. Eventually, I offer this care down into the earth as awakened gratitude and slowly radiate it up toward the sky.

I imagine myself floating on this ocean of awakened care, allowing it to float me into the work that needs to be done. Letting this awakened care hold me, I allow my body to be as it is in the moment. I let sensation come and go and offer it the space to be its most authentic. I do not react. I hold it with care. I am not adjusting, pushing away, or grabbing onto anything. This is the practice of the natural body.

Floating on this ocean eventually leads me to breath.

Breath

Breath is life: the fluid exchange between oxygen and carbon, the maintenance of the physical body buoyed by the tending of the energetic expression of my body or my life force energy. The breath is also an expression of wind. As I breathe, I am praying for air to move and cool others that need to be moved and cooled. I breathe for all those who can't breathe. My breath is a memorial for those whose breath has left them.

I allow my breath to settle into a natural rhythm, like turning on the radio and allowing the current song to play without the option to change stations. I allow my breath to breathe. I connect to the earth, as if I am breathing in and out from it, while at the same time imbuing my breath with awakened care and offering the exhale up to Father Sky. When we notice the breath and let it be, we are practicing natural breath.

Somewhere along the periphery, memories and moments of pain arise.

The Body in Pain

My back is hurting. I am not distracted by it; it is just something I notice. I know enough about my body by now to understand that the aching back is telling me a few things. First, that I am exhausted. Though I am sleeping well, I may not be resting long enough to balance the labor I am doing.

The aching is also telling me that beyond the exhaustion, I am carrying the weight of emotional labor for others in my back. The body holds emotional energy as physical sensation. I feel my ancestors on my back as if they are hanging on for their lives. America was built on our backs. Our backs are strong because they were given no choice to be anything other than strong. My back is strong, and my folks know that they can hang on when they need to because they know I can carry them. But my back aches, and, despite its strength, if I am not careful, my back will break.

The sensation of pain is how my body tells me that my physical body needs attention and tending to. Discomfort is always pointing me to places that need care. I send awakened care into my back, letting the pain float on the ocean of care. I imagine releasing this experience of pain down into the earth while simultaneously breathing it out of my body and up to the sky to disperse. I ask my body what else it needs, and it tells me it simply needs to be tended to in the way I am tending to it now.

What Is the Clarity of the Body?

The clarity of the body means that the body is here and present, not wandering in the past or lost in the future. To return to the body is to journey back to the present moment. But returning to the body also means returning to the reasons we left the body to begin with. We go back to the trauma and the forgone narratives, the things left unreconciled and unattended to.

We can't get free in the past or in the future because neither is happening in the moment. To attempt to do so is like trying to catch a speeding train. We can't board the train until it stops and lets us on; then it can take us to where we need to go. Returning to the present moment, to what's happening now, is to return to the presentness of our bodies held by the solidity of the earth. When our awareness unites with the body, mind and body move toward awakening together.

Enlightenment is possible in the body because the body, as an extension of the earth, can hold and ground the intensity of the pure clarity of the mind. Without the body, and certainly without rigorous meditation training, the fluidity and boundlessness of the mind can seem chaotic and overwhelming. Our awareness needs the anchor of the body in order to gradually begin to focus into emptiness. If there is no holding or anchoring, our awareness will not be stabilized enough to hold the material of the mind without being distracted by it.

Anorexia

I don't remember how my disorder started, but I know that I wanted to be seen, loved, and, most importantly, desired. Being fat often felt like two extremes trying to kiss each other. On one hand I felt too seen: the object of people's disgust and judgment. On the other

hand I felt invisible. My fatness gave people an excuse to dehuman-
ize me, to get a break from caring for me. My fat body reminded
people of what it meant to be disliked.

My fatness felt like a moral failure. When people gain weight, we
assume that they are failing or that they have given up. We label fat
people sinful. Sometimes when people looked at me, it felt like I was
causing them harm or that my body was testifying against them,
as if those who loved me had failed me by allowing me to get fat.

For about eight months during my mid-thirties, I starved myself
Monday through Friday and worked out at the gym at least six
days a week. Sometimes I would be exercising and would feel like
I was about to pass out. The pressure I was placing on my body felt
productive. Pain, I believed, meant that I was getting somewhere.

People praised me for my rapid weight loss; I became valued
and seen. I adored hearing people say, "Wow, you look good" or "I
see you're losing some weight, good for you." I was held differently,
more tenderly, and was taken more seriously because I was doing
something that was supposedly commendable.

But during the early days of graduate school, I understood that
my body could not maintain my abuse while surviving a rigorous
academic schedule. School distracted me away from my body, and
it was free from my violence

Now, floating on and in this ocean of care, I ask my body for
forgiveness and pray that this care restores everything that I have
taken from it. I apologize. I send the energy of awakened care back
to the person I used to be, freeing my painful memories. I imagine
that this care restores everything that my choices have depleted
from my body.

Ancestors and the Body

My body is an expression of everyone who has come before me.

My body is big, tall, and relatively strong. I have inherited my
father's physical body, including his height, large hands, long,
slightly knee-knocked legs, long arms, big feet, and round head.

I have been gifted with most of my mother's facial features, as well as her skin tone. My mother and father were both athletes; what has manifested in my body is the opposite. Instead of moving, I have gravitated toward being settled. Instead of being thrilled by competition, I am turned off by it. In Ayurveda, my dosha—or body type—is the union of water and earth. I am mud.

I am more attuned to my mother's body, as it was her body that formed mine. When I was little, I would cuddle up with her or come lie on her chest. It's strange to think that I was once smaller than her or that our bodies would meet in such tenderness. Of course, she gave birth to me, and my body formed from the material of her body. I am descended from a woman and remember that it is because of my mother that I am here.

My mother is a minister, and she once preached about the biblical story of a woman suffering from a bleeding disorder. Doctors were not able to help her and having nowhere else to turn, she sought out Jesus, wanting only to touch his garment. But my mother did more than preach; she became the woman in her sermon. She knelt on the floor and crawled in front of the pulpit, helping the congregation understand what it must have been like for this woman.

How can I allow my body to transmit teaching and prophecy? What does it mean to become clarity itself? My mother's medicine has anointed me—where do I go from here? Where and how do I move?

I offer all of this to the ocean of care and pray that as my body heals it awakens to its capacity for prophecy and teaching, remembering that we are expressions of all who came before us.

Hands

My hands are big and callused—the hands of someone who grows food or builds things. My hands have not labored like the hands of the elders in my family, but still I have their hands.

I have the hands of people who had to mold survival out of earth; who touched the earth and prayed for food, built shelter from wood and brick, washed clothes by the creek, hauled and sewed, kneaded and braided, held babies, and dug graves for their dead.

My ancestors and I link hands together across realms.

My hands are the hands of every Black man whose hand I have ever shook. We meet each other in the handshake and offer each other care, channeling the respect of countless men before us. I miss those handshakes, those rituals that remind us that we belong to people, that those people are holding on.

My hands are also the hands of my grandfather, Moses. I do not remember him in life, but he was said to have the gift of healing people by laying his hands on them.

My hands are my favorite expression of my body, and they draw me to other men in intimacy. Whoever has the hands of my grandfather or the men I grew up with will easily have my heart.

I imagine my hands and all the hands of my ancestors and descendants filling with awakened care, releasing us from labor that is not joyful, generative, or necessary. I offer care to my people. May our hands be healed, may the labor our hands continue to do be blessed, and may our hands one day come to rest.

Feet

My feet are often praised, which is strange, because as a Black boy, I was raised with the notion that my feet should never be exposed. In high school swim class, I had a Black friend who swam with his socks on! I have been the recipient of many *look at this nigga with his toes hanging out* glances from other Black men because I have absolutely adored the freedom of sandals and flip-flops when the weather is appropriate. Actually, that's a lie—it can be raining cats and dogs and I'll still be in flip-flops.

I love massaging and caressing my feet. I bought a foot massager years ago, and it is one of the more special treats in my life. Once, someone found me caressing my feet and asked sarcastically if I had a foot fetish. While there is nothing strange about foot fetishes, I responded saying that I just like my feet a lot.

When people ask me how I keep my feet looking good, I disclose that I pay other people to keep them looking good for me. I started frequenting nail salons in my late thirties, after wanting the experience for years. In places like Boston where I lived or in smaller towns I visited, I would often be the only man in a salon until I moved to Atlanta, where I sashayed into shops that were sometimes mostly populated by men. Many of our sensory nerves run through our feet, so applying pressure to certain points in the foot can have a dramatic impact on our physical and emotional health. Even at an early age, I intuitively sensed that.

I love my feet because they keep me connected to the earth. They have carried me through deserts, up mountains, and through swamps. They have supported a large, busy body with no complaints. And like my hands, these feet are the feet of my ancestors. I feel the journeys of my people in my soles.

I allow the energy of awakened care to tend to my feet, releasing the pain of all of my ancestors' long journeys down into the earth. My feet continue to carry me through the journey of this life.

Movement

Any movement cradled in awareness with the intention of getting free is called asana.

In asana, I move in and out of the illusion of time. My body leads the mind. Each stretch upward expresses a desire to touch the Divine. I am not trying to escape my body but to offer it the space to grant me permission to transcend. I find myself constantly reaching up and up into the unseen but deeply felt energy of the Divine, which feels like space and warmth. At the beginning of my practice, I believed that the Divine meant the absence of suffering. Now I understand that my suffering is as much an expression of the Divine as my pleasure.

The upward stretch is freedom embodied. My body is flowing with the tides of energies in and around me. The energetic expression of phenomenal reality is waves of energy gliding over yet deeper oceans of still energies. Asana is a cosmic dance that recognizes that everything is ecstatic flux. My mind contains everything, as my mind is the nature of everything.

My body wanders through space, bumping into other bodies. In the collision, it figures out what it is, where it stops, and where the phenomenal world begins. It is only by naming the end of its territory that it knows it exists. My body, like the sense of self that possesses it, is addicted to the world, to the end of one territory and the beginning of others. From this sense of self, we begin caring about the world, not because we want it to be free but because we need to manipulate it to figure out who we are—and, unfortunately, how to invade other bodies because ours seems too small. The ego only survives in contraction, even though it seems to expand. Its expansion is an aching desperation to endure. We believe that the expansion will soothe our aching, which actually masks the desire to let go and return to emptiness.

And then the truth: There is no movement. No intention. No body. No breath. No exhaustion. No focus. In emptiness, there is only stillness.

I imagine that my movement is filled with awakened care. My pose is cared for. The earth holds my movement, and I pray that it helps ease my desire to claim other bodies without consent. May my movement become a prayer that frees all beings.

Touch

Touch is a ritual action. It is the colliding of bodies not necessarily for sexual intent but for a basic recognition.

There is something transferred through the act of human contact. When I am touched by others, they are transferring the essence of their lineage into my body. Just through one touch, I know what they have survived and what their songs are. I can feel their joy, how they have cried in their life, how they have wanted to be free. How we touch is an expression of how other people have touched us.

The space beyond my body is a territory that I have learned to navigate with caution. I have not always been touched or held with kindness. My body still remembers the touches that have left scars and invisible wounds that I am still healing from. I don't trust everyone to touch me with the intention of freeing me from suffering. Still, I go on trying to understand who to be open to and how to offer permission to be touched. When I am touched in care by others, they are touching my tenderness. My deepest sensations arise as emotions, and in this touch my body says thank you.

I imagine awakened care anointing my touch and pray that my touch will only sooth and calm others, making it more possible for them to experience liberation.

Sex and Pleasure

The erotic is not just the hardening of my penis, but the activation of space and fluidity, of how my body starts to bend and open to another body. The excitement builds not necessarily into sex but into the reality of connection. For a moment, loneliness ceases and yields to the warmth of companionship.

Sex is how I attempt to return home to the experience of union. The pleasure I experience is what it feels like to rest in and with the experience of others.

I have confided in lovers that I am afraid to touch my body, to experience its pleasure, because I have convinced myself that pleasure betrays the countless beings who cannot enjoy pleasure. My resistance to pleasure is how I maintain solidarity with the most disenfranchised. But what is really happening is that when I sit still enough, I hear the quiet sobbing of thousands of gay men who died alone and invisible during the height of the AIDS epidemic. They are crying from within my body. Somehow, I have taught myself to hold their trauma in my flesh. They walk with me down the street, shop with me, and sleep with me. They are my only consistent lovers.

The ones who could not survive the labors and violent demands of this world live in and around me, their spirits calling for memorial and reconciliation. They are with me when I fuck; when I fuck, we are fucking together, and when I cum, they cum with me. I intentionally offer what is good to them.

When I experience the erotic, I imagine that I am experiencing it on behalf of any being who has never felt the liberation of the erotic. When the erotic opens into pleasure and sex, I imagine that I am having sex for all those who could not enjoy the sensations of their bodies. In the very moment of orgasm, I imagine my body and mind erupting in thick sweet floods of the most profound care for my partners and all beings.

I pray for the healing of my pleasure body. I imagine awakened care flooding into the wounds and sadness that prevent me from fully embodying pleasure. I release this same care to heal the sexual wounds of my ancestors, my lovers, and all beings who depend on me for healing. I release the hurt into the earth on behalf of all beings struggling to claim liberatory pleasure.

Dick

Of all the parts of my body, my dick has demanded the most attention and care. When I first realized I had a right to pleasure, I knew that we would forever be yoked together.

I no longer believe my dick makes me a man. I no longer know what a man is. Everything that I was told I should be as a boy transitioning into a man was based on how my dick needed to be handled and the right it had to thrust into anything it wanted.

I have lost count of how many men have prostrated to my dick, worshipping it, inviting it in. When the beautiful ones worshipped it, it was as if they were worshipping me. But I now know that they were only worshipping what my dick could give them, what it could anoint them with in the same way I have worshipped other men's dicks and received sacrament and anointing.

My dick is pulsating with the worship and anointing of many other men, and I feel that power circulating in me. I'm not interested in using this power to become a god, to lie perpetually in my own temple, or to subjugate others to bend to me. This power is the energy that I return to all bodies, wanting them to vibrate with agency and worship, becoming familiar with being seen and held. My dick is more than a site of pleasure; it reminds me to transcend the limitation of pleasure and displeasure, to awaken to the essence through awareness of power.

I imagine that awakened care releases me from the worship of my dick and any harm it has done to others. On behalf of all people with dicks, I release the violence that dicks have symbolized to the earth and pray that all woundedness is healed. May my dick become an expression of liberation.

Lips

My lips are one of my favorite physical features. They are soft, pliable, and thick like everyone's lips in my family. I love kissing. Lips are also one of my favorite features on other men. Full lips have a feeling of richness and decadence. Kissing and being kissed feels like the warmest care and the most intimate exchange.

The first time I kissed anyone was when I was seven or eight. She was barely older than me. We were with two other girls, and she dared me to kiss her. I was scared. I felt the trembling in my body. Our lips met. She seemed like she had done this before. It didn't feel like it looked on TV. Her arms wrapped around me, and my hands wandered down her back. This was the first time I had touched anyone like this. The kiss lasted a few seconds. Afterward I felt like I did something wrong because it felt so uninteresting.

Thirteen or fourteen years later, I would kiss a boy who looked like me, with thick, full lips, and I realized what a kiss was supposed to feel like. That kiss stays with me even now. But my lips remember so many other lips I have kissed in pleasure, in friendship, or as blessing. My kisses have adorned so many bodies. The only reason to have lips is for this adornment.

Even now, I imagine my lips awakening old pleasant memories of past kisses and even those kisses yet to come. May my kissing become a blessing, an extension of the care I hold for myself.

Eyes

I have never thought too much about my eyes. They have been a functional sensory organ used to gather visual data about the world around me. I am not someone who has often been complimented for having pretty eyes, since my eyes are not blue or green. But when I gaze into a mirror, it is my eyes that draw me the most. They are like invitations into other worlds.

My eyes are reflective brown pools that have carried as much despair as joy. They are like portals opening into the most tender parts of me. I sense the care that I practice radiating out into the world through my eyes, and I find myself being cared for when I gaze into my own reflection.

My eyes are doing more than gazing out into the world—they are gazing through the world, through light and shadow. I am gazing into the heart of things and people. What I see are their hopes and fears. I see their hidden cravings. I see what most people overlook. To see is to know, to be aware of. I see the multiple layers of realities folded on top of each other and because of this, reality becomes rich and complex. All of this is reflected in my eyes, and I am moved.

I allow awakened care to tend to my eyes as I think of Chenrezig, the one who holds us all in an unconditional gaze. May my eyes become like Chenrezig's divine eyes, gazing across the universe, liberating all beings with unconditional care.

Teeth

I never liked my teeth. For most of my life I would stand in front of the mirror with my mouth wide open, wishing that my wide, gapped-tooth smile would magically transform into a straight, tight smile. Though my teeth have always been strong, I haven't been satisfied.

My gapped smile reminded me of being Black and poor, of having lived in the projects, of being raised by a single mother. My teeth made me look country and unsophisticated. I felt judged by others because oral hygiene is often associated with class, and I believed that I would never achieve class mobility with my teeth giving me away. Even as I transitioned into being a spiritual teacher and let go of that thinking, I still felt embarrassed about my teeth.

Yet as my spiritual practices deepened, I began to understand that my teeth ground me. When I feel ungrounded, and things get too abstract or blurred, I can turn my attention to my teeth to usher me back to something that feels tangible.

I decided to get braces to further care for my teeth. It was an act of care for myself, and I have noticed how much more I smile and let the world see my teeth. Sometimes we need to do things like this because of how it can help support our work of helping others. I wish that I could use my practice to transcend anxiety about my teeth, but sometimes we can take a quicker, more worldly path to reduce suffering.

I offer awakened care to my teeth as an expression of gratitude for everything they do to support my well-being and happiness. I release anxiety about my teeth to the earth along with the anxiety of all beings.

Voice

I never cared much for my voice. I never thought it was anything special. In elementary school, I worked with a speech therapist because there were a few sounds I couldn't form, which resulted in a heightened awareness of my speech patterns. It took me years to become comfortable with speaking, and it was getting involved in competitive speaking competitions in high school and college that boosted my confidence.

I have always loved to sing and was one of countless little gay boys who expressed my creativity and need to perform in a gospel choir. I never believed I was a good singer until very recently, even despite all the years I sang in ensembles. I never sounded like my favorite singers. I sounded like what some people think queer men sound like: lispy, soft, and timid.

When I started teaching professionally, I decided to record myself and listen to my talks. This helped me to gain more confidence speaking as a spiritual teacher. Then I started singing more informally, for fun, and as other folks heard, they encouraged me to sing more.

As Black gospel is my root music, I imagine that as I am singing gospel, I am tapping into the voices of all of my ancestors, and I begin to feel them sing with me. My voice is a rich baritone with a little breathiness. I feel as if I speak from the heart of the earth. When I speak, I am speaking with the care that I have been cultivating for years. When I sing, I am singing with all the beings who love me. I am no longer ashamed of my voice but understand it as an expression of my heart.

May awakened care continue to blossom in my voice and lead countless beings to liberation.

It is easy for the body to get left behind in liberation work. It makes sense because we struggle to understand what the body is attempting to tell us about what it needs. Like the Buddha, we have to learn to ally with our bodies which means caring for it and tending to its pain which is our pain as well. However, tending to our bodies is the work of liberation and important work of the New Saint.

Loving God

Recently I wandered around the grocery store yearning to love God. I didn't know what I was doing or what was happening. Yet nonetheless I paced the long aisles, searching for cleaning sprays, toilet tissue, beer, and BBQ sauce almost on the verge of tears because I was allowing my heart to open to an experience of spaciousness, safety, and warmth. It felt like I was connecting to an intense experience of being enveloped in care, and I knew that this was what God felt like, this experience of profound, simple acceptance wrapping me up, restoring everything that hate and judgment from others has depleted. In that moment I wished that all beings could experience God like this.

It's strange at this point in my life to say that I love God and to practice loving God. I ran away from Christianity after having broken up with God in college and thought I would never understand God. Yet after twenty years of practicing Buddhism, I began to hear God calling me back into loving.

I no longer see God as the personification of people's weaponized pain, sorrow, and trauma. God is no longer a psychological terrorist restricting me from the love that I deserve because of my queerness or belief in justice. At this point I know God as an experience of the essence of all phenomena. God is the expression of my mind, which is to say the expression of the union of emptiness, space, and energy potential. This union is, of course, the very state of freedom itself. It is where spiritual abolitionism points to. God is everything. To dwell in God is to dwell in the heart of everything at once. This dwelling without threat or judgment is to be loved by God.

Loving God in this way has also been an experience of unconditional abiding. Unconditional abiding means I allow myself to dwell in this experience of openheartedness. It is very much like the last stage of SNOELL, when we let material float in the spaciousness of the mind. Yet in this case, I am the material floating in the liberated heart space of God. This openness connects me into the experience of all phenomena. In this way I disrupt isolation and experience connection and a deep sense of belonging to everything. When I experience belonging, then I am experiencing being loved. And whatever pain arises, I can trust myself to hold it because I am being held by everything. In this way, God offers me permission to rest and surrender to being cared for.

This experience of God has helped me take care of one of my traumas as a Black person. Part of the white supremacist capitalist conditioning of my body has dictated that I must always be in motion, that my body must always be producing something that is consumable. When I am not in motion producing something—be it entertainment, pleasure, comfort for White folks, or tangible goods—I have no purpose and am rendered lazy and therefore dangerous and worthy of annihilation. It has been my experience that Black folks being still or resting is viewed as threatening at worst and not useful at best. However, when we choose to rest, to produce resources and experiences for our own care and liberation, we become more than just lazy; we become uppity and hardheaded. When I continue to make this choice, I enter into fugitivity. God invites me into simply being and resting within this experience of everything, and in doing so, I disrupt the expectations of the system. Although I may lose the validation of the system along with resources that I have relied on to maintain the illusion of safety (because safety within any system of violence is an illusion), I gain the love of God, which is the experience of being a part of and being held by everything. This is the experience that great changemakers like Mother Harriet and Mother Sojourner relied on to love and free Black people.

Deities

I never thought much about the multiplicity of gods when I was younger. Growing up in a Christian denomination, my monotheistic indoctrination left very little room to consider any other presence than God as the Father. The belief of other gods was idolatry, a very grave sin indeed. I did well in maintaining my monogamy with God until I broke up with God in college. Having left a long-term monogamous relationship with a somewhat jealous and controlling daddy, I started getting curious as to what I had been missing.

I soon landed in a world religions class that ended up feeling like speed dating as we explored multiple religions, spiritualities, and philosophies that I had never been exposed to. I was never curious about other paths before because I had never allowed the space to explore those other paths for fear of going to hell. Now I had permission to explore and wonder about different ways of experiencing the Divine. I especially loved the exposure I received to Islam, Buddhism, and Hinduism and felt particularly strong about Islam as a faith I could explore because of my love for Malcolm X and my understanding of how the Islamic path had transformed his life.

I was also really interested in Hinduism, and, more specifically, I felt a tender and warm pull toward the deity Ganesh, which would eventually evolve into a profound devotion to the deity ten years later. However, sitting in class learning about Ganesh felt like developing a crush. I was enthralled by him. He felt familiar and evocative with his elephant head, round tummy, and rat companion. He was called the Lord of Obstacles, which means that he removed obstacles and was often prayed to at the beginning of any work, project, or practice or just to get the day started. I didn't pray to him back then. I was not a praying person as a college student. Yet, it was the first time I fell in love with a deity.

Within three years after that initial awakening to Ganesh in college, I found myself passing through India on a multicountry trip, spending as much time as possible chasing after Ganesh in temples, feeling mesmerized by all the statues and iconography of him. I just wanted to gaze at him like I would at any cute guy. It was on that first visit to India that I bought my first of what would become many statutes of Ganesh.

After that initial trip, I landed in Tibetan Buddhism, and once I was grounded in a stable meditation practice, I was introduced to an overwhelming assortment of deities. As I mentioned earlier, the first deity I began formally practicing with was Chenrezig, the great deity of love. I learned my lineage's formal chanting and visualization practice for Chenrezig and began to experience the opening of my heart to authentic love. Soon after there came Tara, the female buddha of compassion, followed by Medicine Buddha. This opening to multiple deities felt liberating, but at the time, I didn't have the language or the understanding to talk about what these beings really were. Even after becoming a lama, it was hard to explain, and it became even more intense when I started being drawn to deities from other paths like Kali Ma and Mother Oshun.

It wasn't until recently that I came to my personal understanding of deities. To begin with, everything emerges from the boundless ocean of the essence. There is a class of beings who are conscious, intelligent, and multidimensional and who resonate in higher frequencies outside of our material and physical world. When beings in this class exercise power in our material world and choose to be in relationship with us, they are called deities. I separate deities into two categories: wisdom deities and worldly deities. One or both kinds of deities manifest in many spiritual and religious paths.

Wisdom deities, or celestial deities, are expressions of the essence itself or enlightened beings that have transcended a sense of self. They are inherently compassionate because they emerge from truth itself. They can embody any form in this world and can be associated with elements, emotions, or mental states. These beings are considered buddhas. Tara is said to have been a being like us until she achieved enlightenment and chose to embody compassion to help us understand and be liberated into the essence.

Worldly deities, though still manifesting in higher frequencies, are not enlightened, so they still have some attachment to the self and have free range to show up as compassionate or malicious. These deities are the most difficult to relate to. Because of their relationship to ego, they still have needs and desires that are only met through relationship with us. That relationship is based on our belief in them, along with rituals and ceremonies dedicated to them to sustain their needs. I believe that wisdom deities have the capacity to help us achieve ultimate freedom because they are completely free. Some benevolent worldly deities can do a lot for us and can be instrumental in helping us experience everything from healing and having good fortune, to being freed from harm, but they can't really take us all the way to enlightenment.

Worldly deities have the capacity to appear anywhere in our material reality. However, there is a class of beings called local deities that are connected to stretches of land, mountains, bodies of water, caves, and so on. Basically, worldly deities are everywhere we live. When we live in locations with worldly deities, it becomes important to recognize them and develop some relationship with them. This has been the foundation of many spiritual traditions all over the world. We acknowledge the spiritual ecology of a place and live consciously with these beings who are also connected to energies like weather or occurrences like illnesses. We can pray to them and make offerings, asking them to bring about change in the physical environment.

The closer any being gets to experiencing the illusion of ego, the more powerful they become. So wisdom deities will always be the most powerful beings in the universe. Worldly beings who are benevolent and are working toward complete enlightenment can choose to take on the forms of wisdom deities to help us on behalf of those deities. They can also make wisdom deities more accessible to us. Wisdom deities can also take on the forms of worldly deities if it's of benefit to others.

Heart Sutra

There are multiple paths by which to experience the essence. When I was growing up in church, I only knew God as the Father, and it was a tough time as the violence of white supremacy and patriarchy was conflated with the notion of God's love. So, God as the Father ended up being a turnoff. After my conversion to Buddhism, I was introduced to the female buddha Tara, who was God as the Mother, and through whom I began to experience space, deeper care, and glimpses of the essence. Through Tara as God as the Mother, I could name the trauma I held around how God as the Father was taught to me. That recognition promoted profound healing—so much healing, in fact, that I have returned to practicing God as the Father through deities like Mahakala and Ganesh.

When the Buddha offered the teaching of the Heart Sutra, he offered one of the most important teachings of Buddhism, which was that all phenomena are just expressions of the essence—that form was emptiness and that emptiness was form. He taught that there was a relative truth of phenomena and the ultimate truth of emptiness.

I also interpret the sutra to be a teaching on the sacred duality between the Mother and the Father. The sacred Father is expressed as form while the Mother is expressed as emptiness and space. If form is nothing other than emptiness, and emptiness is nothing other than form, then the Mother is nothing other than the Father, and the Father is nothing other than the Mother. They are reflections of one another while also being expressions of one another. In union they are the expression of God, the total essence.

God as the Mother and God as the Father are dualistic paths diverging from the essence that is God and leading back to the essence of God. This is an example of sacred dualism taught in the Heart Sutra. The universe is driven through a sacred duality that spins us into the essence. Everything is an expression of the essence. Duality is necessary for most of us because we don't have the capacity to just rest in the essence. Duality points us in a direction that can be held, and duality becomes sacred when we allow it to lead us into holding space and that space leads us to the essence.

Using dualities like this expresses another theme of the Heart Sutra, which is the potential of liberation through contradictions. The Heart Sutra is nothing but a contradiction. Sacred duality is a contradiction because ultimately, there is no duality as there are no phenomena. However, until we awaken fully, duality must be skillfully used and related to in order to return to the realization of the essence.

Dualities generate a tension that, through practice, we can ride back into the essence. The tension itself keeps us activated, which in turn keeps us from sinking into a lull or numbness from which it is difficult to break out. The tension of light and dark invites us to do the labor of moving beyond our notions of what either is as the dualism highlights the wisdom of the other. And we can rest in our awareness of phenomena, which is the expression of the Father and then from that resting expand outward into space, which is the Mother. We can use the tension to energize the power of our awareness to keep expanding and holding everything until our awareness boundlessly sinks into our consciousness and back into the essence.

However, what all this really means is that we can notice which stream of conscious energy from the essence we can get with. I spent many years working intensely with expressions of both the Father and Mother. And while Divine Mother practices, often in the forms of Tara or Kali, have been deeply liberating, I am also noticing how I am deeply embodying practices of the Divine Father. In any case, we figure out what resonates with us, always understanding that both streams are reflections of the other and lead back to the essence.

Even from this duality, other kinds of expressions from the essence can occur. In Tantric Buddhism, we talk about how an awakened being can manifest in three forms: a physical being, a pure energy form, and a direct expression of the essence, which is a direct experience of the essence. These three forms, or bodies, are dimensions we can arise in to be accessible for other beings. Another example is the Holy Trinity in Christianity. There is God as the Father, as the essence itself; the Holy Spirit, as the energy of the essence; and, Jesus, as the physical being consciously emanating from God and the Holy Spirit and acting as an accessible path for Christians to experience both. So many spiritual and religious paths are founded on the realization of a person connected to higher states of consciousness becoming vehicles that can channel and translate these higher states into teachings and other experiences more ordinary beings can connect to.

Getting to the Mother never meant bypassing the Father, and understanding God was never about restricting God to the expression of either the Mother or the Father. Balance has never meant extremism. It has meant letting go of wherever we have been put and allowing things to be as they are. The union of the Mother and the Father as God awakens and God becomes what God has always been: the primordial expression of space and energy that has no experience of suffering or violence but only of the purest love.

The Divine Mother

The Mother is everything. We are born from the Mother. We live and die in the Mother. The Mother is the expression of space and without space nothing could arise. This is why this expression of God and essence is called the Mother. To experience the Mother is to experience space, which can be overwhelmingly disorienting because we are oriented toward contraction. To open into the spaciousness of the Mother is to begin letting go of the suffering we choose and refocusing on the space that holds everything and the joy arising from that space.

I first met Mother through Mother Tara. As I mentioned in the "Awakened Care" chapter, in Sanskrit, *Tara* means "star." In the Tibetan language, she is called Dolma, which means "Mother Liberator." As an expression of space, she is the mother of all deities. Her principal quality is compassion, as compassion is the space to care and to understand that we are already free. Her compassion shines bright like a star guiding us into deep and transformative empathy and liberation work. In Buddhist Tantra, there are several visual representations of her, as is true for most deity representations. These variations in representation are intended to represent all the various and nuanced energies that can materialize. Tara has several representations to help us understand how to embody all the various expressions of compassion.

Tara is the only female buddha in the Tibetan Buddhist pantheon. I spent years practicing her sadhana in long retreats. Yet, like most of the practices back then, I struggled to develop a personal relationship with Tara herself. My early practice with deities felt mechanical, pointlessly repetitive, and, well, dull. This was not the fault of my teachers or lineage. It was more that I was unsure of how to relate to Tara. Years ago, a female teacher taught me that we have a right to think of Tara as a dear close friend—a homegirl in a sense. This felt true and engaging, yet I still struggled to make sense of this simple, inviting teaching.

After a time of practicing with Tara, I was led to articulate my sadness. It was heartbreaking and liberating at the same time. Most of us will never start the path of liberation until we admit our brokenheartedness to ourselves in whatever way we experience it. I had to learn that it's okay to say, "The world is fucked up, my life is hard, and I'm sad." When we can say that, we are able to start leaning into the experience of sadness and disappointment. That was what Tara began to teach me.

The practice of the Mother can be triggering for many of us because we relate this practice to our relationships with our own mothers, caretakers, or birth parents. It takes time to push through our trauma from parental relationships. When I find myself struggling with this hurt, I practice offering it at the feet of the Mother, which is to say I offer my suffering back into the space and emptiness that it arises from. I do this over and over again until I reconnect to the experience of space and fluidity.

The Divine Father

My root teacher's nickname for me was Gönpo. When he first called me this, we were outside on the monastery grounds taking an afternoon walk with a group of other monastics. I was new to the monastery and was slowly getting used to the monastic community. As we strolled, my teacher, Norlha Rinpoche, seemed to be in a good mood. I was walking about ten feet in front of him when I heard him saying, "Oh, Gönpo." I glanced behind me to catch him looking at me and caught the nervous gestures and whispers of others as if he had said something offensive. It was explained to me in the moment that *Gönpo* was a Tibetan word that meant "protector" and was another name for the great Dharma protector, the wisdom deity called Mahakala, and particularly the manifestation of this deity that was Black. The anxiety from other monastics came from their belief that because I was this big Black man, Rinpoche was maybe teasing me. I didn't feel offended, and somehow I knew it had nothing to do with my physicality either. Later I would understand that the name referred to the power of my practice.

The experience of the Father arises as the illusion of form, but form is deceiving. The world of phenomena seems real, and its illusionary nature is not evident. God as the Father in this understanding creates structures and containers and holds us so that we can have a foundation to do the work of freedom. Form was never meant to be taken seriously or worshipped because that relationship makes form and structure too real, rigid, and material. When something becomes real, it becomes hard and rigid, losing fluidity, flexibility, and movement. When the expression of the Father becomes hardened and rigid, we lose contact with the expression of the Mother. This loss leads to violence because when there is no contact with the Mother, we lose our relationship to space, and when space is lost, we contract and contraction means habitual reactivity from a place of being trapped. We are confined to the illusion of no room, and we get claustrophobic.

The Father has been calling me back for some time now, but every time I attempt to turn toward the Father, I meet my own hurt and violence around what the misunderstanding of the Father has created for me and this world. With the support of Mother Tara, I attempt to touch the Father, to open my heart to an experience of divine masculinity, which means that I have to first learn how to touch myself. I have to name my body in this world and how this sacred energy has touched me and how I have lived terrified of it. This is more than just calling myself a man. It is more than just renouncing the violence of rigidity while overconsuming the Mother. It is more than shutting up, repressing the articulation of my conditioning, smiling, and keeping it all to myself. It is more than performing allyship with women and femme-centered, gender-nonconforming, and nonbinary folks. It is more than giving up masculine pronouns for neutral pronouns. It is more than hating other men who make us feel like hell. More than any of that, it is telling myself the truth that I can be free and reduce violence while learning how to be myself rather than whom I am expected to be.

It was the Father who taught me that to find him, I had to stop being afraid of myself. All along it was the fear that drove me into running away from myself into the performance of manhood. The supreme practice was accepting everything I struggled with — the trauma, the violence, rage, addiction to power over others—and in accepting it all, loving it all, and in loving it, releasing myself from a compulsive relationship to it all.

The Roots of Patriarchy

The carceral state is nothing if not the expression of rigidity. God as the Mother and the Father are both expressions of space and fluidity; while the Mother is an expression of the emptiness of space, the Father is an expression of the potentiality of space to become the illusion of form. Yet when we get confused and lose connection to the Mother as space, we become desperate to find something to stabilize us, and we begin using form to solidify a sense of self. Form becomes solidified as well through our belief in its realness, and this is the birth of rigidity.

This belief in form and the rigidity and reactivity that arise from this belief as it has historically been expressed through men is the root of patriarchy. Patriarchy disconnects men from fluidity and subjects us to the trauma of rigidity and constriction. The driving force of patriarchy has been the cisgender male body, although it can be witnessed and reproduced in all bodies. Mother bell hooks, who is an ancestor now but who in life was a prolific scholar, teacher, writer, and elder, wrote about patriarchy, teaching that "patriarchy has no gender." This means that patriarchy can be expressed by anyone regardless of our gender identification.

Patriarchy expresses itself on three levels: outer, inner, and secret.

— OUTER LEVEL —

The outer level of patriarchy is a political, social, and mental system that perpetuates the myth that men should be dominant. Patriarchy polices men's emotional expressions, labeling such expressions as weak or feminine. Such conditioning has depleted men's access to a fuller, more expressive life that is in more alignment with the feminine.

— INNER LEVEL —

The inner level of patriarchy is the duality between power and weakness. The essence of the Mother as an expression of fluidity and space, which is essentially liberation itself, is a mirror reflecting back to men our own incarceration in rigidity and, even more, our perceived helplessness to transcend it. Patriarchy is a full-spirited expression of dominance, hegemony, and rigidity fueled by emotional distance and a limited experience of self-empathy. This lack of self-empathy feels like being suffocated and slowly killed. Patriarchy encourages people to react to this pain by enacting violence against anyone who reminds them of it. Thus, interpersonal and systemic patriarchal violence is born.

— SECRET LEVEL —

The secret level of patriarchy is the loss of belief in change and the secret worship of rigidity. It is the embodiment of incarceration, which is the experience of being trapped in decisions made without our consent. Although hopelessness is felt, it goes unnamed. We feel as if we have no option but to choose violence against ourselves and/or against others who remind us that we are not free.

Freedom from Patriarchy

Several years ago, I was told by a spiritual advisor that I needed to disrupt what was being passed down to me from my male ancestors, that I needed to disrupt the transference of the violence of patriarchy. My advisor helped me to understand that I descend from a lineage of men who never had the chance to be truly free because they were forced into a system meant to annihilate them and anyone in relationship with them.

I have thought about the lineage of men I descend from for a while now. I have struggled so much with the trauma of being conditioned into manhood by other men that I have let the hurt convince me that I have received nothing of value from this lineage. I understand now that this is not true. Yes, there has been the trauma of being forced to abide by a gender performance that has been the root of so much violence against everyone, including men themselves, but as I write this I feel my male ancestors surround me with the most tender care, reminding me that I have also inherited their capacity to care, along with a fierce dedication to being free. My body is their body, and I am here because of their labor. Most importantly, I am doing this work because they didn't have what they needed to be free from patriarchy. Their care right now reminds me that their longing for freedom has gifted me with this capacity to experience freedom in a way they never could, and because I can experience this, I can offer this liberation back to them.

Patriarchy is what happens when wounds aren't tended to—when heartbreak expresses itself as intense violence against ourselves and the fiercest subjugation of all other beings. It is a state of trauma that guards itself against empathy with emotional distance and overreactivity. It is the suffering of never being allowed to be yourself, of being forced to measure every thought, action, or word against a standard that does not care for us. The imperative to be strong results in the terror of seeming weak or vulnerable.

Patriarchy is forgetting that what I need most is to allow myself to be reflected by all beings, especially other men—to see myself in their eyes, feel myself in their touch, and hear myself in their speech while having the courage and tenderness to allow other men to be reflected, gently, in me. When I resist patriarchy, when I feel this tenderness, when I am being touched and touching other men for the first time, I experience freedom from shame, and freedom to care for and heal all those whom my violence has harmed.

Sacred Masculinity and the Masculine Erotic

Over the course of many years, I have been trying to understand sacred masculinity, which is an awakened state of masculinity, freed from patriarchy. I have, understandably, been met with resistance by folks who have been so deeply hurt by patriarchal violence that the phrase "sacred masculinity" sounds like an oxymoron. This is mostly because of how patriarchy has been entwined with masculinity. However, although we have come to conflate the two, patriarchy and masculinity are actually different expressions.

The sacred masculine is an expression of beauty, intimacy, fluidity, and connection driven by the masculine erotic. In its awakened state, the masculine erotic—as well as the feminine erotic—is an expression of God, or the essence.

Traditionally in Western cultures, we have defined masculinity by the traits and behaviors attributed to boys and men or anyone identifying as male. These traits have included assertiveness and objectivity. But these traits are socially constructed. They are rituals that arise as a means of relating to and navigating the illusion of form and identity. Masculinity, like femininity, is an expression of energies that are labeled and reacted to in the carceral state and give rise to gender expressions imbued with certain meanings that play into how we relate to one another. Masculinity is not a system, but patriarchy has absorbed it as a means of maintaining systems of violence.

Still, I crave the energy of masculinity, which isn't about sex or gender but the energy of form and structure that is trying to lure me into the essence. Masculinity is fluid, even in its play as form, but when it is expressed through patriarchy, it solidifies, just as molten lava turns to rock.

The masculine erotic is like the Holy Spirit or the energy form in Tantra because it energizes and awakens us. The erotic is what excites and inspires us. It wakes us up and invites us to dance with the phenomenal world. The erotic opens our hearts, reduces fear, and lets awakened care flood our experience of life. The erotic is transformative because it is speaking from the deepest and most vulnerable essence of who we are.

I feel the erotic when I close my eyes and shift my attention to my heartbeat and the way it reverberates within the essence of all phenomenal reality. The whole world is alive with my pounding heart.

The masculine erotic is a life force; it is the point at which I start believing that things are workable and changeable. I begin to think that where I have been told to stay is a lie, a story that I have cocreated. When I begin to challenge this story, I find spaciousness. This spaciousness is evocative; it turns me on. I see potential; I can become what I need to become.

The masculine erotic is how men begin to do liberatory emotional labor, which is a form of awakened care. When phenomena, including thoughts and emotions, become more fluid, we have room to choose other ways of being. We get the space to name our hurt, experience it, let it go, and make choices that deepen joy, creativity, belonging, and authenticity, which results in a reduction of violence against ourselves and others. This reduction of violence also means we are divesting ourselves of the rigidity of patriarchy and becoming emotionally fluid. When our minds are fluid, our bodies become fluid. In this fluidity, I feel resourced enough to break through barriers with other men to tend to them.

When I pass other men on the sidewalk or walking through a door, I often attempt to touch them empathetically. Sometimes I am met with a smile or nod or a "How ya doing?" or a "sup." Other times I am met with a warning as mild as a blank stare or as intense as a "What the fuck are you looking at!" In these moments, I take a breath and pull my awareness inward to take care of my fear and the disappointment beneath it. I notice how my fear is attempting to shut down my heart. I notice thoughts like *Fuck you too* or *Maybe I should give up on connecting to other men*. Then I breathe again and reflect on how this interaction wasn't about me. It was about the pain of another person. With this reflection, I soften some and try again.

I must be clear about this: I am not saying that the masculine erotic is directly related to the act of sex. Rather, it is an expression of intimacy. It is when two men feel into one another and are not afraid. We are letting our hearts and minds be seen and tended to through emotional or empathetic touching. We can touch each other's bodies, but that touching does not need to be about desire or physical pleasure. I suffer when my reaching out is not appreciated or seen because my reaching out is an extension of my own vulnerability. Vulnerability is my willingness to show you what I need and how I need it.

Too many men are little boys that need to be held, who are struggling to convince their fathers to hold them. This is part of the masculine erotic: doing the emotional labor of tending to our broken hearts while also tending to the broken hearts of our fathers. Our unmet longing devolves into violence; we react to the hurt in order to kill it. When we externalize our hurt and project it onto other men, we annihilate them. Healing means we disrupt this cycle of violence, redefining what it means to be descended from men. The work we do to embody the sacred masculine reduces the violence we transmit to our male descendants.

Queerness is also an expression of the sacred and is also an expression of sacred masculinity. Here, I define queerness as the intentional blurring of the boundaries between what the world has told us we are and who we are in our most liberated expression. Queerness is dangerous. It is a risk because the carceral state demands that we stay put and consent to how it categorizes us. The state is disrupted by resisting any category that does not mean the practice of care and freedom.

Queerness isn't necessarily about sex either; it's about choosing the way we want to be free, which means choosing a reduction of violence and deep care for ourselves and collectives as well as our liberatory emotional well-being, which releases us from constricting mental suffering.

The secret expression of the sacred masculine is the desire to connect to the energy of beauty. I want to enjoy beauty. I want to be cracked open by the beauty of my body and experience as well as the beauty of other people and the world. Patriarchy has stolen men's capacity to abide in the beauty of things and left a craving expressed as a frustrated, unconscious grieving. I want to be a part of beauty, but I have too often found myself trying to dominate beauty instead.

Maybe this helps: If you identify as a man, what would it be like to wear a glowing yellow daisy tucked behind your ear? Imagine walking around in public, having people see you. What would that be like? How are people reacting? Are people smiling? Do you feel beautiful? Do you believe you have a right to feel and experience beauty? Are you beautiful? How are you desired? What may be uncomfortable about adorning your body with pretty flowers, sweet-smelling perfumes, powders and rouges, about making yourself precious and fantastic, pristine, delicate, and simple? Can you name the rigidity that arises and all the stories that keep you from imagining this and enjoying this kind of presentation and relationship to beauty? Or can you perhaps define what beauty is for you and imagine embodying it for others to see?

Patriarchy is forgetting who I am and in that forgetting, becoming unknowingly devoted to violence, participating in relegating any being not rigid and brokenhearted to the feminine to be ritually and systematically erased while repressing other men into the psychic terrorism of patriarchal carcerality. To remember, we must submit ourselves to the care of sacred masculinity and the erotic and surrender to the care of collectives who want us to be free. We must choose to allow our hearts to break and be cared for. In doing this, we can be released from the violence that emerges from pushing away all the ways we have been threatened not to be.

LINEAGE OF MEN PRACTICE

To begin, call on the earth to hold you. Notice the weight of your body making contact with your seat or feel your feet resting on the floor.

Now, generate the intention to start this practice to benefit yourself and your lineage of men and male ancestors.

Next, move through the awakened care practice, eventually feeling awakened care streaming through your body. Rest in this experience of care for as long as you need to.

When you're ready, imagine calling on the men in your family, all your male ancestors as well as your future male descendants. Imagine that they gather around you in a circle. This is your lineage of men.

Reflect on their pain and all the choices they made to manage their pain, which often resulted in harm against themselves and countless others. Reflect on how you share the same pain and have made the same choices they have.

Allow yourself to feel your brokenheartedness and then extend it out to meet the brokenheartedness of the men around you.

Speak to the men around you saying, "I acknowledge that this is the pain of our lineage born from rigidity, insecurity, and confusion and transmitted from generation to generation as patriarchal trauma. I want to free all of us from this suffering."

Now, imagine that your body becomes a conduit channeling all the awakened care in your body into their experience as light, warmth, or any expression of energy that feels appropriate. Imagine all the pain of the lineage dissolving into the care, leaving a sense of lightness and joy in the lineage.

At the end of the practice, imagine that your lineage has been completely freed and invite the lineage to return to where they came from to join you.

SPIRITUAL PRACTICES FOR DIVESTING ONESELF OF PATRIARCHY FOR MEN

When you don't know what to say, be silent. When you are silent, listen. When you are listening, hold space for everything.

Build your altars to the sacred feminine in your private space. Offer prayers and make offerings. Pray that the sacred feminine reveals itself in you.

Reflection: In what ways am I loyal to patriarchy?

Return to your body. Feel it. Feel your hurt.

Allow your heart to break.

Reflection: How has patriarchy broken my heart?

Breathe.

Remember that you are a part of a lineage of men and that compassion for ourselves and the world means that we disrupt the violence that has been passed down through our lineage.

Figure out what forgiveness means.

Forgive yourself.

Forgive your father.

Forgive his father.

Forgive your children.

Forgive all the men who hurt you.

Breathe.

Reflection: What is a man?

Instead of blaming your broken heart on everyone else, see it as the teacher. Let it teach you that this is what many others are feeling right now along with you.

Instead of saying, "Other men . . .," say instead, "This man here," placing your hand on your heart center and gently acknowledging that you are the other men you are afraid of.

Reflection: I am both an individual and a representation of a system.

Develop rituals with other men that allow you to touch each other.

To be an ally, ask women and gender-expansive people where you should be and then go there. Take other men with you.

Reflection: How innocent am I?

Build your altar to the sacred masculine. Offer prayers and make offerings. Pray for the sacred masculine to be revealed.

Take any man who has loved you and allowed you to be free as your teacher.

Reflection: I am the problem.

To be an ally, figure out what your front line is and go there.

Train to do emotional labor with other men.

Breathe.

Reflection: Why don't I give a shit?

Make crying a regular practice. Let the pain you experience soften your heart.

Reflection: Why am I so angry?

Place your hand over your heart center and silently chant to yourself, *I am the Beloved.*

Keep your hand on your heart center and call yourself precious, sweet, and beautiful.

Reflection: Why don't I believe women?

Surround yourself in a field of benefactors that love you. Let them love you.

Allow the world to love and care for you.

Reflection: To be gendered as a cisgender man means that I am traumatized.

Speak about your hurt. Make art about it. Write about it. Express it to other men.

Reflection: What am I so afraid of?

Listen to people when they say they are afraid of you.

Reflection: You are both victim and perpetrator.

Be angry. Feel the anger. Let your anger point you back to your broken heart.

Reflection: What do you need?

Surrendering to the Dark

Darkness is difficult to grapple with on the path of liberation. Many of us have been taught to relate to the dark as dangerous or deceitful. However, in the tradition of the New Saint, darkness becomes yet another experience we must learn to ally with to get free.

I used to be afraid of the dark and what I thought darkness meant. So many of us are afraid of the dark, but what exactly is darkness? For me, darkness was fear, but it was the fear of losing agency over everything, submitting to something that disrupted my senses, disarming me and leaving me open to harm. Darkness did not allow me to know things. How could I survive if I did not know?

Darkness can be an expression of a different kind of clarity—one that invites us to consider how darkness isn't necessarily asking us to figure it out but instead is asking us to take care of it. We can and must hold, sense, and experience darkness without reacting to it, or else we get consumed by it. Evil is the loss of clarity, and when clarity is lost, we lose the space and start feeling trapped by the illusion of rigidity. Feeling trapped, we start to strike out, thinking that's how we should alleviate the suffering.

Light and dark depend on each other to maintain sacred and necessary balance. Reflecting on the Heart Sutra, I believe that the relative world is driven by the balance of two extremes. This is the balance of sacred duality. There is no relative experience without this sacred balance. The tension is meant to jolt us toward the realization of the essence of everything, which is the experience of dualities emanating from the essence. Therefore, there is no light without darkness—or, in the language of the Heart Sutra, light is dark, dark is light, light is none other than darkness, darkness is none other than light. Darkness is not meant to overwhelm the light, nor is the light meant to overwhelm the darkness. In the relative, imbalance is the root of suffering.

Once, I believed in evil and then there was a time when I didn't believe in it. Presently, I believe evil is more than just the opposite of good. I believe it is the experience of reacting to the loss of the experience of the essence. Darkness is not inherently evil. Evil arises when we lose that relationship to the essence and start reacting to the ambiguity of darkness. That reactivity creates more confusion, which leads to violence.

Those we label evil are people who have lost agency with darkness and how the darkness has agency over them. They have lost contact with sacred balance and are reacting to the fear that comes with such a loss. They have collapsed into selfishness and struggle to empathize with others.

I have always been both fond and afraid of dark things. I have always felt at home with the dark, especially learning about things we attribute to the dark, studying evil things and having a fair curiosity about the devil. I was raised with the belief that if we didn't understand something or if it wasn't overtly Christian, it was evil. "Naw baby, we don't do that" or "That sounds like the devil's work" was how I heard people responding to things far outside their experience. Anything sinful was obviously the devil's domain, which included any challenge to our fixed and rigid notions of gender and sexuality. If you weren't a God-fearing Christian cisgender man or woman, you were considered dark—even though white supremacist culture had categorized the whole African race as dark and evil, which opened the door to our oppression.

Though no one would admit this, my home community had a decent distrust of anything that didn't align with the Christianity taught to our enslaved ancestors by our captors and policers. Anything outside of how they taught us to behave and accept a theology of subservience was probably a liberatory praxis aimed at disrupting the institution of slavery, its anti-Blackness, and the white supremacy that founded all of it. Even how we learned and studied the Exodus fell short because it wasn't just about us getting free, it was also about abolishing any state, including ancient Egypt, that would attempt to curtail anyone's right to be free. Eventually, I began to feel that anything that really helped Black folks get free and disrupt white supremacy was considered evil, especially by White people.

Unfortunately, this sentiment also extended to the practices of our ancestors. Though my spiritual ancestry is quite vast and inclusive, my biological ancestry is largely Nigerian, so I know that my ancestors practiced Ifa and Vodou and supplicated the orishas. I also know that some of my enslaved ancestors practiced Hoodoo as well. I felt extremely divorced from these practices because I was taught that these beliefs were evil. And despite my natural curiosity and open mind, even after I became interested in the study of religion, I avoided all these ancestral practices, believing that they were indeed tied to the devil, which, for me, meant violence.

I believe that the practice of fearing God can lead to self-harm and harm against others. I practice loving and respecting God as the expression of the essence. I find that I don't want to deal with the things that I am afraid of, and it is even harder to attempt to love something that I am essentially terrified of. Fearing God disrupts the transmission of deep care from the essence. It creates a carceral dynamic where we are motivated to practice goodness because we are afraid of being punished or going to hell instead of embodying goodness because we have cultivated awakened care for ourselves and all beings. So, our motivation to help others is rooted in wanting everyone, including ourselves, to be liberated from the causes and conditions of suffering to experience the essence. Motivation through fear is not sustainable or spacious. Fear will have the impact of forcing contraction, and that contraction will always be a source of reactivity resulting in using violence and fear of violence to control people in the way we are inherently being controlled. Loving God is the only way to God in the same way love is the only path to liberation.

Tantra and Darkness

While the experience of light has always been about clarity and goodness, light isn't always that clear because even light can be complex in the carceral state. Consider all the times religion has been used to exert violence and reinforce the suffering of incarceration, from the Crusades to witch hunts, slavery, mass genocides, restrictions of agency over our bodies, and all the forms of discrimination in the name of God's will and the purging of what is dark and evil. Darkness has often been considered ambiguous, dangerous, and bad, but it can also offer clarity and safety. For the most part, darkness is misunderstood and aligned with what is evil; those of us who are Black have been aligned with the darkness.

One of the many practices that drew me to Tantric Buddhism is learning to speak to the darkness. In this practice, the darkness is made real for us, snatched from the hypothetical or from being labeled evil and unworkable. It is personified into all manner of demons and monsters dripping with blood and guts, wielding sharp teeth, and swinging weapons. They are fearsome representations that invite us to disrupt fear and see these images as expressions of the essence. When that starts to happen, we experience freedom.

Moreover, when I started studying the iconography of these wrathful beings, I felt galvanized, awakened, enraged, terrified, excited, and, frankly, aroused. These images are supposed to make us feel these things because they are engaging the deeply buried, heavily guarded, uncomfortable emotions and energetic states that we are often ashamed of or feel we have no agency over and are too afraid to look at. The iconography of these beings attempts to summon these energies into our awareness so we can start tending to them instead of running away from them or reacting to them. The horror we feel is a reflection of what we refuse to tend to. But we need to tend to it, to start to care for and befriend this expression of ourselves. Without this labor, we cannot be free from ourselves or our reactivity.

The six-armed Mahakala, or Chadrupa, is one of my principal deities and protectors. In Tantric traditions, as well as magic and shamanic paths, we need strong spirit protectors against the harmful energies we may attract as we work with potent energies. Our protectors form barriers around us, countering energies from other beings sent to harm us. We take vows with these beings and are initiated into the path of practice that sustains our connection with them. I was given permission by my primary teacher to take Chadrupa not only as a protector but also as one of my principal or tutelary deities.

He is represented as a big black fearsome demon, with a wide face snarling like a rabid dog. He is vicious and seems out of control. He has six arms, some of which hold weapons dripping with blood and flesh. He is often depicted dancing on corpses of different kinds of beings. He's not a being you want to fuck with, and yet still plenty of beings who want to hurt me attempt to. I love Chadrupa. I experience him as an intensely strong energy around me in the form of wrath. When I look at him, I see an expression of love. I see a being mirroring back parts of my experience that seem shameful and dangerous as he offers profound care to help me to integrate these fears into my conscious awareness so I can start offering them awakened care. When I can tend to these experiences, I can be freed from reactivity and transition into experiencing these energies and releasing them.

When the Darkness Lives Inside

I have told this story so many times in the past that I find myself believing it. The story is about how I am a survivor of severe depression. I have used this tale as my origin story, depicting how I was introduced to Buddhist practice. I have spoken about how in my early twenties, I felt as if I was losing all sense of connection to life. My joy evaporated, sleep became hard, my appetite changed, my view of the world dulled into black and white and various shades of gray. I started avoiding people. But the hardest experience was this feeling that my life was being slowly drained. It felt like I was slowly evaporating.

The story continues with me seeking out the council of mentors, who all offered helpful suggestions. Yet it was after one mentor encouraged me to explore medications that a sharp urge in me to keep exploring other modalities arose. This urge eventually found me sitting with a Christian psychic healer. This is where I have deviated in the past from the true story. I used to talk about how this healer saw the suffering I was experiencing and gave me a set of practices to work with my condition, which included mindfulness meditation and prayer. Eventually I worked through everything and embraced Buddhism and meditation as a spiritual path of liberation. This is all true.

However, let's rewind back to this initial meeting and add one detail. I called this healer to set up an appointment, got their voicemail, and left a message. About ten minutes later, they called me back, urging me to see them later that afternoon. Arriving at their place, they looked at me and explained that I had a demonic presence and that we had to begin immediately extracting it. Almost twenty years went by before I had enough courage to name what I was moving through, which was an exorcism.

Instead of one or a few sessions of attempting to cast the demon out, we worked to draw it out of me and transfer it into another object. I was instructed to do a set of practices in my session with the healer, which included prayer and meditation, as well as practices that promoted cleansing of negative energy. I would eventually learn how to sense the frequency of the presence in me as we were drawing it out. After the work was done, I entered a brand-new experience of connectedness, joy, and vitality. I had this incredible energy for the first time in my life, which I dedicated to my Buddhist practice.

What I know about demons has come from surviving demonic possession. After moving through the exorcism, I was left with an acute ability to sense evil in spaces around me and within other people. Soon after the exorcism my friend was sleeping in another room one night when I woke up to find a dark shadow hovering over me. I knew that it was a demonic presence trying to harm me. I also knew for certain that it was emanating from my sleeping friend. I realized that I wasn't afraid. I just sat up in bed and stared at it. A gentle feeling of being protected came over me, and I lay back down and fell asleep. The next morning, I confided in my friend, and they shared that they had indeed been feeling something strange in their sleep.

Mother Toni Morrison wrote that "if you surrendered to the air, you could ride it." Likewise, when we surrender to the dark, it can set you free.

I wrote a prayer that I often use in my yearly Diwali ceremonies. Diwali is one of the most important holidays in India. It is observed as a celebration of light and everything it represents. I often rely on prayer when I feel as if I am being consumed by the darkness of the world represented as delusion, hate, and apathy.

I am praying for the light today. When I say that I am praying for the light what I mean is that I am deciding to become the light. I also accept that there is darkness in the world. I understand that the darkness I see in the world is also the darkness I see in myself. There is no darkness in the world that does not also abide in some form in me. When I acknowledge the dark, I am also acknowledging that I could not know the blessing of light without first naming the darkness. Therefore, while I pray for and love the light, I will also love the darkness because whatever I choose to authentically love, I allow it to be free. I choose to let my darkness be free so it can stand next to the light. When they are standing together, they will tell the true story of my life, and in that truth telling I will accept both the light and the dark and know that the dark is only a place where the light has not learned to live. As I decide to become light, I am also praying that I develop the courage to learn to live in the dark places.

Forgiveness

Candy Ferocity is a character played by the incomparable Angelica Ross on the hit show *Pose*. *Pose* explores the ballroom culture in New York City in the late 1980s and early 1990s. Ballroom is an underground subculture where mostly Black and Latinx LGBTQIA+ folks compete in a variety of categories for prizes. In season two, Candy, a Black transgender woman, is murdered while engaging in sex work.

When the episode aired, my circle of Black and Brown trans, nonbinary, and queer friends felt mixed. We loved Candy and how the show embraced both love and joy in the epicenter of struggle. Yet with her death, some of my beloveds questioned why Black trans women and femme violence needed to be portrayed when that violence is already so prevalent for survivors and allies. The show writers and producers made the decision to shoot the episode because it reflected real life.

By now, I have watched this episode countless times. Often, I sob through the episode. The violence against the trans community and especially Black and Brown trans women mirrors the violence many of us face each day as individuals, especially those of us surviving multiple disprivileged identities. When we survive harm, we work to move from being survivors to becoming thrivers—people who are no longer defined by the violence we've survived, and who are experiencing restoration through self and collective care.

The episode in which Candy is murdered takes place primarily at a funeral home, a location that was then a place to celebrate and mourn not only those dying from violence but also from AIDS-related illness.

During the opening moment of silence at her memorial, Candy appears and sits with one of the other main characters, Pray Tell, portrayed by Billy Porter. Candy sits with Pray Tell, an emcee and leader of the ballroom scene, and asks him why he was so hostile toward her in life. But before she confronts him, she declares her forgiveness. "I forgive you," she says. "That's right, bitch! I said I forgive you." What follows is a series of moving moments of emotional labor by Candy where she processes the difficult experiences with several characters, beginning with Pray Tell, and comes to something that feels like final resolution with each character. It is this labor that rips my heart open; so many of us need this labor from others to reconcile our broken hearts. This episode opens the door to thinking about the crucial work of forgiveness necessary for the New Saint on the path of liberation for themselves and others.

Real Forgiveness

Forgiveness is one of the hardest practices to pull off. Growing up, I always struggled with the way that I was being taught to forgive. I always heard phrases like "Turn the other cheek" or "Forgive and forget." As I got older, I understood that this way of forgiving seemed unkind to me. It was as if I had to privilege the experience of offenders' feelings over mine.

We are all survivors and perpetrators of harm. This is why forgiveness work is complex; it's all too easy to identify as a survivor of harm, and very difficult to recognize the harm we engage in. In truth, we impact each other in ways that are beneficial and harmful. At this point in the exploration of forgiveness in the New Saint's tradition, I am interested in how we experience care for ourselves as survivors of harm, and how we might eventually extend that care to our offenders.

Many of us have been taught to forgive others as quickly as possible for a couple of reasons. First, we forgive because often we feel pressured to assuage the guilt or other discomfort of the offender. Second, we have been taught that to be a good person or the better person, even as a survivor, we should get to forgiving as quickly as possible. All of this points to our struggle to hold the experience of discomfort that comes with being harmed and harming others.

Two days after a mass shooting several years ago, a parent whose child was killed went on national TV and forgave the shooter. I didn't believe them. I *couldn't* believe them. Something seemed so rushed and performative about the whole thing; it felt as if this public forgiveness was happening to fulfill the prescribed modes of forgiveness that many of us were raised with. It seemed as if the parents needed us to know that they were good people and wanted to model forgiveness for the world to see. All of it felt very inauthentic.

What Is Forgiveness?

In the New Saint's tradition, I define forgiveness as the experience of wanting the person that hurt me to experience the care they need to be well. Traditionally, many of us think that forgiving means letting go of the resentment we feel toward an offender. However, I want more than to move past being harmed; I want the offender to be resourced, which means that I want them to experience care and have what they need to be well. If they had what they needed, then maybe they would have had the capacity to hold space for themselves and others, reducing their potential to enact harm.

However, forgiveness begins with learning to forgive ourselves. We often skip over ourselves after being hurt, and so forgiveness becomes a tool for bypassing our own hurt. Forgiveness should first be about the care we offer to ourselves. It involves recognizing that we have survived harm and learning what we need to feel resourced again. Only when we feel resourced will we have the capacity to extend care to the offender. If I don't take care of myself first, then my attempts at forgiving the offender will be at best performative and at worst saturated with resentment and hate, which may turn the attempted forgiveness into revenge or wanting the offender to hurt as much as they hurt you.

Wanting the offender to experience care does not mean they should not be held accountable—they should. However, I believe that offenders are not held accountable by others but must choose accountability for themselves after recognizing the harm they have caused. Even when they are called in by survivors of harm to bring awareness to the experience of that harm, they deserve to be resourced because we are often at our most violent when we are underresourced. Accountability and being called in with care is a resource for offenders because it can disrupt the harm they cause to themselves and others around them. Caring accountability can be a channel of care for survivors as well because the harm they experienced is being held in caring awareness by offenders.

Sometimes, as survivors of harm, we blame ourselves for surviving. We convince ourselves that somehow we deserved what happened and that there was nothing we could do about it. So much of this thinking comes from the ways in which offender-driven forgiveness culture attempts to blame others for getting hurt. It sets up the notion that offenders are less to blame for their actions because the unskillfulness of survivors forced them to react in ways that created harm.

Ultimately, although we are open to support from others, we must do the actual labor of healing ourselves. After surviving harm, I wish that the offender's apology could take all the hurt away. And even more, I wish that my apologies as an offender could completely take the hurt of others away. Although authentic apologies do alleviate some of the hurt we feel, we still must tend to our own wounds.

Oppression and Forgiveness

As a member of multiple disprivileged communities, I am sensitive to how those communities are expected to do the extra emotional labor of forgiving privileged offender communities. I often reflect on my experience of some of the teachings of the Black church that emphasize forgiving White folks, parroting the last words of

Jesus when he asked God to forgive the people because they had no idea what they were really doing. That belief was fed to our ancestors by their overseers as a way to train them to continually bypass their hurt and need for care and to instead care for their White oppressors. This indoctrination is folded up within the psyche of those of us who descend from enslaved people. Again, this mode of forgiving is weaponized to care for offenders, while keeping survivors underresourced.

Of course, disprivileged communities have had to develop a sensitivity to the needs of dominant groups to survive. Maybe we didn't really forgive dominant offender groups, but we had to pretend to in order to make the dominant groups reduce violence against us.

I often feel unsafe reflecting to those in offender-dominant communities the harm I have experienced. When they feel uncomfortable, they sometimes react to it by expressing violence against me in ways that they may be unconscious of because of how being comfortable is normalized as part of their identity. Because they experience discomfort as a fundamental challenge to who they are, I run the risk of disrupting their identity. And if they consider themselves basically good people (as most people do), I am seen as the bad agent that needs to be annihilated. Blackness through the lens of white supremacy is positioned as antigood.

One of the most caring things that I can do for myself and for others who occupy positions of dominance is to center caring for myself over caring for them. I likewise appreciate it when I hurt people, and they do not immediately forgive me because I need the space to reflect on the harm I have caused, hold the discomfort that arises to generate genuine regret for the harm, and offer an authentic apology.

As survivors, we often feel the need to do emotional labor for ourselves and also for offenders. Even when an offender is held accountable, we may wind up doing the emotional labor of holding them as we try to hold ourselves. This is why community is important to support both survivors and offenders. Communities can keep survivors from taking on more labor than is appropriate and can support offenders as they do the emotional labor of recognizing the harm they have caused.

THE STAGES OF RESTORATIVE FORGIVENESS

Restorative forgiveness helps to ensure we are tending to our own hurt and to understand that when this hurt is not being tended to, it can turn into anger, which may disrupt our attempts at care and harm ourselves or others.

Forgiving others is an expression of caretaking for both us and the offender. Restorative forgiveness does not mean that the hurt or anger goes away. It *does* mean that we are able to hold space for both without reacting to them. Holding this space allows us to experience care for ourselves and the offender.

Restorative forgiveness takes time and practice. We need time to restore what has been impacted. The healing that restorative forgiveness yields is lasting and sustainable. As we work through the stages of restorative forgiveness, we are developing and practicing strategies of healing, which are at the same time practices of liberation.

First: Take Your Space

After you have been hurt, you need to take space to assess the hurt. Sometimes this can't happen immediately, but we can, at the very least, notice how we are responding to the hurt. At this point, you should engage with the offender only if you feel safe enough to do so, or if you have enough space to respond in a way that doesn't compound the hurt already present.

Taking space is the first step in caring for ourselves. Then we can begin the work of connecting to our hurt.

Second: Empathize with and Metabolize Your Hurt

Once you begin holding space for yourself, notice your hurt and allow the hurt to be there. At this stage, you are not thinking about who hurt you or how to get back at them. You are just present with your hurt, breathing with it and expanding around it. This is the labor of metabolizing our hurt. This is the heart of our embodiment work as we practice restorative forgiveness.

Sometimes, the hurt is too much to bear, especially if it produces a trauma sensation as opposed to a hurt feeling. You can briefly touch this experience and then back off it, as if you were trying to climb into cold water. You may dip a toe in and then a calf, slowly getting used to the temperature. But sometimes the temperature is too extreme, and you give up on getting into the water altogether.

Rest is an important practice here. Sometimes, I need an anchor to rest my attention on before returning to the labor of noticing and holding difficult material. Below are a few of the preferred anchors I use as I metabolize hurt.

- Rest your attention on the feeling of the ground under your feet or under your body.
- Rest your attention on the palms of your hands.
- Rest your attention on your fingers gently tapping somewhere on your body. I like tapping my knees.
- Rest your attention on the sensation of massaging your feet. Connecting your hands and feet can be grounding.

- Rest your attention on the feeling of holding something. I like to use precious and sacred stones.
- Rest your attention on a scent. I do this with subtle scents like palo santo.
- Rest your attention on a sound. I often use opera vocalists like Jessye Norman or Sweet Honey in the Rock.
- Rest your attention on the experience of walking meditation.

As we touch difficult hurt, we can use these anchors to help us slowly submerge ourselves in the hurt, offering it space through nonreactivity.

Third: Set Boundaries

Boundaries are a natural extension of care for you and the offender. Setting boundaries means that we take into consideration what we need to experience safety. Boundaries communicate to the offender that there is something they need to look deeply at, that these boundaries didn't just appear for no reason. Boundaries should also give you space to begin and continue to practice care and to help you potentially forgive the offender. The work of forgiving the offender may take years; you may never fully complete it. In those cases, all you can do is put the boundary up and practice care for yourself.

Boundary setting should come from a place of care and should not be used as a means of hurting the offender. Boundaries provide the space for us to practice caring for ourselves and reducing further harm against ourselves and our offenders.

Fourth: Take Care of Yourself

As you touch more into your hurt, you start to get a
sense of how to best take care of yourself. Taking
care of yourself means making decisions and doing
things that help you to hold space for the hurt. What
will help support you? For me, when I am taking care
of my hurt, meditation and awakened care practice are
both important. The resting practices above are also
important. Do something that is a source of joy for you.
The care we are engaging with is a source of energy that
supports our holding of the hurt not a distraction away
from it.

Fifth: Express Awakened Care for Yourself
(Forgive Yourself)

At this stage, you can generate awakened care for
yourself. Begin by opening to the streams of love,
compassion, and joy, and allow these streams to flow
down into your heart center. From the heart center,
awakened care flows throughout the body. Imagine
floating on top of this ocean of care. Allow this ocean to
hold the hurt you are experiencing. This is an expression
of care for yourself.

To move deeper into the practice, imagine that awakened
care is saturating the hurt itself. When the hurt is tended
to by awakened care, you may experience balance,
felt as euphoria or contentment, regardless of what is
happening around you.

At this point, it is beneficial to offer yourself some
healing confirmations. I like to tell myself, *It's OK. I am
feeling safe, grounded, and cared for. I am not the only
one who is experiencing hurt right now.* I continue by

wishing, *May I continue receiving the care I need right now and forever.* This is the dawning of self-forgiveness: we develop the wish for ourselves to experience care. The hurt is still there, but we are holding the space for it and have allowed it to receive care.

If you are feeling resourced enough, make a wish by saying to yourself, *May I receive this care and healing on behalf of all beings that are not able to practice with their hurt right now.* And a final, even more powerful aspiration, *May I take on the hurt of all beings right now and liberate it into the ocean of awakened care.*

As this stage of the practice ends, keep resting in the energy of awakened care and offer whatever doubts or judgments arise out into the ocean.

Sixth: Empathize with the Offender

At this stage, you are resourced enough to start considering the experience of the offender. I advise that you not start this empathizing labor until you are very grounded and are experiencing awakened care and forgiveness for yourself. This self-love is the primary resource that supports us as we turn our attention to the offender.

You can wonder about some of the conditions in their life that have informed this experience of hurt. If the hurt was unintentional, you could ask yourself if the person had insight into what they were doing in the moment. Would they have stopped the harm from happening if they could? Regardless of this, you can still understand that the person struggles just like you to be OK and to do their best to limit the harm they do with the resources they have. In this stage, allow the offender to be complex and multidimensional.

Seventh: Develop Care for the Offender

When you start developing empathy for the offender, you are extending your experience of awakened care to the offender. You start wishing for them to be resourced, safe, happy, and cared for.

Allow this wish to extend from your ocean of care. You don't have to be afraid of care running out. We extend this wish that the offender be free from suffering because no one deserves to suffer. The less discomfort someone is in, the less violent they may be. This care also helps you to understand that the offender may need support in empathizing with themselves and in disrupting the violence they are doing to themselves and others. The motivation to support others in cutting through their discomfort is what informs how you think the offender should be held accountable for their actions.

Letting Go of the Lover
I Used to Be

Trauma is not easy to write about, think about, or read about. It is not a linear progression, and though it may have a starting point, it never follows a trajectory that makes sense. Trauma is the heartbeat of the carceral state, and to transcend the carceral state, we have to start getting clear about what's happening and then make different choices that lead to liberation not deeper suffering.

For me, sexual trauma and the trauma experienced from trying to love without that feeling being reciprocated have been the hardest forms of suffering to heal. I suspect that this may be the case for most people who read this. So I invite you into my healing process, returning back into sites and moments of trauma to name what has happened, forgive, and open to the space that is trying to care for me. This labor of healing is supposed to be messy. I have never known authentic healing to be pretty and organized.

I start with two men who have been supporting me in my efforts to get free from this trauma. Join me as I close my eyes and return to that night I met them in Corona, Queens, New York City, November 2006, a year before my three years of solitude in retreat. I was twenty-seven years a man. A friend took me to a gay Latino bar whose name I forget. I wanted to drink but didn't have much money. I noticed two men dancing slowly together to a song in Spanish. I found myself transfixed, gazing at them pressed together, hugging, caressing, needing to become one.

I remember standing in the corner in my reddish plaid Hilfiger shirt. I was crying but do not remember tears. In the moment of watching this couple, I knew that they were living something I had never lived because somewhere early in my life I had learned to distrust the care of other bodies as well as the intimacy of what this kind of closeness I was now witnessing could offer. I am trapped in memories I can't transcend because somewhere I learned that I do not have a right to experience freedom through pleasure.

As I stood in the corner experiencing these thoughts and feelings, I imagined what these two men might say to me if we actually met, and they knew what was going through my mind as I watched them:

"This is already sounding very intense, my friend," says one of the men, looking over at me as I stare back at them. The music has stopped, and they are no longer dancing. The bar is empty.

I smile anxiously. "Well, I guess," I admit, "But trauma is intense."

"Perhaps," the other partner adds. We three are sitting at the bar now. They are holding hands, eyes gazing lovingly into mine. I think to myself that this could be the start of a fun threesome.

"Corazón, we are not here for that right now," one of them points out. "Maybe later!" He winks, and we grin mischievously at each other, the way queer men do when we know a joke masks real desire.

"Corazón, what do you need to say? What can we hold for you? What is your heart full of right now?" one of the partners asks.

"Maybe this," I reply. "The thing that I have always wanted and needed is to be touched by another man, to allow another man to touch me. I am queer like you, so our craving of other men has been a central theme for us. I have touched many men before, and I cannot assume that you have, too. But I think you have touched enough.

"There were times when I wasn't so alone, when the prospect of a long night seemed exciting because there was someone with me, wading into stretches of silence, sharing space, listening to my stories, holding me. These memories of past love sprout fields of lush, green vegetation and trees of ripe, sweet fruit that gush in my mouth when I bite into them.

"But where to go with this? Probably back to my little boy years, before I knew the sophisticated language of sexuality and the erotic. What was it for me? Probably the warmth that would flood my body

around other boys. The warmth that filled every crevice of my body, feeding on itself while giving birth to itself."

The First Touch: Church Camp

I remember the first time another boy touched me, that day at church summer camp when he slipped his little brown fingers down my thigh, glanced at me, and smiled as we sang about Jesus. Jesus! Maybe this was why all the mothers were jumping up and shouting—maybe Jesus was slipping his hand down their thighs!

When he touched the inside of my inner thigh, my whole body rocked shut. As if in response to an unwanted visitor knocking at the front door, my body demanded, *What are you doing here? I don't need what you're trying to offer.* I had never thought about sex and craving until that touch. No one ever talked about sex or sexuality, so I had no idea what I was feeling. Since my body was trembling, I thought I was terrified.

When he gazed into me, something warned *dangerous*. At the same time, I knew that there was something about him that I craved. His touch was full of something both exciting and threatening. Why did I see him as a threat? Why did I react to his touch as if it were poison? Why was his touch so confusing?

But I remember his fingers—short and rough but strong. His hands knew me, wanted me. Or maybe he saw me as a victim. Why was I so afraid?

"Then what happened, corazón?" one of the partners interrupts.

"He just stopped," I respond. "Looking back, I wish I could have experienced more with him, but I was too overwhelmed. And I forgot the whole incident for years."

Touch has always been dangerous for me. I think that it has been dangerous for many queer folks, especially little queer boys, because it was never safe for us to express our longing for touch with other boys. Like older men, we learned to create elaborate rituals—sports and rough play—to mask our erotic longing for each other.

To be touched not just on the surface of things but to caress the soft, tender places that pulsated beneath our skins that no one ever tended to: that peculiar interaction of maleness and queerness collided for me and resulted in a feeling of being suffocated for most of my adolescence. I wanted to experience intimacy with other boys but knew that any effort to do so would be met with severe punishment from my community.

The Second Touch: A Rainy Night

Though young men, we were still little boys when I met you. I didn't know who you were at first. A friend found me to explain that you were trying to flirt with me. I was the first boy who ever touched you and, in many ways, you were the first boy I ever let touch me. You were everything I thought I needed, and the world was finally exciting because I had someone for me in it. But the world becomes different when you kiss another boy for the first time. People see and attempt to annihilate you. You were new to this violence. Before I knew it, you had freaked out and shrunk into yourself like a turtle retreating into its shell.

The last time I reached for you, it was raining, and I was going away and asked if you would miss me. After a long pause you said, "No." That was it.

The next day, I flew to Northern California and sat in front of the Buddha and cried well into the night.

Memories of us sustained me through the years of loneliness during my long retreat. I still needed you, but I struggled to get rid of you because remembering you felt like hell. And I still love you, even if I am forgetting how to say your name.

"I have never forgotten you two," I say now to the partners in my mind. "Ever since that night you gave me a vision that I have never fully embodied."

"And it feels like you have never left that bar or that night," one of the partners reveals.

"I guess not. There have been so few experiences that seemed as real as that moment."

"Because you felt our intimacy?"

"Yes."

"Because we let you in. We offered you some of the good stuff between us."

"And then you became my teachers and my sustainers."

"And we moved into your head rent free!"

"Yes, you did!" I respond, laughing.

"But maybe it's time for us to move on."

"Maybe."

"Keep going. We are still giving you the good stuff."

I'm always looking for intimacy, which I experience as connection. A knowingness. Feeling safe enough to relax my boundaries and let someone cross my personal territory into my most tender and sweet place. I am naked and vulnerable and when I invite someone in, I am trusting them to hold me. I know that anxiety always arises to possibly shut me down because this person can kill me with a simple flinch or recoil. And when they arrive offering this care, I have what I need to offer them the same tending of their tender and sweet place.

This is the moment when we awaken within each other and remember that we have always been naked, and we see each other's nudity, and we offer each other grace. That offering of grace is the experience of returning home to God.

The Third Touch: Trash

I tried running away from the shame of intimacy and found you one night at the bar. I was still a young man but preparing to enter the holy life, and you were beautiful. Your beauty was marked by a shyness and an inquisitiveness that drew me to you.

It felt like I had won something. I was the fat Black boy whom all the White boys sidestepped, and then there was you, Black like me, desired, stepping to me. I knew you were a transgender man and although I hadn't had much experience dating trans men at the time, my lack of experience didn't seem to hinder my desire for you.

However, I had not learned how to be as free as you were then, as much as I hope I am now. When we found ourselves alone that first night, I froze. I was swallowed by my unwillingness to hold what my attraction to you meant.

I couldn't tell you how your honesty and beauty threw my transphobia back in my face and forced me to glimpse all the ways I was performing who I thought I was. I couldn't negotiate the shame I felt for not having the capacity to understand who you were outside of what I needed you to be to firm up my identity as a cisgender man attracted to other men. What I saw in that moment was that I didn't see you as a man but as an experience for me to have, which was an act of violence toward you. I couldn't take this. You felt too dangerous. So I did what I had been taught to do: walk away and forget about you.

Like many men before me and many men after me, I was a terrorist. A terrorist who couldn't tend to their own insecurity and chose to annihilate you. I was trash.

I have changed and I apologize.

"There has been a lot of shutting down, walking away, and forgetting," one of the partners points out.

"Yeah. No one ever taught me how to deal with trauma and all these reactions seemed like the best I could do."

"If you could go back, what would you do differently?"

"I don't feel like going back."

But there is this: There is all the fear that must be negotiated. I fear my intimacy being flooded by the hurt. I fear the old kinds of policing I do with others. I fear how we police ourselves because despite our queerness, we are still not who we need to be.

I fear how my queerness masks misogyny, ableism, transphobia, and fatphobia. I fear how intimacy is performed in the gaze of whiteness. I fear how I struggle to name that the trauma is always my invisible lover. I fear that I am not able to touch other men without hurting them.

Sometimes I don't know how to tend to the aching that arises between me and a lover or the loneliness that sits curtly around the corner. Sometimes I fuck all this up and start shrinking into myself as the numbness blooms, and I become a thing using others to cum as quickly as possible so I can move on to somewhere that doesn't remind me of how much this hurts.

The Fourth Touch: Bad Hip Hop

I am not sure why I loved you like I did or why my body leaned toward yours or gave way like tall grass being parted by a smooth breeze. The way your mouth and nostrils opened to breathe me in or how your eyes widened when you smiled, weighed down on the edges by decades of the streets using you to survive. How you were so particular about the music we listened to together, how you couldn't stand that hip-hop shit, and how you cringed when any of that mess came up on the playlist. Rap was the only prophecy that fed you. Hip hop was too . . . gay.

"Man, what's this we listening to!" you said, as you shot up a raised eyebrow of condemnation.

You reminded me of my mother in the way you would cast a challenging smirk back at anyone or anything that didn't align with your understanding of the world. And because you are not my mother, I let myself wonder, *Who the hell is this nigga rolling up in my house talking shit!*

You were one way when I met you on the streets and became another when my bedroom held us tight against the hostility of the world. You became more yourself: soft, delicate, kind, a little more full of light. And you would smile at me. I felt like I had won the lottery. I wasn't hooked on you, but somehow you were hooked inside of me.

And though it was like it was, I knew you were never mine, and I would never be yours. We were just having moments together that always turned into suffering when the moment passed. And after each moment, I lost you and had no idea where you had gone.

"Like you two were just a moment that stuck to me," I explain to the partners, *"and it became easier to wade through your pleasant moment instead of finding moments that could grow into experiences of truly belonging to someone who also belonged to me."*

"That belonging is the intimacy," both seemed to exhale together.

Even after all these years, there is no other way to say this: I love you, but I don't trust you. I don't know how to say that when I look into your eyes. All I see are all my own unmet needs for belonging looking back at me. I know it was never more than just a moment, or a cuddle and orgasm, and yet I still want to run away from this. I get it now. I need more than what I taught myself to settle for.

It takes so much loving and truth telling to escape Giovanni's room, passing through the walls that protect the safety of pleasure and fantasy against the passionless imaginary of the world. I want my fuchsia-and-gold-colored intimacy with a lover to survive the brutality of a predictable black and white arrangement of love. I was told that I could only survive somewhere over the rainbow. But what if somewhere over the rainbow is really right here, right now?

The Fifth Touch: Heartbreak and Confusion

We were lying in bed one afternoon when you began talking about a party you worked where a group of men crossed your boundaries. As you spoke, your voice trailed off and gave way to a plot of silence with a wide stream of unspoken pain flowing through it. You shivered in my arms, and I felt you leave your body and float down that river back into the helpless night where you would once again fight to escape. I met that stream with my own brokenheartedness because I loved you and would never hurt you. I held you closely and in that holding I stepped into that stream, feeling what seemed like lifetimes of being reduced to a body and site of other men's pleasure.

Later, you called me and in the first breath said you loved me, but you took it back in the second breath. I said it was OK, that we all have a right to change our minds. I was able to let you go not because I was suffering or because you had hurt me but because I understood that I had touched you and didn't hurt you and that without each other we would still survive.

Intimacy is not the cliché closeness or friendliness that we seem to perform in our daily lives, passing through the world, through bodies and spaces believing that we are close to others, that we practice a sacred transparency that is true loving or truthfulness. What I mean to say about intimacy is that two bodies know each other and that knowing often renders them speechless. It is difficult to articulate the feeling of being inside another person because it will be like being inside of you, and you will say that I know you; your joy bubbles through my experience just as the sorrow wades through as well.

The Sixth Touch: Violence

I never knew how this worked until it worked on me.

I have tried to forget this because I didn't want to deal with surviving another act of violence. I never wanted to hate you; I did for a while, but then the hate gave way to a quiet sadness that dissipated into an intentional forgetfulness.

I don't want to call myself a survivor because each time I replay that afternoon I find fault with myself.

Yes, I invited you over with the understanding that we would be having sex. Yes, I led you to my bedroom. Yes, I wanted you. Yes, my body uncurled toward yours as yours uncurled toward mine.

And I told you what I didn't want.

You decided that you would give it to me anyway.

And then my body stopped uncurling and started saying no.

No, I don't fuck without a condom.

No, I can't just slide it in.

No, I don't want you to get closer.

No, I'm not into this anymore.

And it was the pressure that felt like all the stories I had ever been told, and the pushing, the breaking of boundaries, how no is only understood as yes.

You wanted what you wanted. I led you on, and it was my fault. I shouldn't have been afraid of you; I was bigger than you. But why does any of this matter?

And you were Brown like me, a queer man like me. Into the same ideas and freedom that I was. You talked a good game. You were a good guy. And I realized how easy it was for this to happen to anyone. Maybe this even happened to you once.

And yes, it could've been worse.

And at the end of the day, what did I survive?

You finally jerked yourself off and left.

I have no idea what to do with the sadness right now. I was told Black boys had no right to the aching. Even now I wonder why. Maybe because we believe we cannot survive the mountain of aching that is ours to experience, tend to, and release.

The Last Touch: Haunting and Healing

I am haunted by how we are born into this world beautiful ones and how that beauty gets broken up into little pieces. And then, broken up, we go about trying to collect the little pieces of our beauty while calling the gathering a life. It is the labor of re-membering not *being* that occupies our living.

I close my eyes and our ancestors appear, the Black men and boys, dark skin and light, who survived moments and ages of never being enough. We harbor these legacies in our blood, on our backs, in our hearts, between our legs. And the trauma I speak to is the trauma of never living who we are, which is only to say how we have never transcended the limitations of gender and self-constructions that have meant liberation. At some point we must name that our bodies have been playgrounds for so many others.

Once I dreamed that we were trying to get free, gathered into a large circle, crying and wailing, our bodies heaving and shaking, releasing the sorrow and traumas, the rage, and making room to ignite in joy. And we were holding each other, wiping one another's tears. We were falling into each other in a way we couldn't in this timeline because of how we have been taught to hate our bodies and thus hate anyone who reflected us. And a voice kept saying, *It can be this simple. It can be this simple.* Why isn't it this simple?

Sometimes, it is too much to hold. I am crying as I write this. Soon, I will be balled up on the floor, weeping for all these beautiful ones. I will let myself cry, a labor I now understand I have little consent in. Often, I have had to choose the labor I am forced to do, or the labor chooses me and thus consumes me. To choose the work I have no choice in doing means that I can disrupt some of the violence that comes from resisting the work I know I must do. This is the story of our ancestors, and it becomes the story of me and my body and mind. But I write all of this only to say that I consent to this labor because I have chosen it. I chose it not just for you but for me as well because somehow there is freedom for us here if I can hold on long enough to survive the grief. Maybe I believe that I can meet you in our collective grief and pull you out.

We disrupt narratives of trauma and policing when we make different choices and finally, I am making my choice to be free.

"You have been quiet," I say to the pair in my head.

"We are just here witnessing, listening, remembering all that we have survived. But you don't need us anymore, corazón. You don't need to stay here."

"Yeah, I think that I can move on."

"What do you finally need to say?"

"Just this: I want more than the quick, easy pleasure of sweat and bodies, heaving heavy things tumbling against each other. I want more than the shadows and the back alleys and the shade and the bitter reads and the tired stunts. We have to be more than histories of disease and trajectories of interpersonal violence. We have to be more than maps of trauma leading only to rounds of rebirth in sorrow. I need to be more than a body or playground for those *who take the good stuff and run. I want to know your name, and I want you to tell me my name. I want us to walk away from each other having known each other and having done what we could to disrupt the policing that keeps us from touching each other. I want our ancestors to consent to our loving. And if our ancestors cannot consent to this loving, then I need for us to have the courage to uninvite them."*

It's not just about me and this life or this moment; it's about everything. We have a responsibility to remember we are in debt to the beautiful ones who have made our living possible and full of potential. This recognition is how I choose to continue. My heart is full of sorrow and at the same time my heart is a vast ocean of care that can tend to the sorrow. If you don't get this, you will never understand why I do the things that I do.

I don't know if this will change anything. I don't know if I am different after writing this. Nor do I have any idea if I have risked enough. I can't even be certain if I am really telling the truth. But I am certain that I love you—all of you I have mentioned here—and because I love you, I want you to be both free and happy.

Karmapa, Think of Me

It seems as if I have stopped and started this reflection a million times for a million different reasons. Sometimes I feel I am yet again overreacting to something and making it a much bigger deal than it is. Other times, I feel ashamed because I feel like I'm missing something profound that at this point in my practice, I should be connecting to instead of ranting about. None of this is helped by the overt judgment of colleagues and communities, which I internalize as self-criticism, bolstering a narrative of how I am a bad practitioner or, even worse, creating division in the community, making it more difficult for people to practice and trust the teachings.

Once, while traveling with my lama in India, I started getting curious about the preparation of chai from a chaiwallah, or tea vendor, wandering over to his cart checking out his workspace. I remember my teacher yelling over to me to leave him alone and stop making trouble. I wasn't trying to make trouble; I was only curious. I have reflected on that experience often and the ways that he and others in my monastery steered me away from uncovering the sexual abuse happening in our community. It is true. I am a troublemaker. In the language of my ancestors, I trouble the water, and I do this troubling because I want people to be free and happy. How can we get free if we don't reveal where liberation needs to happen? Troubling to get people free is an expression of love.

I am offering the troubling of this reflection to you, my Karmapa, known as the 17th Gyalwang Karmapa, Ogyen Trinley Dorje, the one who first taught me how to love and trust. So much has happened. More and more, the harm that teachers are directing toward students is being exposed in the lineage. Though you are the leader of our school and lineage, you, along with many of my male teachers from lamas to shamans, have been accused of harming students through sexual misconduct, and these abuses have been documented and covered by media outlets. I have also sat with many survivors of abuse from within our lineage, and I hold their stories as well as their pain with me as I continue this writing.

I have finally decided to write this to you, my Karmapa, and all the teachers I love. Though our path of liberation is profound, it is also messy because we have legitimized violence and called it skillful means. Though we can argue that in the absolute, everything is perfect, I also must state that anything considered solely as an expression of the absolute without the counterbalance of the relative will often become an expression of violence. The absolute view is so easy to fall into as a gorgeous performance with no real intelligence or earned realization. There is no labor here. The real labor is touching the ground of the relative and gently pulling the heaven-like absolute view down to kiss the earth. That kissing gives birth to a truer skillfulness—one that does not privilege one extreme over another but binds both together.

I am also writing this because I need to hear my voice making sense of a uniquely complex relationship that we develop in this tradition. I need to think through what I have consented to and struggle with each day. And I admit that my attempts in the past to speak of my relationship with teachers have maybe been lacking because I did not have the insight or the audacity to make sense of this relationship for those outside of the tradition.

When I first met you, I offered you a poem I wrote called "Karmapa, Think of Me"—it was the best of what I had to give then. I offer it to you again, along with a narrative of how my heart and mind have changed through all these years of being in love with you.

> In the tender adolescence of morning, I rise
> bruised beneath jagged debris of the loneliest empire.
>   Soon

my head is to the floor to chant your name in offering.
I pray your perfect blessing rains blissful shades

of pastel harmony. When the ripening sun
  marks the morning's puberty,
I will bloom in the spring of your seduction. Till then,

Karmapa, think of me.

When I first saw you, time and breath danced away from me. You pulled me into emptiness, and I floated there, needing nothing else but to offer you what little devotion I knew to give. And then I felt you, and it was like experiencing the embodiment of tranquility. You were the sweet stillness awakened in the heart of the world's chaos. At that moment, I remembered that I had always loved you, well before this lifetime, and will continue loving you long after this life fades. It is a cosmic love that in this moment is still pulsating within the complexity of the phenomenal world.

This was the time when there was nothing but you.

The samsaric daydream of this flesh rules from
a throne of broken hearts. Its aching is an arrow
  that pierces

memories of your cool honey
  radiance. Beyond fantasies
of immortality, these youthful bones will decay

into a mala of worn beads, you will count the springs
I have offered to you. Before this illusion ends,

Karmapa, think of me.

In the first dream you were sitting on a high throne draped in bright-colored fabrics, chanting from long rectangular sheets of prayers written in Tibetan script. Around you sat a sea of practitioners with heads buried in copies of the prayers, struggling to keep up. From your throne I noticed you staring out across this sea of struggling chanters, becoming noticeably frustrated. And then you looked at me, suddenly demanding, "Follow me, not that piece of paper!" In that moment I felt as if you were reaching out your hand and asking me to take it as you encouraged me to understand that devotion wasn't about chanting a practice perfectly but more about whether I could trust you to show me how to be with you in the moment.

That dream gave me permission to trust my love for you. This deepening of love wasn't about fixation, but it was an experience of something intensely erotic. You are physically beautiful, and I began to learn that my physical attraction to you and other teachers was a hook for me because it forced me to pay attention. It is a function of the politic of beauty that we are drawn to those we find attractive. That attraction also means that I unconsciously surrender my personal agency to you. I knew what was happening, and I am no longer ashamed to admit that I gladly submitted to my fair share of sexual fantasies about you. My fantasies became a skillful and controlled means of helping me to work with the naturally arising erotic energy that was a part of this deepening devotion: a sweet intimacy and tenderness with another man.

And despite my fantasies and attractions, I was very clear about my boundaries—not just with you, but with all my teachers. I surrendered to this because I wanted a teacher to show me how to deepen my capacity for compassion and wisdom leading to absolute liberation. I wasn't looking for a lover, a best friend, a dad, or anything like that. I already had those relationships. My relationship with a teacher is about the business of liberation. It is about a sacred commitment where the teacher pledges to help get the student free while the student pledges to follow the instruction of the teacher and to do the labor of liberation. Yet it's more than us doing the work we have been instructed to do. It is also about offering back to the teacher what is appropriate to sustain their care so they may continue helping others get free.

It was the act of stepping into a deeply felt experience of my heart opening for the first time for someone I believed could never break it.

> Believing I have nothing left to give, my
> > prayers for rain leave my
> mouth a desert, my skin piles of dust.

> These tears, having cried their own rivers,
> > persuade my eyes to confess
> thirst in a language older than speech itself. I pray you

> once more dip your finger beneath my
> > shadowed skin of sorrow and sow
> a new prophecy of spring rain. Please, in this time
> > of drought,

> Karmapa, think of me.

When I first started training in devotion, it felt dangerous to trust someone so much with my mental, emotional, and spiritual well-being. I came into all of this with a good amount of distrust for authority, influenced by my early allegiance to anarchism, which has always been grounded in the questioning of power and authority. Anarchism and devotion can seem like mixing oil and water together, but now I understand that my practice of anarchism is about dreaming and working toward a liberated future. Liberation is not possible without first trusting others to help me get free and trusting that I am able to be freed. That's what my devotion for you began to feel like.

When I began the traditional practices to open my heart and mind to you, I closed shut. My senses and perception clouded.

Not only was I clouded and shutdown, but I also felt like a vast desert—dusty, hot, and barren. At the time, I had no idea what was happening. I prayed to Saint John of the Cross, asking him to deliver me from what felt like a dark night of my soul. Yet I continued with the mantras and visualizations. I continued seeing you as the Buddha himself, while my awareness wandered like a ghost through the contracted barrenness of my mind and body.

I didn't know what transmission meant back then outside of what I had read in the commentaries by great masters centuries dead. Even those reflections felt either lacking or too dramatic. Yet what I did know was that the practice felt like hell. And I slowly noticed that the more I reached for you, the more I seemed to be reaching for myself. When I imagined gazing into your eyes to experience your nature, I kept getting glances of my nature. It wasn't just you reflecting my shit back to me; it was you reflecting my good sweet stuff back to me. I saw this clearly, and it was overwhelming because no one had ever shown me who I really was. No matter what shit I gave, you only returned my inherent sweetness back to me. That was the moment when I understood what love was. You were nothing but a mirror reflecting to me what was good about me.

Over time I learned to trust this reflection more and more. I began to feel that this devotion was only the labor of learning to trust myself. It's trusting that I am enough and have enough to get free. It's realizing that I will never trust you until I can trust myself. Maybe devotion isn't about my love for you. Maybe it is actually not about you at all. Maybe it is about how deeply I can trust myself in order to love myself.

You taught me that practicing real devotion is also consenting wholeheartedly to freedom. In loving you and myself so intensely, I experienced true spaciousness, and I was learning to let go and let that space hold me. As I let go, glimpses of my true nature, or essence, began to emerge, and I was learning to trust it and to take refuge in it.

In the evening, when the melody of
     sun cools itself deep within
the symphony of shadow's breast, I find myself
     a fatherless child

bathed in hues of glistening starlight.
     How can there be anyone
to remember my name or to remind these homeless

thoughts of their pilgrimage back to the
     cradle of your compassion? Above
my head you sing a sweet lullaby called spring.

Karmapa, think of me.

Although I have spent years trying to understand you and experience your clarity through the love you have transmitted, I still do not know you or what it's like to *be* you. At this moment, I am not a refugee. My homeland has not been invaded, and my community and culture have not been disrupted. I haven't had to escape from my home and students to get free from another nation's occupation. I don't know what it's like to miss home and not be able to return. I don't know what it's like to experience anxiety about the future of my religion and culture. I have not had to contemplate what it means to authorize people of other cultures and races into the sacredness of my religion and history.

Nor do I know what it is like to be abducted from your life and told you are a realized master who was consciously reincarnated to set us all free. What was it like being born with a clearly defined agenda for your life? As an adolescent, what was it like to be called savior? I can't fathom what having this responsibility as a child must have been and what it caused you to miss, bypass, or speed through. And being a child, what was taken away from you even though you were who you were? What was it that can never be replaced? What did you survive that may never be able to be named?

I used to call you Yeshin Norbu, a Tibetan name that means "wish fulfilling jewel" because I believed that you had no other agency or needs outside of getting me free. Did people really love you, or did they just see you as a fulfillment of their own unmet needs? Maybe I was doing to you what had been done to me—denying you personhood, making you something other than human.

In some ways, I understand what it is like for pieces of boyhood to be snatched away. When I was a little boy, the world saw me as dangerous, lacking innocence or anything gentle. White supremacist culture renders little Black boys, and all Black children, mature, because to offer us the innocence of childhood makes us too much of a mirror, reflecting the reality of white supremacist violence back to White folks and their institutions.

I wasn't called a savior. I was viewed as a threat by the culture and called slow, dumb, fat, and often detached most of my life. I wonder what it would have been like for me and all other Black children if we were called saviors, or if our births were celebrated as the coming of hope and vision into the world. But maybe I didn't need any of that.

Moreover, I do know what it is like to be perpetually under surveillance as a form of control by a culture with a particular agenda: yours to make sure you become the savior, mine to ensure erasure. You were intended to roar, and I was intended to shut the hell up. Yet even in your roaring, you are silent. You may proclaim the truth of dharma but struggle to name your needs and wants as a human being.

No matter how awakened we are, we still need and want things because we are human and are still susceptible to the mechanisms of humanity. We still have preferences. We will miss our families and teachers. We will long for our homelands. We will still have people we belong to, cultures we wear like outfits. This is the consequence of staying close to ego. I suppose that longing, not the physical body, is what makes us—and even the awakened ones—human. Yet in the longing lies the risk.

However, I do understand the obligations we have as incarnate embodied beings moving through the relative world. Though our view may be high and pure and cast deep into the effervescent heart of the absolute, we are still here on the earth in the swirling confusion of the carceral state, and we are mandated to focus our view into this world to understand that our realization demands the labor of reducing violence here and now. I do know that neither of us is a victim. Though holding this complexity is challenging, we always knew what we were getting into. We chose to walk this earth as a vow to free all beings.

In these hands slumber another lifetime of loving
and needing to be loved. Another lifetime of
    hurricanes and fire,

floods, scars from battles I do not want to
    fight. Another lifetime of being full
while fasting, of begging while having too much,
    of interpreting life

but acting death. Since there is no life
    without craving nor spring
without winter's prelude,

Karmapa, think of me.

I wanted a perfect teacher and when I realized that there was no such thing, my heart broke and I blamed you. I felt betrayed because you were not what the books told me you would be. You were too much like me. You were too human, and I couldn't fathom how humanity and enlightenment could live in the same body. I believed in your perfection, and I worshipped it. And I knew what I was doing. By worshipping your enlightenment, I was trying to bypass all the ways I was imperfect, namely the very precise ways I still hated myself. I needed to be distracted. And with you being who you were and are, I needed to at least lose myself in you for a bit.

I understand now that enlightenment does not equal perfection. Perfection is one of the biggest scams in the contemporary spirituality/wellness industrial complex. Perfection is advertised and sold as the great destination of our invested labor. Yet the worship of perfection becomes yet another way that my own self-hate is further weaponized against me, resulting in my willingness to relinquish agency to some self-proclaimed guru who themselves are only performing perfection. There are way more actors than authentic teachers in the industry.

And then I did what any heartbroken person does in a relationship: I left you. Not only that, I left everyone who loved you because I kept seeing you in everyone connected to you. And all of this was too much. Being with a teacher is like sitting next to a fire. At the right distance, the fire is warming and comforting. The closer you get, the hotter it gets, and if you step into it, you will be burned up. I got too close to you and wasn't ready for the burn. So, leaving was my way of tending to the burns.

There are two truths here: I love you, and we all make mistakes. But these are more than just mistakes; they are deliberate and calculated maneuvers meant to manipulate others into getting your unmet needs met. You lost your boyhood and what remains is a poignant regret that is yet unmourned and, thus, unmetabolized.

Despite our awakening, we still must be allowed to be ourselves, and if that doesn't happen, what are the consequences? Maybe we perform our way through life attempting to meet everyone else's needs except our own. It seems like we will get resentful after a while of doing this. I think this resentment makes us dangerous.

> In this hungry mind, the blue-black
> trembling of a storm heavy sky marches victoriously
>   through

songs of you. Beneath my tongue mantras lie obscured,
suffocated within the dense fabric of the coldest winter.

In my chest pulses a rock-hard heart that
*   fears falling in love with you.*
While spring reaches out to set me free,

Karmapa, think of me.

My practice of devotion has meant that I see any enlightened person as a human first and an expression of God second. There is something violent about robbing people of their humanity through degradation or overvaluing. I see you as human because if I can't relate to you as a human like me and the billions of other humans on this planet, how can I understand how possible it is to achieve awakening in this world? And if I bypass your humanity, your very human mistakes will feel overwhelmingly cruel because I still believe that an enlightened being is perfect. If I see you as a god, an ineffable distance arises between us that I can't reach across because I am a flawed human, and you are perfect. This is nothing but a power differential that ends up with me ceding my agency to you because I fall back into a habitual pattern of worshipping gods. I do not worship you. I cannot worship you. My love for you is clarity that helps me to understand what is possible in this body and world through diligent and authentic practice. Your enlightened mind mirrors back to me the qualities of my own enlightened mind.

This is what I am trying to say: if I let you be human, you can reflect my humanity back to me. But it's more than this; letting you be human reminds me that we all fuck up, and it reminds me that we can still forget who we are and take from others what is not freely offered. Your transgressions are also a mirror for me, teaching me that I must make different choices.

If beings like you struggle, what hope is there for the rest of us who are less extraordinary? The hope is in the fact that I am not you. Maybe my karma isn't to be as awake as you are, but my karma has created a life where I have been acutely interested in how to live in community while reducing violence to myself and others. And yes, I still struggle with this. Yet as long as we touch this earth in these bodies, we will all struggle, and the struggle is real. But we have to know that we struggle, and we have to name the struggle in our practice and prayers while asking for the resources to help us manage the struggle.

> In dreams you glide along the pavement
>   of my fears. Your footprints are pools
> of silver moonlight, your breath streaks of
>   gold against
>
> a midnight canvas. Dakinis glitter along
>   the horizon recalling my million
> incarnations of love in you. You turn and gaze into me,
>   I prostrate
>
> into an ocean of your beautiful emanations.
>
> I wake in the arms of Mother
> Liberator, who whispers, "always with the Father,
>   we abide."
>
> Offering this sign of spring,
>
> Karmapa, think of me.

It has taken me a while to figure out how to finish this. I feel like I've said too much, made assumptions that are at best exaggeration and at worst wrong. I don't know how to hide my broken heart anymore.

I have not given up on you or our lineage. I am just disappointed about how we normalize and justify institutional violence against young monastics and incarnate teachers and violence from teachers toward students. I am disappointed about being blamed by our lineage for talking about the violence many of us participate in. I am disappointed about being called divisive or being told that I lack devotion. I am disappointed in a lineage of people I love but who confuse their trauma with devotion and weaponize it against survivors of sexual misconduct and anyone questioning the violence that has been masked as skillful means. I am disappointed in the many male teachers who remain silent because they know how much they benefit from the ongoing violence. Mother Audre always taught that our silence will not save us. In this case, our silence is full of violence. I gave up trying to be a "good lama" years ago and decided to choose speaking over silence.

I love you, and my heart has broken, and somewhere in all this I am being pushed to break through the aching and fear to say finally that I know I must make different choices. If I am to embody the sacred masculine, to awaken God as the Father in me, I do it bowing to the feet of the Mother. In this remembering, I choose to be myself—human—and willing to disclose where I struggle, what I need, and what my boundaries are so that I can protect those seeking me to get them free. I am not perfect, and I will make mistakes, and even these mistakes I lay at the feet of the Mother. I am willing to be held accountable, and I submit myself to being held by communities that love me.

Epilogue

Despite this rainy night in Georgia, the street is quiet. It feels resolved and settled like streets do when people forget about them. Rain tends to capture random energies and dissolve them. The earth rises to absorb and neutralize what has been dissolved by the rain. The night feels like things are being tucked in and settled.

I am not being called to the pipe and the offering of tobacco, which is for the best because who knows what young men there will be to kiss later tonight—having tobacco on my breath has traditionally been a turnoff for potential lovers. It doesn't help to explain that tobacco and smoke offerings are an important part of my spiritual practice. This language is inconvenient for most people. Being a holy man has often gotten in the way of frolicking.

In my headphones, Dinah Washington sings about this bitter earth and the fruit it bears. The lush orchestration lifting her voice like prayer to her descendants, like me articulating for us what we struggle to name for ourselves, that this living has been hard.

I feel the kindness of the night and the gentleness of the rain begin to tend to the pain of this world. The pain isn't bitter but disappointed. It, like all things, shall pass.

The end is near, but I have lived long enough to give up believing in endings. Instead, the beginning is near. The old demons once celebrating their hold on our minds and bodies are losing their grip, and discarded gods are remembering their sacred vows to the living. And although it feels like the darkness of delusion grows thicker and longer, it is only the experience of labor as the new world prepares to be born.

Regardless of this truth, I am experiencing sadness. There are still long, hard days ahead of us, but I'm not sad about this. These days must come, and I have survived many such days before. I suppose I feel sadness because no matter how much I work, there will be many people who will not survive the long days ahead, and I find myself mourning this. This lesson has taken me decades to even articulate without harsh denial. I can't save everyone. Neither can you.

How do we hold on until the darkest night passes? How do those of us who will survive say goodbye to those who will not make it through the long night? What kind of sweet grace and uncomplicated compassion will let us kiss the foreheads of our most beloved ones as we wake into an age they cannot join us in? What kind of love helps us to know that no one is ever truly lost but only waiting until they are ready to get free? The door to liberation is never closed because we are already free beings just trying to remember who we are.

When I was young in the late 1980s, every Friday morning our favorite Black radio station would play "Oh Happy Day" to express the joy many Black folks felt getting to the end of the workweek and, particularly, to payday. I was always moved by the lyrics, about Jesus teaching us to watch, fight, and pray. Jesus was teaching how to wage spiritual warfare and part of me knew that this was incredibly important to do. It sounded like a battle cry to me. As I grew older and found myself on a spiritual path, I realized that much of my practice is to mourn, to be in silence, to fast, and to pray. This orientation is older than this life.

This is an age of the spirit, or rather a return to the spirit. There will always be the business of justice and freedom to attend to here while we are being called to attend to our spirits and minds, to the tenderness of our hearts, and to the truth that at the end of the day, this world is not our home.

I will continue loving, praying, and struggling through my trauma to drink from the Divine, offering everything I can to those transitioning into the spirit realms, offering what I can to those who remain in this realm.

The Salt Eaters, a novel by Toni Cade Bambara, centers around two women named Velma Henry and Minnie Ransom. Velma is a longtime activist but has recently succumbed to the years of stress accumulated between her activism, marriage, and job and has been hospitalized for attempting to take her own life. Minnie is probably the most gifted healer in the community and is called to the hospital to heal Velma. However, Velma seems to be resisting. She wants no part of it. Minnie eventually asks Velma, "Are you sure, sweetheart, that you want to be well? . . . Just so's you're sure, sweetheart, and ready to be healed, 'cause wholeness is no trifling matter. A lot of weight when you're well."

I hear Minnie asking me this question right now, asking if I am ready to get more than just healed, asking if I am ready to get free. It seems like my whole life has been an answer to this question. And though sometimes I am confused about what freedom feels like or if I am as free as I think I am, I know this for sure: I consent to this sacred work. I consent to the brokenheartedness, the rage, and the hopelessness, as well as to the joy, the gratitude, and the care. I consent to the weight of being healed and the responsibility I choose to get others well and free. This has been the only choice for me in this life. With the help of the saints, both old and new, I keep moving on.

Acknowledgments

This book found me soon after my last book, *Love and Rage*, was published in June of 2020. It offered me visions of what it needed to be and the work I would have to undertake to channel its spirit into the material world. I knew it was a book that needed to be here, so I consented to be the channel through which *The New Saints* would take form.

This labor has demanded everything from me. It has sent me to the Amazon jungle multiple times, wrestling with the expression of the Mother as ayahuasca. It has asked me to walk the floors of my home, weeping into the gentle darkness in the middle of the night. I have gone to the waters to pray to Mothers Yemoja and Oshun. I have retreated to the mountains to consult the local deities and have sat at the fire praying for all the obstacles to be burned away. I've journeyed back into old trauma and listened to its stories and desire to finally be free. I have sat with the elder spirits in the great lodge. I have had to remember things that I never knew I knew, channel energies that I never thought could be channeled, and grieve more than I thought was possible. I did this and much more with a grateful heart because this book was never for me but for those who dream of liberation.

However, it has taken the support and collaboration of many beings in both the seen and unseen worlds to support this labor.

I offer immense gratitude to the land and earth, especially the lands I have written and prayed on, including my homeland, the traditional lands of the Creek, Cherokee, and Muscogee people, who are also my spiritual ancestors and elders. I bow to the medicines they have led me to, whose allyship I have relied on, including ayahuasca, psilocybin, tobacco, cannabis, sage, palo santo, chamomile, lavender, and rose.

I offer the deepest appreciation to all the spiritual lineages I practice, including the Kagyu school of Tibetan Buddhism as well as the Kashi lineage. I offer appreciation to all my teachers for holding me through this process, especially Acharya Swami Jaya Devi, and equal appreciation for the blessings of Lama Willa Baker, Lama Tsering Wangdu Rinpoche, Lama Norlha Rinpoche, and Ma Jaya Sati Bhagavati.

I am indebted to my home, including its spirits and protectors, for tending to me through the long process of this writing.

This book emerges from countless thinkers, writers, artists, activists, and abolitionists whom I have been in conversation with, including Harriet Tubman, Sojourner Truth, Frederick Douglas, Toni Morrison, Alice Walker, bell hooks, James Baldwin, Dr. Martin Luther King, Jr., Ntozake Shange, Cornell West, John Deere, Samuel Delany, Essex Hemphill, Joseph Beam, Alvin Ailey, Marsha P. Johnson, Tony Kushner, Emma Goldman, Toni Cade Bambara, Audre Lorde, Fannie Lou Hamer, Reginald Shepherd, André Leon Talley, Carrie Sealine, Jessye Norman, Kathleen Battle, and Sweet Honey in the Rock.

There are no words to express my debt to the ancestors for their constant support and clarity, as well as their willingness to change. I am grateful for my ancestral deities who have been both kind and firm in our relationship. I am also grateful for the continuous blessing of my protector deities, helping gather the resources needed to complete this work.

There are many people who are responsible for this work being in the world. First, I am beyond grateful for the care of my literary agent, Stephanie Tade, for believing in the importance of my voice and the necessity for this text to be in the world.

I am immensely grateful for the care of Sounds True, for Jennifer Brown for inviting me to Sounds True and for Sarah Stanton for her holding this process with care. I am especially grateful to my friend, elder, and publisher Tami Simon for her fierce love and encouragement during this process.

I offer so much appreciation to my friend Marcus Rogers for creating the stunning artwork for this book.

I am deeply moved by Maya Binyam, who worked closely with me and this text as the lead editor, helping the text express itself as clearly as possible.

I am not sure if there would even be a book without the overwhelming care and skill of my dear sister and spiritual advisor Leah Tioxon, whom I consider the godmother of this book and who has consistently made herself available to support me in what has often been an intense and frustrating experience of channeling this book into the world. I am also grateful for Luana Morales, Lauren Greiner, Corrie Roberson, Anna Gallagher, and Emily Carson for offering their healing medicine for this work.

I am deeply grateful to all the spiritual communities that have held me in this process, especially my own community, Bhumisparsha, and particularly the Medicine Buddha community where many of these teachings were first shared publicly.

I am especially grateful for the constant care and support of my team including Ericka Phillips, who has been a staunch supporter, friend, and confidant, and Daniel Sutton-Johanson, whose love and sensitivity are an inspiration. I also extend deep gratitude to Vivian Mac, Seth Freedman, River Molloy, Nia Austin-Edwards, Eric Busse, and Sesalli Castillo, as well as the past support of Marisol Ybarra, Andi Nyiradi, and Tanzanite Msola.

I thank my family for all their support, especially my mom, Rev. Wendy Owens, and my dad, Dr. Hershel Holiday.

I am grateful for the care and prayers of my elders in this writing, especially the support of Karen Zeigler, Randa McNamara, Colevia Carter, Cheryl Giles, Kathe McKenna, Metta McGarvey, Rehena Harilall, Ayesha Ali, Brenda Collins, Rachael Wooten, and Acharya Yashoda.

I am indebted to my dear brother Charles Stephens for his twenty years of friendship and the many hours of conversation and feedback on this writing.

I owe so much to my dear sister friend Sister Sadada Jackson for her fierce love and loyalty.

I am grateful for the care of my dear friends and colleagues Lama Justin Von Bujdoss and Spring Washam. And special thanks to Jamie Fergerson, Joshua Bogart, and Evan Hemphill for the many years of support and friendship.

I am also grateful for the spiritual friendship and care of Rev. angel Kyodo williams, Jasmine Syedullah, Shanté Paradigm Smalls, Aishah Shahidah Simmons, Sanah Ahsan, Nova Reed, Andrea Wright, Stacie Graham, Marcel Foster, Swami Jaya Das, Swami Agni Ma, and Acharya Swami Durga Das.

Finally, I offer appreciation to Tim McKee and North Atlantic Books for their continued care and support of my previous works, *Radical Dharma* and *Love and Rage*.

May whatever blessings are awakened with this labor be first dedicated to all beings who have made this work possible then shared with all beings everywhere so that we will all be liberated as quickly as possible.

About
the Author

Lama Rod Owens is a Black Buddhist Southern Queen. He is an international influencer with a master of divinity degree in Buddhist studies from Harvard Divinity School with a focus on the intersection of social change, identity, and spiritual practice. Author of *Love and Rage: The Path of Liberation Through Anger* and coauthor of *Radical Dharma: Talking Race, Love, and Liberation*, his teachings center on freedom, self-expression, and radical self-care. Highly sought after for talks, retreats, and workshops, his mission is showing you how to heal and free yourself.

A leading voice in a new generation of Buddhist teachers, Lama Rod is highly respected among his peers and the communities that he serves. "It can be confusing for people to hear Tantric Buddhist teachings coming from someone who's Black and queer, southern and fat; it's who I am," he says. From these intersections, he creates a platform that is very natural, engaging, and inclusive.

Applauded for his mastery in balancing weighty topics with a sense of lightness while still speaking truth to power, this queen has been featured by CNN, *Good Morning America*, the BBC, the *Washington Post*, PBS, NPR, *Ebony*, *Out*, and more. Connection is Lama Rod's second language; authenticity is his first. Meeting people where they are and speaking to them rather than at them with words they can relate to makes his delivery digestible and highly sought after.

Honoring his southern roots, he refers to his healing approach as "laying hands." His laying of hands, however, is showing you how to do the work of making the necessary choices in your day-to-day relationships and routines to heal and free yourself from the traumas that bind you to self-sabotaging behaviors. He teaches you how to continuously choose clarity and light and how to transform emotions such as grief and anger into liberation.

In 2018, Lama Rod cofounded Bhumisparsha, a spiritual community with a mission of making Tantra accessible and inclusive for North American practitioners while serving as a catalyst for transformative social change. He is the cohost of the podcast series *The Spirit Underground* with fellow Buddhist teacher Spring Washam where they explore spiritual abolition through the framework of Black and Indigenous spiritualities. Prior engagements from this Buddhist minister, author, activist, yoga instructor, and authorized Lama in the Kagyu school of Tibetan Buddhism include talks, retreats, and workshops for organizations, businesses, and universities, including Calm, New York University, Yale University, Massachusetts Institute of Technology, Harvard University, Google, Columbia University, Northwestern University, and Stanford University. He can be contacted through his website lamarod.com.

About
Sounds True

Sounds True was founded in 1985 by Tami Simon with a clear mission: to disseminate spiritual wisdom. Since starting out as a project with one woman and her tape recorder, we have grown into a multimedia publishing company with a catalog of more than 3,000 titles by some of the leading teachers and visionaries of our time, and an ever-expanding family of beloved customers from across the world.

In more than three decades of evolution, Sounds True has maintained our focus on our overriding purpose and mission: to wake up the world. We offer books, audio programs, online learning experiences, and in-person events to support your personal growth and awakening, and to unlock our greatest human capacities to love and serve.

At SoundsTrue.com you'll find a wealth of resources to enrich your journey, including our weekly Insights at the Edge podcast, free downloads, and information about our nonprofit Sounds True Foundation, where we strive to remove financial barriers to the materials we publish through scholarships and donations worldwide.

To learn more, please visit SoundsTrue.com/freegifts or call us toll free at 800.333.9185.

Together, we can wake up the world.